E U L I S !

THE HISTORY OF LOVE:

ITS WONDROUS MAGIC, CHEMISTRY, RULES, LAWS, MODES, MOODS AND RATIONALE;

BEING THE

THIRD REVELATION OF SOUL AND SEX.

ALSO, REPLY TO

"WHY IS MAN IMMORTAL?"

THE SOLUTION OF THE DARWIN PROBLEM.

AN ENTIRELY NEW THEORY.

BY

PASCHAL BEVERLY RANDOLPH, M.D.

SECOND EDITION.

TOLEDO, OHIO:
RANDOLPH PUBLISHING CO.
1874.

TO

JOHN F. KAPP; L. H. McLAUGHLIN;

ALBERT BURPEE; JOHN TEMPLE;

GUSTAV SCHRADER; LEWIS AND JONATHAN KIRK;

E. A. PERCEVAL, JR; ABU-ID-DURR

DJUNDUB OF THE ANSAIREH; OTHMAN ASWAD EL

KINDEE; HER GRACIOUS PURITY,

FAIROOZ SHIRWAN AFRIDOON,

and to every man, woman or child besides, whoever, as the named great, because GOOD Souls, ever did me a kindness or spoke me fairly in the dark hour,
and through them to all human kind, for the firm and steady rebuilding of a right
and true system of social ethics, based upon the purity of woman, the nobleness of man and the honor of the race, one wholly free from all abnormalism;
devoted to the everlasting discomfiture of all who aim to pervert the higher,
better, purer, nobler instincts of our common human nature; to the speedy down-
fall of all false systems and shams, whether in Physics, Morals, Politics or
Faith; and to the corresponding advance, thrift and triumph of the Good, the
Beautiful and the True, and to the assured success of the Superlative Order
of Men and Women who constitute the E. W. A. S., this present Edition of

MY WORK OR RELIGIO-MEDICI

IS GRATEFULLY DEDICATED BY THE

RE-FOUNDER AND HIERARCH OF EULIS,

TOLEDO, OHIO, 1874.   P. B. RANDOLPH.

———————

AFFECTIONAL ALCHEMY.

PART I.

READER, mine, I am about to treat herein the grandest subject that ever engaged or challenged human thought. In doing so it is likely that I may repeat some things elsewhere, by myself or others, said before; but even if so, I have struck upon many things now given to the race for the first time.

A vast amount of "physiological" chaff is current in the world, originating in the pulpy brains of certain people with "M.D." after their names; folks who eke out a good living by putting medicines, of which they know little, into bodies whereof they know less.

A still larger amount of "chaff" labelled "philosophy" is afloat, generated for the most part in the angular heads of people, whom a chronic prostatitis or ovarian fever has so deranged that they really imagine themselves philosophers, --being only shams, --who propose to revolutionize the world, especially the domain of Marriage-land, by inculcating pudacious sophistries, better calculated to kill than to cure the victims, on either side. One thing is certain: Light is needed; and this work (originally intended to be called by a different title, but which intent was abandon-ed, owing to the vastly larger scope of the completed and rewritten volume) is meant to afford exactly what is required; and

I. What a tremendous deal of suffering, horror, crime, wretchedness and des-pair there is in this beautiful, but badly misused world of ours!--most of which might be prevented in the first instance, or remedied in the second, were there less consummate and confounded ignorance afloat up and down the earth's strong tides of human life, with its strangely, wildly surging ebbs and flows, heats and snows, in reference to matters pertaining to, and concerning the, relations, wise and otherwise, subsisting between the separate genders of the human race; especially that portion of it located in the so-called "civilized" lands, and particularly in the cis-Atlantic portion of the Lord's exceedingly immoral vineyard.

Now, whoever supposes that the ignorance alluded to is confined solely to the masses,--sometimes spellable as "them asses," according to Carlyle,--or that the sum total of non-knowledge must be looked for among the unread, unlettered and un-washed crowds that throng the great highways of the world, and whose struggles for life, and clamors for bread, occupy most of their time and attention,--will find him or herself most wofully mistaken; for a far less dense and conglobate ignorance upon matters of vital import to every human being exists among the people--the rude crowd who jostle each other everywhere, and which is the plastic material that the brain-ful few mould into voters, hero-worshippers, or send to fight their battles against each other, armed with ploughs or rifles, pitchforks or bayonets, cannons or spades --than is to be found in circles making very lofty pretensions, not only to knowledge, but to morality also, from its geologic base to its astronomic summit.

For gross and culpable non-knowledge, especially upon all the vital points that cluster round the one word "sex," you must look, not amidst the untaught hosts, the democratic underlayer of society, but right squarely among the so-called "learned," professional, much-boasted, highly-cultured upper-strata, especially in those centres of population whence newspapers by myriads are scattered broadcast over all the lands.

Were not this a painful fact, such classes of "reformers" as now march over the world were in utter impossibility.

They are an unhealthy set, the fungi of a flase civilization, regnant for a time, but certain to disappear with the advent of common sense among the people as a general thing.

Sex is a thing of soul; most people think it but a mere matter of earthly form and physical structure. True, there are some unsexed souls; some no sex at all, and others still claiming one gender, and manifesting its exact opposite. But its laws, offices, utilities, and its deeper and diviner meanings are sealed books to all but about two in a million; yet they ought to have the attentive study of every rational human being, every aspirant to immortality beyond the grave.

In some sense this matter has been, and is, the subject of thought, but only in its outer phases, or its grosser aspects; seldom in its higher ones, and never, until now, in any of its loftier and mystical bearings. Books by ship-loads on one or two, and always either its physiological or sentimental sides of the subject, have been put forth by ambitious M.D.'s, or motoriety-seeking empirics; books which mainly satisfied a prurient taste or morbid curiosity, gave but little light, and generally left their readers practically as ignorant as before.

Other books, in other millions, vile, atrocious, cancerous, abounding with death in every line, fraught with ruin on every page, have been, still are being, scattered everywhere across the nations, till the flower of the world's youth has been blighted, and the morality of earth sapped dry. Oh, that literature, foul, disgusting beyond belief! terrible as the cobra's fang, keener than the dagger's edge, monstrous as a drunkard's dream, more devastating than the spotted plague! until between the two millstones--quackery, pseudo-professional literature on the one hand, and the execrable, libidinous abominations on the other--one-half of the manhood and womanhood of our nation has been ground into the very dust. No punishment can be too severe for the disseminators of the latter; no contempt too great for the authors of the former.

Not one of the very many respectable people, including fifty French, a score of English, about as many Americans, and a few German authors, who have stained reams of good white paper, and spilled gallons of ink in writing anent the sublime subject of sex, have taken the trouble to go one inch below the surface; but have been content to copy each other, and repeat the same old worn-out story,--else concealed a few good ideas in barrels of words. They have taken man and woman, shown us their anatomy; explained something of physical gender; said something about function and periods, and there left us, because they knew nothing further themselves.

For example, there are ten thousand treatises extant concerning what the doctors call the sin of one Onan, meaning, thereby, a certain nameless solitary vice. But the man alluded to in the Bible never was guilty of that sin at all. Albeit his crime was equally bad, equally disastrous and hateful. In these days it is politely called "conjugal fraud," and in plain terms consists of the nuptive union to the orgasmal climax, which was allowed to occur only in a manner never intended by the Infinite God. "He wasted his seed upon the ground, that he might not beget children to inherit his brother's name." (See Bible.) Millions do the accursed thing to-day that they may be childless, as indeed they deserve to be; for he who does that heinous wrong commits a quadruple crime, against his wife, himself, nature and God; to say nothing about the right of all souls to be incarnated by the act of man.

Now the doctors truly say that the sin solitary, and the fraud conjugal are both bad; but fail to give us even half the reasons why.

-2-

Here let me make a point for the doctors, and all others besides. In the normal proper nuptive union, a term I invent expressive of the most sacred and intimate <u>fact</u> of marriage, there is a certain amount of the male vital life in fluid form (semen) voided; exactly the same by actual weight or volume may be wasted in a lascivious dream,--a spontaneous ejection of superfluous vital force in the same form; 3d, the same may be lost by the abominable conjugal fraud; or by the heinous sin against ones self--solitary vice. But note the tremendous difference in the results that follow in each of the four cases 1st. In the reciprocal and normal one, only joy results, positive and pronounced; and never is follow^{ed} by any particularly sombre feelings; happiness ensues, and the man's soul is at perfect peace with his physical form.

In the second case, resulting from spermatic plethora, a relief follows, but leaves a weakness after it, requiring phosphoric food to recuperate from. There's a little shame-facedness too, but not much. In the third case the whole being is <u>shocked</u>, and the man feels himself to be contemptible and mean; and so he is. In the fourth case, a bitter, poignant <u>remorse</u> haunts the self-sinner day and night, for sometimes weeks together; and the results of his dreadful sin stands by him like an accusing goblin from the deeps. Now why? Remember, we suppose, what is true, that weights and reasures are the same in all four instances; that the exact amount of fluid life is lost; yet one launches its victim into steepdown gulfs of remorseful, mental torture, and the others do not.

The physiologists have not answered that question. I will. In case first, the normal one, waste is occasioned by the magnetic action of the electric lymph, the absorption of which by the masculine compensates the vital loss on one side; and the absorption by the feminine parietes of the exudation from Cowper's gland compensates on the other side; and here I give the doctors a new discovery--to them, not me-- which is, that just within the vulva are two little glands, called glands of Duvernay, from their French discoverer. That much the doctors were aware of. But they did <u>not</u> know that those glands are the seat of all vaginal and uterine life; nor that trouble seals them up; Love only keeps them open. When sealed there is no exudation of magnetic lymph, which <u>must</u> be present, else marital rites mean death to her sooner or later. That's what ails half the wives of Christendom. Now another new thing for the doctors. Just forward of the prostate gland is what is known as Cowper's gland; but they know not its use. I have just explained it. It is to collect, store up, and discharge the magnetic fluid of the body in liquid form. It precedes both the semen and prostatic lymph; and upon contact with the lochia--Duvennay--they fuse; the result of which is the fulfilment of God's purpose in bi-sexing man. I hope this thought will be carefully studied and understood. Now in the case of the <u>solitaire</u> there is but <u>one</u> force at work. The result is from imaginative and mechanical forces; not from electric, magnetic or spiritual ones; hence he draws upon his very soul itself; violates and disobeys the fundamental law of LOVE, and <u>that</u> is why he pays the dreadful penalty. Love resides in the soul; the basic law of that soul he deliberately prostitutes, wherefore his soul, as well as his body, must and does suffer.

AN EPISODE.--A SINGULAR EXPERIENCE.

II. One day as I went walking up and down the town in soliloquent mood, I met a man, whose woe-begone countenance betokened great griefs tugging at his heart-strings; and that soul-pangs were racking the very foundations of his being. I MET THE MAN. No, I did <u>not</u> say that--it was my <u>alter ego</u> encountering myself!--and I learned his sad story, pondering deeply upon which, I pursued my way to where sleep and I were wont to woo each other; and there, throwing myself upon a lounge, drank some fresh, sweet milk, brought me by a chunky little germanesque neighbor of mine, of say nine years, pretty, as all children are, and loquacious and talkative as all children should be.

As I lay there I thought of the man,--a lone, and lonely man; for she whom he loved and trusted, many years younger than himself, was afar off, among strange people, where amid the rounds of gayety, in fashion's tide, she had no time to think of him,--the delving toiler; and far too many follow the example of that thoughtless girl.

She was wondrously fair, and heedless as beautiful; with fashions to air and conquests to achieve; poor, sweet little lady! And as I pictured her beauty and bloom, I could but justify her vanity, and on that basis condone her apparent heart-less coldness in never deigning to write to him, who was suffering daily deaths by reason of her cold silence--and --contempt.

And so I lay upon the lounge and quaffed the sweet, delicious milk, and I thought about the Woman and the Man; and, as I did so, I fell into a sort of magnetic trance and clairvoyance--a habit familiar, seeing that the power to do wo was born with me; and by its means I have a thousand times been able to see afar off, and to glimpse things denied to mortal vision. On this occasion I fell into it from hav-ing incidentally cast my eyes upon a third class triune, or magic mirror, such as for years I have used expressly to induce the state of psycho-vision. It hung over the table against the wall, where I had placed it after polishing it, preparatory to sending it to a lady in Brooklyn, N. Y., to whom impecuniosity had compelled me to sell it.

It was a fine one, though not the best or most costly; yet was capable of mighty things when in the humor; for, be it known, they like watches, razors, loco-motives and women, are very set in their ways, and will not work unless well treated, and coaxed besides; then they operate well enough, as did the one alluded to. Its power ranged to the aerial spaces above, and to the vaulted deeps below; and on its surface the dead could, and often did, cast cognizable pictures of themselves and surroundings then and THEN again. On the morning alluded to, as I breathed upon it, a thick, heavy, black, portentous cloud obscured its face, followed by a silvery sheen indicative of coming trouble, hatred, folly, error, succeeded by happiness and contentment; but I actually forgot all that, nor recalled it till after the approach-ing drama was ended,--a drama strange and weird, fraught with pain unutterable, in-expressible, almost unendurable; yet whose results or fruitage was as ripe pome-granates are to the thirsty pilgrims, or the cool, bubbling waters to the parched lips of the Arab on the burning sands of Sahara. Little did I dream that the strange experience was full of true light to others than myself; yet such it is, and was,; and with grateful heart I thank the Most Compassionate God, the Ineffable Lord, that I was found worthy to become the vessel for the conveyance of so grand a lesson to my brethren of the wide and wasteful world.

In an instant, as my eyes fell on it--that wondrous glyphae--the outer world sight receded, and the soul-sight came in play. Child, table, chairs, lounge--all were gone and unheeded, and on the face of that marvellous glass I beheld a scene which at the time, and for six weeks afterwards, I religiously believed was at that very instant being enacted far away, in, to the man in Toledo, dreadful reality. The sequel--far along in this book--will show whether it was the shadow of an enacted fact, or a figment of fancy woven of mist, and conjured up out of the cellars of suspicion. I loved the man, at all events; hence what I saw froze my blood with horror, and made my nerves fairly tingle with excitement and pain. I saw the lady, whom the MAN loved so well, and for whom he yearned, and mourned, and wept bitter tears, revealed before the eyes of my soul. She was just emerging from a dormitory,

-4-

evidently, judging by appearances, both a dishonest and dishonored wife and woman. She was gaily chatting with her paramour, a gallant young fellow, who stood near her, and on whom she gazed with unutterable tenderness, volupty and love. I shuddered with mortal anguish; for I loved my friend, and that woman bore his name. Until that hour I and he had believed, her to be pure as an angel from heaven; and now did I, through sympathy for him, suffer,—ay, the agonies of the nether hell. Presently you will see whether the vision was a lesson or a fact; and whether jealousy is, and is not, sometimes based on solid ground, sometimes empty air.

On the day I met the man; he had told me that she had asked him very singular questions: "Is it possible for a husband to discover if his wife goes astray during an absence, without the ordinary evidence that establishes such facts? Can he find it out without seeing or hearing of it?" I don't know what answer was given; but I do know that the words sunk deep, like hot iron, into his soul; and he pondered on them till he grew morbid, and every day, in his loneliness, he imagined all sorts of things, which now bodied themselves in palpable form before my soul's gaze.

Subsequently she had written to say that her yearnings were great, and she was dying from the mere fact of prolonged absence; yet within a week wrote that she was supremely happy, and longed for nothing. This was ground for suspecting her to be a truant wife, and my friend a deceived husband; and all the more in that she was thrown in contact with some very popular agitators of the marriage and fidelity questions,—on what I regarded as the wrong side.

As I gazed on the scene upon the mystic mirror's face, I saw the lady and her lover as before, and beheld his burning kisses fall thick and fast upon her rich, ripe, and alluring lips; saw her languish in voluptuous death in his strong arms, and watched her return his fiery salutation. I heard his love expressions, and her warm replies; but the most cruel thing of all was their combined laugh and "joke" they were playing on my friend, by making his slender purse bear the cost of their guiltful amours. He loved that woman as mothers love the babes God sends through wailing agony to their longing hearts.

I leaped from the couch; rushed to my friend's place; and told him the tragic tale; fired his soul with vengeance dire; and, putting a loaded revolver in his pocket, bade him swiftly traverse the 1,100 miles intervening betwixt him and his deep revenge. This done, I went to a grocery hard by, to drink beer to drown out the agony felt for the man,—the detestation of the woman. "Man proposes," but God upsets his calculations; or Destiny does. So now, on my way to Grambrins Halle, I encountered my little friend, the German child, at play. She strangely interested me; and I left the Halle with but one glass, where I had intended to drink at least a dozen. The child saved me! Returning, I caught her up, seated her jauntily on my head, and marched back to the lonely house on the hill, where I threw myself on the lounge, kissed this little child goodby, and, as she ran off trippingly home, at her little brother's call, who was just then having dreadful trouble with his rabbits, I caught sight of a scintillant flash of white light issuant from her head, like the radiant gleam of a peerless diamond, when all the lamps are brightly burning; and a glowing, streaming iridescence flowed from her lips. I had drawn her to me, and pressed her rosy, childish face to mine, inhaling the balmy aroma of her pure, fresh, joyous soul; and a portion of the roseate fire of her sweet lips had clung to mine. I saw it, like a thin cloud of opalescence, waving gently to and fro, as I moved my head, or breathed. I began to study the meaning of a kiss.

There are but few among the many who know the meaning of a kiss;—or that the soul, from its seat in the brain, is in telegraphic unity with the lips,—affectional, friendly, filial, parental, general, in the upper one; sensuous, magnetic, passional, in the lower; nor that, when loving lips meet lips that love, there is a magnetic discharge of soul-flame, and each party gives and receives large measures of magnetic life and fluid love at the instant of impact or contact, which measures are greater or less according to the love-fulness or emptiness of each respectively. While pondering on this, and marvelling at the beautiful irradiation alluded to above, I chanced to recur in thought in the mirror scene, and to the woman and the man, the wierdly strange phantorama already described; again that strange numbness of the outer being came over me, and in another instant I lay there, rapt, entranced, transfigured, and for the time being was as are the newly dead. Clearly, distinctly, did my soul's vision penetrate the spaces and localize itself in that far-off room, where still stood the recalcitrant wife and her new-found lover, and the woman stood on this side, the man upon that, hands on shoulders, and mutual kisses, accompanied with glowing red passion-fires from lip to lip; and as I thought of my friend, _her_ husband, I exclaimed, "Guilty! by the Lord of Hosts!" But as I said so and gazed, a great change came over my feelings and my soul. I put myself in my friend's, her husband's place, by means of the three principles, Posism, Volantia and Decretism, hereinafter alluded to, and then, far more clearly comprehending the situation, I would not, as before, have slain her, spattered his heart's blood upon the walls and floor, or have sent a leaden bullet crashing through his brains, for the whole world, or millions more just like it; for whereas before I had observed effects, I now beheld their producing, hidden causes. A great cloud rolled away from before my gaze into the vague, dim AEth, and my soul, representing my friend, the man said unto my soul, She did not love you; if she had, this scene could never have occurred. It is but one of millions, this very day, transpiring in thousands of places the wide world over, and is the legitmate result of the wrong relations subsisting between the mated, or rather, mismated marriagees of the earth! Love only can keep souls, and the bodies they wear, true and faithful! Where it does not mutually exist there can be, and is, no guaranty of fidelity. Wherefore, it is incumbent on you to face the facts; call to your aid the rare philosophy of COMMON SENSE; struggle manfully against this dreadful, appalling, yet perfectly natural catastrophe; accept the situation; hush the throbbings of your tortured heart; ask God for strength to bear the heavy burden, and be wise.

Still representing my friend, my soul said on: Perchance what you see is, after all, but a fevered dream, begotten of your depressed nervous state, morbidity of fancy and loneliness, combined with the suspicions kindled by the strange questions asked upon the eve of her departure many days ago, and greatly strengthened by unwisely worded letters sent back by her; and made still stronger by her six weeks' utter silence--in itself good cause for suspicion, for every husband has a right to know his wife's whereabouts, her surroundings and the company she keeps; and if she does _not_ keep him thus informed, he has fair and just grounds to infer that her actions are such as ought to be hidden from his gaze, and also from that of humanity at large.

If innocent, she is still guilty of a great folly; while your trouble and pain may really have no more solid foundation than vague and empty air. Let justice rule on both sides; for she was unwise, while your illness tortures things out of shape, till mere phasmas assume forms as solid in appearance as the very truth itself; and it may be your anxiety and sympathy may have conjured up a lie; and this apparently recusant woman really be as unsoiled as the down upon the ring-dove's breast, or the spotless plume of an angel's wing! Oh, _how_ my heart, for my friend, clung to that hope! My soul to my soul went on: They twain, the far-off couple, are young; are adapted to each other; you(my friend, of course) are too old for her. You had no right to subject her to the terrible temptation of being away from your side for months together, in the midst of gay people, where everything appealed to and impressed her young heart and fancy, and made a wider gulf between herself and you. I know your heart is bleeding, that hot tears are streaming down your face, that your poor soul is sweltering amidst the tortuous flames of the fiercest hell of jealousy; yet why? for one who loves you not!--who is heartless to you, heartful to her paramour! Be a man! and remember that she, too, has rights which you are bound to respect;--not the right to dishonor, but to be free from you by laws human and divine, and to make such choice and legal disposal of herself as her youth demands, and her will, soul, and conscience prompt.

If she has fallen, it is the fault of her husband, not altogether her own. She admires him, but probably loves this distant Adonis, and, tempted beyond her strength, she may have forgotten and neglected duty, at the urgence and call of love; the facts of which came rushing through the air to you and took form and shape through the vision of the seer.

Be magnanimous! and if ye twain part, as ye likely will, and forever, do not fail to recognize the end as the legitmate result of the stupid folly of allowing her to dwell so far away in the midst of tempting scenes and people. Guilty, or not guilty, forget and forgive. Voluntarily free this simpleton from the chafing thrall that binds her to one whose purse, not person, is all on earth she cares for. Let her go at the call of affection, and, forsaking you and duty, yield her to the better and nobler law of love. Free her, and they twain will likely wed. Hold her, and she is that nameless thing--a wedded harlot.

My soul had, still as my friend, not myself, gotten thus far in its just reasonings when methought I heard a sweet and silvery voice say, "Behold!" And as the delicious tones rung glorified changes through my spirit I felt that I had grown a century within an hour; and notwithstanding that I actually believed my friend's wife to be guilty, and might probably so believe until my dying day, yet I had charity for her, as well as sorrow and sympathy for him. I put myself in his place, and for the first time in my life not only realized the luxury of forgiveness, but felt capable of even dying a lingering death that the woman so loved might be happy with him she so loved; and greater affection than that can no man show, in that he would lay down his life for a friend. I talked with the husband; persuaded him to lay by the pistols and revenge. He did so, and ceased to be jealous from that hour, caring but little whether the vision was of actual fact or a delirious dream.

"Behold!" I looked, still with that ultra soul-sight which leaps all boundaries cleaves all space, flashes over rivers, mountains, seas, penetrates all bodies, and brings us in actual contact with the whole domain of mystery; and again I saw the little German child, through the walls of both houses, as clearly as if they were of finest crystal or purest glass instead of boards and mortar. And I beheld an ineffably pure, pearly-hued effulgence playing about her little head, undulating in billowy movement all about her infantile shoulders, streaming from her hair, glowing round her waist, and in loving wavelets all around. I watched this with astonishment. It was but the prelude to the celestial cantata that followed. I saw her mother gently chide her, and soon she went to bed, and slept the sweet, delicious slumber of absolute innocence; and as she thus lay I saw the gossamic cloud of pearly aura expand till it filled the room, penetrated the ceiling, the roof, swelling and lengthening out clear into the starlight, and forming to a point shot out and afar off into the very depths of space till I could follow it no more. Then I turned me again to the sleeping child; and what was my astonishment at beholding literally hundreds of bright shining and divinely beautiful forms, as of young children and the virgin dead, come trooping down the lane of pearly light, and, entering the house, gather and dance and play at the bedside of the slumbering little one. Good is catching! That child had enabled me to stave off a fit of jealous rage in sympathy with my friend; and now I was, through her again, about to learn one of the most important lessons of my life. I had kissed that child, and had become suffused with a portion of her own sweet aromal aura or atmosphere, and was, therefore, en _rapport_ with the same bright beings as she was herself, and was played upon by the same celestial, pure and divine influences, whereof Love was the dominant or major element.

A portion of these purer, better, and hyperphysical auras displaced and occupied the room of the grosser aura, earth-born and turbid. I found myself cleaner, better, than before, and comprehended Christ's "Suffer little children to come unto me." Not until that holy hour of rapt contemplation had I realized the immense meaning of a single touch of loving lips; that if it be purely given and received, both participants are blessed, not only directly, but through oblique ways, a myriad fold.

Love in very deed lies at the foot of all, and its mystic and ideal meaning outweighs the material and popular ones by as many degrees as the pure soul of that baby-girl outweighs the corrupt body of the low-lived debauchee. We may be hugged, embraced, kissed into heavenly states, or into their exact opposites! Hence, aside from common relational lip-contacts, they are worse than unwise who touch lips unless love be the underlying prompter; for if the kissed or kisser be bad, just so much of that specific evil is sure to flow from the magnetic poles of either pair of lips to the soul of him or her upon whose mouth they are laid.

I have said the moist lips are batteries charged with our very inmost good or evil. It is utterly impossible for a negress having borne a child to a white father ever to give birth to one perfectly negro,--even though its father, like herself, has never a drop of other blood in him,--for the reason that the blood of the white man, through his child, has mingled in the mother's veins. More than that, her blood under the microscope will not show the same crystalline forms after the birth of the mixed child as it did before. Just so is it impossible for us not to be made better or worse by lip touching.

Harlots invariably descend unless snatched from ruin by a miracle. It is because of the many forms of hell struggling in their veins, combating in their nerves; and as heaven or its opposite attends the kiss so also is it with every other sort of _human_ _contact_--even the ordinary shaking of the hands. Gloves, therefore, have new uses.

I awoke from my slumber a wiser, and, I trust, a better man. I went out and found my soul-harried and victimized friend. I reasoned with him just as I had with my own soul a while before. I told him it was clear as sunlight that the absent woman really cared not a straw for him, but only for what current funds she could extract from him; and that, although to lost her was a bitter draught of gall, yet he had better swallow it, for that he was only loving his own sphere wherewith he had embalmed her. I asked what right had he to hold a woman in duress _couvert_ or non-couvert, whose soul was not attached by love to his; whose compliance, duty only, not affectional. It was clear he ought to give her up at once even if the effort snapped his heart-strings, because the marking of her child was a doubtful question. Why should he pursue a heartless phantom? They were disunited in soul. Behold the folly of continuance! Let her go!

III. As previously remarked herein, writers upon the general topics of love and its offices, uses, abuses, nature, moods, and modes, have, in the main, been content with the merely superficial or external view thereof, and have, as a general thing, utterly ignored most, if not all, of the other and deeper significances attached thereunto; and not one of them has even attempted to tell mankind any more of the principles underlying sex, Love, and their copula passion, or desire, than any one's personal experience suggests; but we have plenty of hard, dry, pseudo-scientific flummery, else a long row or medical platitudes wholly useless, because

-8-

totally indigestible by the average intellectual stomach. Who of them all has given us the rationale of the orgasm--the why and wherefore, or the cause of its being a thing of apparently no moment whatever at certain times, and under circumstances: yet at another will almost shock the human soul out of its earthly tenement, the body--by its keen, incisive, cutting, awful intensity? Which of them all has explained what every one ought to, but does not know to be a fact, i. e., that, as explained in the "New Mola," and elsewhere in this book, human conjugation is or may be triple; that is, it may be of soul, spirit or body, alone, or either, and the binary minglings of the three, in various degrees, even to an infinity; for instance, one part soul, ten spirit, five hundred of mere body, and so on; but never true or normal except in exact equations; even tens or hundreds, according as the participants are high or low. The philosophers never even guessed at this truth.

Who of them has told, or can tell, why the nuptium fairly laps the very soul itself, of each participant, too, in the tenderest, softest, truly human, <u>because strictly human</u>, joy at one time; yet at another gives naught but cruel pain; else is but a nervous spasm, unsatisfactory to one party, and injurious to both; and yet the same people in both instances?

Why is it, O learned anthropologists, that the generative rite will at one time wholly unman one, yet at another--same ones too--will fill him with the most exquisite manly, gallant sensibility; inspire him with the most lofty virtue and high resolve; charge him to the lips with true and royal courage; yet at another time transmute him into an errant coward and miserable poltroon? And, <u>mirabile dictu</u>--same parties still,--bring pain, keen mental agony, shamefacedness, and suicidal thought; yet at another, result in pride, joy, gratefulness, generosity, and mental summer, with physical springtime? Why will this mysterious duty--for such it is in God's sight, who by its means peoples the worlds, and stocks in the starry spaces--plunge us into the deepest "blues," and fang our souls with remorse cruel as the grave, relentless as the Hadean gulf of Milton, and the other poets; yet at another induce a state of feeling in soul and spirit quite approaching the supposed angelic; why? and a myriad gaping crowd of scalpel-drivers repeat the sound, and echo "Why?" The answers: their science don't know, therefore <u>cannot</u> answer; wherefore I must take up my pen to respond to it, for those who need the information it is my lot to impart.

Since Dr. Dixon, of "The Scalpel," printed his great and warning essay on "The organic Law" (of sex), and the anonymous author of "Satan in Society" faintly echoed those stirring notes, nothing has been given to the world on the mighty subject worthy of attention or record. Neither essay filled the required bill, and for that reason I print this series of salvatory counsels. I may, and probably shall, ere long, be numbered with the armies of the dead; and who then will give Randolph's thoughts to the world? I don't know, and therefore give at least a part of them before I leave for good and all; consequently, I shall now convey certain brief and concise forms of certain knowledges, which, if abided by, will prolong many a life, and add immeasurable happiness to mankind. I wish to be clearly understood, and yet not to offend the most delicate or fastidious; for God is my judge that my sole aim is to teach certain truths, whose mission is to stop the tide of crime, misery and wretchedness now devastating our land. I am forced to use similes, but trust to be fully and entirely understood.

IV. Now for the answer to the loud "Whys?" of section three. The states resulting happily from human fusion were because there really <u>was a human fusion</u>, and that's just it! In all the other cases there was either too much body, too much spirit, and too little or no soul at all. They were violations of the love-law, and the suffering was the penalty. It is a pity that ten thousand times the pain was not the direct result of every violation of the organic law; and if every proposed debauchee could or would but die in the attempt, the world would soon be a great deal better off.

Where love sits enshrined over the married man's chamber door, and reason guides his conduct towards his wife therein, peace will reign, and the sale of syphilitic remedies vastly decrease. No pangs follow the celebration of the rites of holy love, nor judicious use of the divine, but abused, faculties of our nature. Unless love equals passion, _marriage rites_ are _never_ right; that's all!

V. The grand mistake made by physiologists and other essayists, writing on the current topic, consists in their persistent overlooking of the fact that man and woman are _not_ the same. The male is an incarnation, so to speak, of one side of Deity; one hemisphere of the Imperial Over SOUL; one section of Nature, MATTER, the Superlative and Infinite Mind of Minds; while the human female represents and is an embodiment of the other; for there _is_ a male and female side to all these, and the two genders correspond to, represent, affiliate with, derive their respective powers from, and are attracted to, those respective sides. Thus either, alone, is an Incompleteness; they belong to opposite side of nature, and it requires a bridge to span the amazing gulf that rolls between them. The magnetic materials for said bridge exists in _nearly_ all human beings. Its name is LOVE. Bridges are in great demand. There's room for more.

VI. No true man can help loving all true women; not in the grosser sense, but in the higher one of soul. Not such as lie a man out of his manhood, run him in debt, empty his purse, and rob him of his peace, until he actually jeopardizes his soul's salvation,--pretending to love him, but meaning not one word of it,--laughing at him in the sleeve, and triumphing in the knowledge of how smart she was, how great a fool was he. That's the sort of women who, from the year one, have driven hard bargains with the masculine portion of the race, and rushed many a good man down the hills of ruin and gloom, and horrid, blank despair. Nor are they all dead yet.

I have neither time, assistance, or inclination for moralizing; but little patience with "Scripture" quoters; none at all with the modern "reform" tribes of the land and age; besides which I cordially despise all women-haters on one side, and Wesnerites (man-haters) on the other; and no words of mine can express my utter abhorrence of the things miscalled Men, who practically regard woman as if she were nothing but a pleasure-vehicle, to be kissed, petted, and ill-treated in alternate slices. But I feel quite as much indignant contempt for that large class of women who are ever ready to use their beauty as a trap to catch male gudgeons; who look on all men as fair game, to be lied to, and played on, generally to the tune of rustling silks, and crisp band notes; and whose utter heartlessness belies the index of their sex. There's quite as many heartless shes as hes in the world; only that one soulless woman is a greater danger to the world than a dozen scoundrelly men; for her sex gives her points of advantage denied to all of the opposite gender. A good, true woman is a diamond; a bad and heartless one worse than Milton's Satan.

Sitting near me in the eating-house where I dined yesterday, were four grave men, deliberately traducing their mother's sex. They went into paroxysms of what they called "Fun" anent pregnancy, menstruation, and sexive matters generally. They, and millions like them everywhere, in every bar-room, hotel, stable, store, grocery, consider it "smart" and manly to, even before young boys, habitually blaspheme Deity and dishonor the mothers that bore them, by irreverent, flippant and obscene speech concerning the sex. Poor wretches who disgrace the forms they bear by speaking of woman as if she were nothing but a target for filthy tongues to hurl their venom at; or, at best, as destined victims to their own abominable lubricity; mere extinguishers of the bile-fires rioting in their own veins,--the venomous fever-passions of their own gross natures, and far more ignoble than those of the four-footed dogs that run our streets. It made me sick; it always did--to listen to the outrageous talk going on everywhere about women, whenever two or more human males of the "civilized" kind happen to get together for an hour. Even stately officials, fathers of families, do; and if not, at least often allow it in their presence, which is almost as bad. So almost universal is this foul talk, to be heard everywhere at any time,--ribald, coarse, obscene, and altogether devilish,--that it is no wonder that the public mind is debauched and totally demoralized.

It is a curious fact that people will talk smut, laugh heartily at coarse jokes and improbable stories concerning the eternal God's method of peopling the worlds, and filling up the starry domes beyond the grave, when of all human deeds it is the most sacred, serious, and laughless. No human being laughs then; for the weight of worlds rests upon human shoulders.

It is a bad sign any man hangs out when he makes "fun" of what ought to challenge his holiest emotions and most profound respect. There was a young man of the fun-making genus,--a fellow whose nature was inflamed nearly a year before his birth, and who kept it up to boiling-point by food and drink, and the secret books he first read, and then so artfully concealed, that the servant-girls were sure to find them,--read, get detected,--of course, by the owner,--result, destruction to poor she,--brag by he, who of course was petted and made much of, while his victim's head, in time hung low, for a bleeding heart was breaking. Well, this Lothario's eyes used to fairly glisten when they rested upon any young female form, and the burden of his talk was the victories he had won over too confiding women. Brag.

It so happened that he was one of a jury of inquest over the dead body of poor Maria Lee, a child of sixteen summers, whom a rich merchant of Loudon had betrayed, and then procured a double murder at the hands of an abortionist. Poor child! she bled to death from a skewer of steel run clean through both the uterus and its contents. The rich merchant paid some money;--some more in charity;--by-and-by joined the church, and his sin was forgotten. The medical practitioner went to jail for six months; was pardoned out in five weeks; and the babe went back to heaven in the arms of its slaughtered mother.

But there she lay, poor child, upon the long work-table of good Simon Scott, the carpenter, all pale and delicate as finest Parian marble or wax-work, and beautiful! O God, how immortally beautiful!--just as Deity had fashioned her before the rich merchant of Loudon and his friends, the doctor and death, had finished the work so fairly begun--finished her for the grave and heaven; for if ever its golden portals swing wide to admit a shining soul, surely its hinges will revolve like lightning to let in a ruined woman.

Well, the autopsy went on; the facts were disclosed; and while the surgeon plied his work, and a strong magnifying glass was handed round among the jurymen, none were so eager and earnest in scrutiny and question, as the fast young man,-- the general lover alluded to. He carefully examined lungs, brain, stomach, breasts, heart, uterus--all; and as he laid down the glass he muttered--and I--with the womb in my hand, and the knife between my teeth--echoed, from the floor of my soul, his words--"Murdered, by GOD! curse him,--THEM! and me, too, if ever I"--and there he stopped; but not till his oath was registered up there where vows are never broken, and nothing is forgotten. If I could, I certainly would have every male over fifteen witness just such a redemptive and impressive scene; and would take every boy through the wards of a hospital for syphilides. I would have every girl taught the long-forgotten truth that her soul is worth, at least, quite as much as her body; something they little dream of, so ardent is their worship at the shrine of Saint Frivole.

Had I been so instructed long years agone, I had escaped very many subsequent mistakes, and consequent misery; but I, like most others, was a long time in learning thoroughly the tremendous difference between the chaste desire of pure love, and the lurid fires of burning lust. I learned it at last; hence this, and my later books, which I trust will serve as beacons to warn mankind off sunken rocks and reefs long after these hands have returned to primal dust, and the soul that animates them is kneeling at the feet of the Redeeming God.

VII. From the earliest historical ages an unnatural custom has prevailed; and its results have been fearful,--sub rosa mainly, for the victims generally grieve, mourn, and die in silence. I refer to the abominable practice of old men marrying young girls. I know that the temptations,--youth and freshness on one side; influence, society, position, money, on the other,--are great indeed; but for all that, it is a something against which that same society ought to turn; and one that God Himself frowns down; for never a marriage among them all produced other fruits than discontent, jealousy, madness and despair.

Campbell, in that odd book "Hermippus, or the Sage's Triumph," lays it down that the old can regain many months or even years of life by consorting and cohabiting with the young. It is, and is not true. If it were possible for two people, one sixty, the other sixteen, to fully and mutually love each other, then the girl would help the man, and the man increase the girl's recuperative power. But, happily, girls of sixteen can't love sixty, nohow you can fix it. I knew a man in New York State, who literally drove his daughter, a thin, pale, waxen child of sixteen, into a hated marriage of sixty-five or thereabouts. Two years afterwards, a child was buried in the West, and four weeks afterwards the father bore his daughter's body to bury it and his happiness together in one grave on the hillside.

Were a man of that age to use means to thus get a daughter of mine, say twenty-five years ago, when I was young, I think there'd have been a third-class funeral in that town; for I regard it as a crime even worse than some sorts of murder; and here are my reasons why: It is safe to say, where occasionally the young girl marries an old man, and good results follow, that such cases are extraordinary, and altogether exceptional to an almost universal rule; because the old man's motive is to prolong his miserable existence at the expense of a fresh young life; and of course his "love!" is one of advantage, either money-wise or from gratitude, and therefore not real love at all; because in the very nature of things she can but feel an utter disgust, an awful and appalling horror and loathing at the bare thought, much less the sickening ordeal of fact.

Happiness is out of the question, and the cases exceedingly rare where they produce anything but misery. Nearly every one will at once see many of the reasons why; but there are some others not quite so self-apparent, and here they are. In marriage and its offices there must be a reciprocal play of electric and magnetic forces; for unless mutual, there's disaster just ahead, and sunken rocks all around, upon which that ship of wedlock is sure, sooner or later, to run aground; and in the wreck that follows some one is sure to be lost,--and that some one is a young wife, tired of an old, besotted worn-out man!

The great disparity of years, magnetism, vitality and life-force between such an ill-starred couple renders it utterly impossible for the young thing to have one single taste or desire in common with the old dotard she calls husband.

She cannot absorb, reciprocate or assimilate him, or aught pertaining to him, magnetically, or in any other way; and she even loathes the food he dotes on, and the liquids he consumes to keep his unnatural fever up.

The magnetic auras issuant from them are unlike, and to her repellent, after a time, if not at once. He consumes, absorbs, and assimilates the totality of her vital life, and at length she dies for sheer want of that whereof he robs her. But a still stronger protest is here: it is found in the well-known fact that the old and coarse magnetism of the man poisons both the body and soul of the young girl; seals up the fountains of her youth and reposive power; shuts the door of amative joy in her face; robs her of her rights as wife; suggests evil thoughts to her mind, and paves the way for her to yield heart and all else to whoever near her own age tries to win her, by giving her a kind of love she needs, and which is proper for one of her tender years.

Where the disparity is even twenty years it is infinitely far too great. Ten years' difference is a deal too much, and five the limit, save in the case of bloodless girls and very magnetic men; in which union the female thrives on the fresh vitality of the man. But, even in such cases, she must be blonde, and he the opposide--always; for if the reverse happens, she's a doomed woman, and he a physical imbecile, in five years' time at the utmost. In the case of ordinary December and May marriages he robs her of life; she gestates horror instead of affection; for in natural marriage souls blend and interfuse more or less perfectly after a time; and those who have lived unhappy lives often find out how well they loved at heart, after death comes tapping at the gate, if not before. Then it is: "Who'd have thought it?" but too late! Such antipodes cannot blend, because the girl is peach-downy, supple, gay, lithe and lightsome, but the man lithy, that is, limy, calcareous; and they cannot, will not mingle in any more intimate relations than that of father and daughter.

Some people have young souls in old bodies, in which case things are not so bad; but where such soul-youth does not exist, and the parties live in passable harmony, still there's great harm done,--in fact, constructive wificide, and this is the reason why,--a wife is apt to become a mother quicker by an old husband than a young one; because the old man's blood is cooler, his passion slower in culmination; and she is likely to conceive from sheer weariness, and physical and mental inability to guard herself; besides which, she never dreams of danger, or of the female finesses she would put in play against a younger husband.

If ever it is right to prevent conception, I believe it is in exceptional cases like this before us; for his old blood, through his child, courses through her veins, making her old prematurely; loading her down with the accumulated mental, physical and moral, magnetic and other diseases of all his long run of years. Besides which, his child is born old;--never knows what babyhood is, or childhood means. It looks, feels, is an oddity; knows no infantile days or pleasures, and is thus, by its own father, robbed and cheated out of its best and most halcyon days. But that's not the worst of it yet; for the offspring of January is sure to be nearly as calcareous as its father. Its bones are harder, firmer, more solid than is right; its cranium is broader, flatter, thicker, and dense as those of a grown man; and if the young mother escapes forceps-delivery, or a still worse operation, she may consider herself a fortunate woman. May God pity all such, and alas! thousands of such there are.

How often we hear the expression, "She tapped the fountains of his love." Well, the thing is possible, yet is seldom realized, for that can only be done when both are maritally conjoined while influenced by a passion born of perfect, deep, soul-founded love; and then! ah, then! the cup of human bliss is indeed full. Why? Because a portion of each soul becomes incorporate in the other, and the mystical blending--"they twain shall be one" --is complete.

But souls can be tapped without reciprocity, for the young wife's soul is drained from her, either directly as a sponge, by her old husband, or indirectly through the uterine and vaginal diseases sure to be her lot sooner or later; for the fluids of the twain will not, <u>cannot</u> blend, except in so far forth as to innoculate the poor young thing with malignant poison, by which I do not here mean syphilis, but I do mean that worse poison resultant from chemical incompatibility, mental and affectional disgust and repulsion, which leave ulcers and corrosions in their train, with death in the foreground. Gentlemen M. D.'s, here's the origin of evil; for even if the husband is not old, but only a hellion to her, she's your patient straightway, and you have a fine chance for the sale of lotions, washes, pessaries, supporters, and all the other vast paraphernalia born of non-love, "in the auld house et hame."

Birth months. Children conceived in May, June, July, August and September, and who, therefore, are born in February, March, April, May, and June, are unquestionably, better constituted and will live longer, have more character and power than when the double events occur in other months; because nature and weather are more propitious at the start. Conceptions occurring in the morning hours are a myriad degrees better than when that event occurs at other periods.

A person's shadow on the wall in a room, by lamp-light, will reveal more of that party's <u>real</u> character than all the phrenology extant, and in its minute phases, too; just as a peculiar smile, observation, movement, or tone of voice will sometimes tell in a second more of a person's real self, than an acquaintance of fifty intimate years would otherwise.

Gender in the human being is a very different thing from gender in the animate kingdoms below the grade of man. In the beasts it means propagation, mainly for food purposes; but in man it stands for, and implies, a great deal more, as will be seen hereinafter.

At this point I wish to pick a flaw or two in the reasonings of the popular physiologists and phrenologists of the day, every one of whom urge their moral pleas mainly upon the ground that the marital-functional nuptive rite of the human being is precisely on a par with the creative act of beasts; that is, that God intended it in man as in animals, to be solely and only a propagative function,--that, and nothing more. It is for generative ends only, and the nervous state precedent to, and succeeding it, is but the natural spur to the God-foreseen result; therefore, say they, the sacred nuptium is permissible <u>only</u> when both parents desire to add one more unit to the great world's population. Now these philosophers either are conscious hypocrites, teaching what they don't believe; else they <u>think</u> us fools, and we <u>know</u> they are.

I have seen a book, of nearly a thousand mortal pages, and that doctrine was the whole gist and burden of its labored and lame argument: lame, for its author shows in a hundred places that he don't believe his own logic; he continually confutes himself, and the completest refutation of the absurdity is to be found in the words: IT IS NOT TRUE! Why? because man is <u>not</u> a beast, and is not governed by identical laws; but comes under, and is played upon, and moved by, higher ones altogether than such as rule in the kingdom of beasts, birds, reptiles, fish and insects.

In those realms, sex is an instinct, a periodical function and appetite. In man, it is a fact of soul; a principle, and a mystical and divine power, altogether superior to the passing furore of beasts that perish and are known no more; and it means more in his case than it does in all other departments of the sentient world, singly or combined.

I here throw down the gauntlet, and state, boldly and squarely, right in the teeth of all the so-called scientists on earth or under heaven, that the sexive principle, habitude, and instinct in the human is not in very many respects identical with that of the non-human inhabitants of the globe we live on; on the contrary, in us it means, implies, and leads to immeasurably more and deeper things than the average thinker ever dreams of or imagines. In the organic kingdoms outside of the human, the instinct is blindly obeyed, and selfseeking there, as everywhere else, and not propagation at all, is the all-powerful impelling motive, if motive there be. Bears and horses, cats and fishes, dogs and flies, and every other living thing bearing gender, invariably trouble themselves not at all concerning increase of family, or prolongation of the species, until such increase appears; by which time Nature has brought a new instinct and passion into play. Parallels between man and beasts are not correct or just; for in beasts sexive and parental instincts are separate affairs,--in man they coexist. In beasts the offspring and parents become disunited at maturity; in the human, the practical relationship lasts not only to the gates of the grave, but leaps the barriers of death, and flourishes in the far-off-heaven; and will till the universe grows old, and Time himself topples with hoary age.

We are gravely told that animals obey the impulse once a year, or season, as the case may be; that man ought to go and do likewise, but he won't; nor will these self-same philosophers,--I'm sure of that!--especially in their own especial and particular cases; because man is a myriad grades or degrees higher and finer in organization than the animals; and his nature calls for more than theirs possibly can, or does.

They obey the instinct; it is the spur to propagation; but the beast, just like man up to a given point, risks all for the spur, and cares nothing for subsequent consequences, but leaves them for nature to attend to; and she does it like the kind, dear old mother that she is! In the average human, the spur is all that's cared for at the time; albeit consequences are foreseen, and due provisions made; for we marry and mate,--beasts only mate, and marriage is unknown to them. Not one human couple in fifty millions propagate on purpose, for as a rule it is impossible; not so with beasts; for one hour seals the origin of the progenal result; and men mark the periods, and know to a day when to look for the new animal; but we can only guess the time when our eyes shall gladden at the sight of the new soul God sends to cheer and bless us.

We are all accidents! --and not a few of us unhappy ones,--I, for instance. To apply rules to man applicable to animals alone, is an insult to the human race. Stirpiculture, or the rearing of better children, will never succeed upon agricultural, stock-farm, or barnyard principles.

True, nature requires a rich soil to produce high grades of fruit, whether human or other sorts; but in the former she requires the richest of fertilizers, and its name is LOVE. Give her that, and she'll make your eyes glisten at the beauty of the work she does; deprive her of it, and crab apples are the result; and a human crab is the gnaliest and most bitter fruit in all God's garden. In the lower kingdoms nature does her best to produce a superior grade of body. In the human world she works wholly to produce a loftier order of soul in its triplicate divisions,--intellect, imagination, emotion; and is never satisfied until success fairly crowns her efforts. A handsomer race, physically, I never saw than the modern Greek; nor such a perfect race of scamps; for your Romaic rascal can discount all others on the earth, if we except these of New York and Boston, who are lords paramount in all sorts of villany, from the picking of a pocket to stealing a railway.

"I guess I'll make an experiment--only just one," says many a man; and he makes it; the upshot being that from the instant he does so, home ceases to be such to him, and any woman's presence and activities is preferable to those of his wife. But why? Simply because his imagination has rendered the other woman's charms five thousand times more important than they actually are, and yet they are sufficient to enable him to draw disparaging estimates between solid wife and fleeting mistress. New fire, strange blood, has inspired him with fresh passion, and he don't care for the old wife, in presence of the new harlot; and so he abuses one, and lavishes all he has on the other. But you just wait a bit; we'll see how it works in the end,--and so will he; and happily, too, if it be not too late. Three weeks' experience with a mistress will cure almost any man of that sort of weakness, if he have not, by that time, buried his wife's love in a grave ten thousand resurrectionless fathoms deep! He did not know that the strange, new, exciting magnetism meant death to his home-love, desolation to his hearth-stone, isolation to his heart, and ruin to his happiness; yet it did and does, and eternally will, because it is scortatory, malign, fiery, and while it effectually displaces and kills home-love, it fails to satisfy; and its end is bitter ashes. In a weak moment, many a man, fired with sudden and electric fire, has fallen into passion's dreadful snare, and for a moment of delirious joy has bartered off a whole life of happiness; for when once one indulges in stolen fruit, which may be sweet, but is never so good as that which grows on one's own trees, the habit becomes fixed, and "just once" lands him--or her--neck-deep in perdition! His talk--or hers--ought to be not "Just once;" but, "It's all very fine, sir or madam--but it won't pay, and--I'll see you in--well, you can guess where--first." That's human talk!

IX. As already said herein, marriage--by which term hereinafter, whenever and wherever printed in italic letters, I mean the nuptive union of the sexes; and it is only really nuptive when love is the prompter; otherwise it is a desecration and worse than beastly profanation--is productive of an entire series of effects and results aside from the perpetuatory or propagative one wherein man and animals are alike, and therein only; for in them sex distinctions are, of course, merely bodily, while in the human it involves and embraces the entire vast domain of both body, soul, and the interwoven spirit. In the non-human races the marriage office ceases when the germ is lodged; but in the human being its offices only begin at that point; for its results continue, whether the rite be propagative or no, not only through an arc or chord of fleeting time; but they, the results, stretch away into and through the infinite and eternal spaces, and probably cease not, but endure forever and forever.

If there is one thing more certain, after death, than another, it is that every immortal man and woman of us is bound and doomed to have all love and lust escapades universally known. We are destined to meet all with whom we have been carnally intimate in any degree, from that of pure and gentle love, to the horror and violence of inhuman rape. Every carnal association affects us, leaves its mark on us and the other; and some there be who will be astonished that their whole career was turned on earth in consequence of such or such an act--fact; and that defeat followed them in after life by reason of the invisible presence of some wronged victims, married or not. Nor is this all, for every escapade mingles magnetisms more or less; and a man in New York in 1875 may feel the life going out of him day by day, himself not even suspecting that a dozen or more women in as many different parts of the earth, or even from the spaces, are at that instant thinking of him, yearning for him, voluntarily or not, and are drawing out his soul just as easily and surely as he drew their life through honeyed lips ten, twenty-or thirty years before; wherefore libertinism and cyprianism are attended with strange penalties.

In the truly human being--the non-savage and non-barbaric specimens of the races --marriage never degrades the parties either in their own or each other's eyes; but it purifies the heart and soul, uplifts them to the Father, is really Pulchritudinem Divitiis Conjunctam, as it ever should be, that is, Beauty and Divinity joined as one; it therefore becomes in this mystic light, instantly, the holiest and most effective of all possible prayers, hence the most potent and tremendous energy in the entire material and hyper-physical universe.

Let me tell you, reader, how and why this is so. But before I do it, just look at Jugurtha, Attila, Nero and the Bonapartes, with scores of other scourges of God and the human world,--called into being in an instant of time to lash the earth to agony,--a prayer of evil-guild, silently, but effectively uttered at the instant of their descent into the matrices that thereafter gave them to the world. Is not this sufficient to prove the truth of what I call a most effective prayer? Turn the page and behold a Christ, St. John, Buddha, Confucius, and see the results of peaceful prayer uttered silently too, exactly as in the other case or cases. But there are other proofs:--

X. That the creative function is the highest force in us, as it is in and of the Deity, admits of no denial; for it ought to be, if it is not, a perfectly self-evident proposition, axiomatic in its nature, and therefore requiring no attempt toward its demonstration; for it is palpably clear that two principles are inter-woven and reciprocally acting and reacting upon each other everywhere and in all things in the universe whereof we know. These principles are male and female, and both alike are manifestations or modes of the superlative and ineffable Master-Potency, Power, Energy, or over-lapping, subtending, underlying, crowning essence of the universal realm, call it by whatever name you will; and it, the bisexive energy, displayed all around, demonstrates itself to be the Imperial Force of all that is. To it all things are subsidiary. To it all things bow, bend, acknowledge the peremptory sway of, and without which the ALL THAT is would become a blank and star-less void, as terrible as eternal Night itself; more cheerless than the grave; a radical nihility, so utterly benumbed and benumbing that destruction itself were tame in comparison.

God is supposed to be a dual being; so is man; but Deity is dual in a double sense; that is to say, God is positively male, and positively female; while also, as in man, all the masculine or electric attributes of God are pervaded by the magnetic feminine principle. We all know that the better side of man is the she or mother side; and that from it spring all the major elements of both his greatness and his goodness; and we admire an intellectual giant, while we adore a loving man; because from his love, not his intellect, arises all of goodness, inspiration, aspiration, generosity of soul which characterizes him. We are pleased with the Platos, but we worship the Christs. It is the softer side of soul that generates moral or any other real grandeur, and makes great deeds possible to man; for it is that alone which has power to transmute man the savage into man the incarnate demi-god.

All sentient and non-sentient being is more or less pervaded, according to capacity, with what I may call the male and female aura or effluence of the great Supreme, the unknown and unknowable Deity; and all these incarnations of the original Life, save only the human, are distinctively and radically either wholly male or female. True, there are among the lower types and forms of organic life, a few seeming exceptions, as the so-called hermaphrodites; but, in reality, such are apparent only; for examination in the light of modern science proves all such organisms to be a union of the two principles in a single body, and not a fusion, by any means; and that the male side fecundates the other. But a human, canine, equine, bovine, or any other bisexed being is an utterly impossible thing, all those affirm-ing to the contrary notwithstanding. There are and have been malformations claimed to be proofs of dual gender, but they were really one or the other.

Below man, while the sexes are distinct, in him, as a principle, not a physical fact, they for the first time fuse and blend, at least on this, and probably upon every other soul-bearing world in the eternal vaults of space. It is this blending of sex in soul that makes us what we are; for were we not half mother, our father's influence upon us would drive the world to chaos in a year; and all that is really excellent in us is the capacity to love and grow; and nothing is capable of love but man.

There is a curious proof of the soundness of the foregoing statement, yet it seems to have escaped the notice of the scientists: I allude to the notorious fact that some womb-bearers, wives and mothers too, are females only physically; while spiritually, mentally, morally, psychically, and every other way but one, they were and are wholly hard, cold, masculine beings, living contradictions of the statements their forms and functions declare to the world. On the other hand, many who wear the Phallic sign of gender are no more men in soul, than is the little romping lass of five brief summers a full-grown, full-blown woman.

Such people are human monstrosities, and were born wrong. If you ask me why and how, listen, and the story shall be fully, fairly, yet briefly told:--

XI. If a human monad, or "zoosperm," from the left side of the father, encounters a ripe ovum from the left side of the mother, that fact determines the gender. It will be male. (See a section on this very point in the sequel.) Reverse the case, and reverse results will follow, invariably,--though how to do it on purpose is a somewhat difficult problem to solve; yet it can be done, and is far more easily accomplished than at first sight may appear.

Now accidents and inversions, aversions and perversions, occur in all departments of nature, but none so glaring and positive as are encountered among human beings; and the mis-sexing of them is one of the most common forms of mal-construction; for it frequently happens that a female zoosperm, which is the living monad, or soul-germ, supplied by the male parent, and clothed in flesh by the mother, is unable to reach a corresponding female ovum, and is compelled to be expurgated, or enter one from the wrong ovarium; in which case the body of the child will be of one gender, its soul and spirit of the opposite one. In a normally peopled world such monstrosities, which now abound all about us, could not possibly be coaxed, drawn or forced into existence as a human incarnation; and it is utterly impossible for such to appear at all upon the world's stage, if parents wholly, or even partially, love each other; and when such miscreations are seen, it is proof stronger than holy writ that love did not rule in the hour of their generation. Now I have affirmed as a truth that true human sex is primarily of soul, and secondarily of body; hence it follows that the post-mortem state of such mixed beings is not a permanent duration of their condition here; for gradually the true sex of the individual asserts its native force and power; the physical, or rather hyper-physical being is gradually toned down or up to his or her true condition; the malformation begins to lessen by slow degrees, its signs to disappear, and then they assume either the perfected states of man, or that of woman; their angularities are worn away, and the beings who on earth belied the story of their true gender become as other normal beings are; the memory of what they once were fades away, and they take rank among the truly human.

XII. The philosophers of my day were generally blind to, or oblivious of, the fact that the greatest degree of human excellence in offspring can never be attained, even though the parents are physically perfect; but that a wife every way inferior except in love, loving and being loved, will give the world such children as will prove themselves, indeed, truly great, and grandly good. The strongest force, mental power, and creative energy in the domains of science, art, philosophy, and literature everywhere, is invariably manifested by those who have the most loved and loving mother in them--people whose feminine or magnetic side entirely balances, or slightly overweighs the electric or masculine moiety of their being. He is everywhere most welcomely greeted, caressed and influential, who is most magnetic, or female,--not in the effeminate sense, but in the glowing, radiant heartfulness of his nature,-- is one who has not the most intellect, but most gentleness, love, affection, comboned with it. Take the real or ideal Nazarene, per example, who perished for loving mankind in the 49th year(see Bunsen); or, going back of his alleged times, leap the chasmal years to the Bo-Tree man, and scores of others equally good, if not so famous; and whenever you find a great soul in a male body, depend upon it he is more than half mother; for it is the woman of such people that gives them power, genius, mental pith, and enables them to write their names in adamantine letters upon the grand facade of the universal human temple! It is equally true, that those are the most glorious and glorified of the other gender, who were, or are, not the most electric, masculine and intellectual, but the most tender, pure, loving and feminine in all respects.

XIII. But you say, "We women are not perfect yet. We want perfect offspring! Some of us have not just such husbands as we wish. We are too pure to sully our souls, no matter how great the temptation may be. We prefer to abide in marriage as we have found it. Some children, the results of such marriage, are not what we would have them; therefore, pray tell us how to improve upon them hereafter."

The answer is simple, the method easy. Never run the risk of conception, except you be mentally and physically prepared,--not for it--but to utterly banish everything but the pure desire of your soul to give him all the love then--at the marriage--that you can, and wish, will, pray, desire, decree, that the result, if such be, may be modelled after your soul's loftiest ideal. Keep up this all the time of gestation if possible, and the operation of the law just revealed will conceive you and the world that nothing equal to it ever fell from human lips or pen.*

Please recall the incident of myself and the little fairy. Well, that is worth worlds to you, for suppose that, instead of wishing, willing, desiring, decreeing perfect offspring, you exert it to redeem your husband, to kindle up his love for you, for home, for his own fireside. But perhaps you care little or naught for all that; still you want health, beauty, strength and long life, all of which are achievable by the same magic means; else in such moments--during power absence--all these

---

* Complaints on both sides -- deep, if not loud -- are made about want of passional fervor, and affectional ardor; and unjustly often in both cases, for each takes especial pains and particular care not to strive in any way to bring about a different nerval condition. I once asked an Arab physician in Egypt, if such things existed among the dark races, in the harems, or amidst the nomads. Yes, he said; but seldom. And when it does, the entire character of the food is changed; abstinence l'amour, is persisted in; and when both these fail, the weak one is by the other mesmerized with a long-fringed feather, tenderly, lightly, slowly drawn down the spine breasts, and across all parts of the well-washed cuticle, so lightly as scarce to touch! There is a peculiar and powerful conducting property in such a feather, and never yet in 2,000 years has it been known to fail. In your cold land (America) the aphrodisiacal treatment should be accompanied with the internal cordials I told you of; and Allah, precious Allah! will speedily bless the unfruitful pair; for a soul begotten without fervor had better never come to earth, for it will be wretched and a curse to itself until its flight toward the Ghillem. There is more on these points, but they cannot be given herein.

are lost, and another nail driven home into your coffin. Obey this grand law, follow out this splendid rule, and ere long you will find that your power will perceptibly augment, most assuredly be felt, and before you are well aware of it will work such a redemptive change as shall bathe your house in pearly glory. This principle will win him from all others, and kindle love where all was cheerless, wintry blasts before. I know it, have seen it tried, and am confident that she who persistently tries cannot by any possibility fail! Of course the same power can be used by husbands. It is simply substituting active soul-will, love, for indifference, passive body and sufferance; but, as sure as death, here is the starting point of a divine life!

XIV. But how about promiscuity or variety in the love relations of life?

Reply: There may be those who can find happiness therein. I never could, and do not want to make the experiment. My reasons will be seen further on in this work; but before we come to that, I wish at this point once for all to say that I believe in free speech, and wide-spread agitation of all questions, social and sexual included; but while I champion the right, I by no means espouse the cause of those champions, for I must abide by the laws of my own individuality, and it is my firm belief that love-variety in any shape is injurious to soul and body, and that the highest point of human power can only be reached by those who are amatively true to each other; for purity alone is the price of power, the secret of soul-might, and it is the coin accepted at God's exchange for such glories as he keeps especially for true and earnest souls. I write these lines here because at this moment a paper lies, in two senses, before me, which distinctly says that I am an advocate of certain opinions which my entire life has been spent in confuting--as witness every book I have ever written, every speech I have ever spoken. Having put this on record, I now drop all that matter,--both the falsehoods and the falsifiers, forever and forevermore, as being beneath either notice or contempt.

The demand for novelty, "variety," or change in love matters, is not a part of being, and only foiled zealots--feminine--and worse things in male shape, ever started such malignant slanders against me,--human perverts of both genders, who, failing to induce me to pervert certain knowledge and powers to their base ends and systems, sought to injure me by the meanest and most contemptible of all possible scandal. But I laughed at the cyprians, and snapped my fingers at the rogues in grain. I am only capable of one love at one time, but that time to me fastens its further end to the eternities just ahead of us all. Temporary attractions departed with my dead years, thank Heaven, and their fruitage was ever bitter, bitter.

XV. So true is the statement concerning the vastly greater and superior relative value of the Feminine Principle, that even in the present lubricious age, when woman is almost everywhere wrongly rated, badly educated, and worse placed than she should be, there is still, deep down in the hearts of most, even the coarsest men, a measure of gallant respect, which occasionally gleams forth in noble deeds, and brace championage of the sex, in such guise as to give great hope for fuller and better things by and by.

The chivalry of all ages has not only proved feal to her and acknowledged its dependence upon her smile and frown, boldly fighting for her right or wrong, then, in the foretime, just as now; but has taken especial pains to celebrate individual women and the universal sex; and this worship of the second, if not the primal element of nature, has been carried further, and been more general, than the modern reader might imagine. For instance, who among those who peruse this essay would believe, save on most indubitable evidence, that the very flower of one, nay, two of the leading nations of the world this day do homage to the emblem of Womanhood? Yet, nevertheless, such is the fact; for the noblest regalia, the highest honor won and worn by

Britain's proudest men, is to be acknowledged to be worthy of wearing the royal insignia of the Garter; while the Fleur-de-lis of France, meaning something precisely similar, has been the boast of her noblest for centuries.

Now what does that same Garter mean? Is there any one so uninformed as to imagine for a moment that it signifies the mere string worn about the leg to keep nice stockings from dragging about fair heels? If so, here let that absurd notion be rectified, for the emblem signifies no such puerile nonsense at all. The motto of the order, Princely and Imperial, is in these days written _Honi_ _soit_ _qui_ _mal_ _y_ _pense_, translated to mean--to the uninitiated, outside world--"Evil to him who evil thinks," which, in a certain sense, is true and correct, for it _does_ mean _that_, but not at all in the manner that people generally think it does. It has no reference to general evil whatever, but it expressly means evil of a certain and peculiar kind; for it so happens that the real first word is not _Honi_ but _Yoni_, and that means nothing more nor less than the feminine organs of generation, coupled with their periodic functions.

Now, while in all ages of the world's known history, a grand majority of all mankind, including all modern Christians, worship brute force, and luxuriate in varied forms of Phallic or Priapic worship, and the Phallus is the male organ of generation and Priapus was its god; while they, I repeat, adored and adore CREATIVE ENERGY as symbolized by the emblem alluded to, of which all steeples, towers, beacons, light-houses, monuments, cenotaphs, and May and liberty poles and flagstaffs, are but symbols; while that form of worship-- of the male god--has been, and still is, almost universal, except in its coarser, grosser forms, in our days, there have been wanting other human hosts who did, and still do, pay homage at the shrine of the Feminine Deity, whose symbol is the rose, discus, arch, oval, and dome; and in some barbaric lands the organ itself, openly, as in all lands _sub_ _rosa_ or secretly; but in civilized America in its most low and disgusting form, for thousands seem to adore no god but Lust, and practically worship at no other shrine. Witness the universal prevalence of concubinage and harlotry, gotten to be even a licensed thing, and everywhere a winked-at adjunct of civilization, to the debasement of man and blasphemy of God and Womanhood, as of yore in Greco-Roman days; but this time entailing dreadful penalties instead of rewards upon its multitudinous devotees; for not even the triplicate king evils, opium, alcohol, and tobacco, inflict such awful punishments upon their votaries as Cypriana, the salacious Diva of Harlotdom. To return to the point at issue: In some form or other, most of us worship the disc symbol; and four-fifths of the intelligent world is to-day agitated, not merely concerning the symbol and its nature, but about the tremendous mysteries it shadows, and the vast volume of meanings that underlie and are embosomed within it. I trust, before this task of mine is finished, to demonstrate it to be in very truth what it claims,--a new revelation of sex, and to make one successful effort to remove the subject far above the muck, slime and filth hitherto attendant upon it; for if there is a divine thing on earth, it ought to be LOVE--its laws, rules, phases and moods, --knowledge of which is a redeeming power.

I alluded to the universality of sex emblems, and will close this section by calling attention to our national banner; for the American flag floating from a staff is one of the finest illustrations of the double glory in the world; because the staff symbolizes the Phallus; its cord represents the chain of love binding the sexes together; the folds of bunting are emblems of woman's floating drapery; the blue means his, her, _their_ mutual truth and fidelity; the white; her purity; the red symbolizes her periodicity and ability to defy death by repeopling the world. I shall allude to other colors in another section.

XVI. A true negro never reaches a stage of mental development enabling him to master metaphysics; nor at maturity does he ever surpass in capacity the adolescent average Anglo Saxon; but in the power of maintaining love at high tide he can discount all the white races of the globe! I make this observation at this point for two reasons: first, to draw a parallel; second, to tell the reader that in my medical practice, in nervo-vital diseases, I often prescribe. "Negro meetings, and fifty cents in the plate" for being thereby benefited. They did so, these pale, haggard wives and chlorotic girls, shout, get glorious, and fill the room with a rich and healthy magnetism, every inhalation of which, to the sick ones, is worth a month's life, and a ton of doctor's stuff thrown in. Now for the other point: No sooner does an American boy get on his first pair of pants than he has prurient notions right straight alone, and takes good care to demonstrate them with chalk upon the walls and fences everywhere. Now this is not so dreadful after all,--for such antics characterize all young animals, -- provided his elders would take him in hand and teach him the true meaning of the origin of the strange ideas which from morbid nature, inculcation, precept and example of his associates he has imbibed, but does not comprehend.

I have said that this nation was the most passional one on earth. But then you know that nations and individuals are exactly alike; moved by the same forces, governed by the same principles, prompted by the same motives; and remember too, that this nation is but a boy yet, not out of its teens; hence, its universal pudicity is not to be wondered at; nor that its principal, most sincere and best-paid-for worship is, and for some time to come yet will be, at the passional shrine, in or out of wedlock. The same thing prevails all over the globe, and likely for the same reason; i. e., because as yet it is but a baby-world! At all events its worship is of the character already set forth; and its best men have been the most earnest devotees; for somehow or other, there is not and never has been a really great man in it but who has been more or less chargeable with practices not accordant with the strictest rules of nun-ship or monk-hood--which is oftener--in results--monkey-hood instead.

XVII. Hargrave Jennings, of England, the eminent Rosicrucian, writing upon the subject of the Garter, and before quoting Ashmole in regard to the same matter, observes: "All the world knows the chivalric origin of the Most Noble of the Garter. It arose in a princely act, rightly considered princely, when the real, delicate, inexpressibly high-bred motive and its circumstances are understood, which motive is systematically and properly concealed. Our great King Edward III. picked from the floor, with the famous words of the motto of the Order of the Garter, the "garter," or, as we interpret it, by adding a new construction with hidden meanings, the "garder" (gaurder, P. B. R.), (or especial cestus, shall we call it?) of the beautiful and celebrated Countess of Salisbury, with whom, it is supposed King Edward was in love." In other words she dropped a cloth which men ought never to behold; and Edward acted the part of a true gentleman, in preserving her from ridicule and shame, by turning an accident fools would giggle at, into one commanding profound reverence and chivalric respect from all who pride themselves on being men.

Old Elias Ashmole, the very highest British authority on the points here involved, writing about them, says: "The Order of the Garter, by its motto, seems to challenge inquiry, and defy reproach. Everybody must know the story that refers the origin of the name to a piece of gallantry; either the Queen or the Countess of Salisbury having been supposed to have dropped one of those very useful pieces of female attire at a dance. (Here follows some Latin, the gist of which I have already given in the conclusion of the last section. P. B. R.) The ensign of the order, in jewelry or enamel, was worn originally on the left arm. Being in the form of a bracelet to the arm, it might possibly divert the attention of the men from the reputed original; it might be dropped and resumed without confusion; and the only objection I can see to the use of such an ornament is the hazard of mistake from the double meaning of the term periscelis, which signifies not only a _garter_, but _breeches_, which our English ladies never wear."

That settles the point. The garter was a _girder_, which the lady dropped; and the true gentleman picked it up, pinned it to his breast, and challenged the world's respect for himself and woman forever and forevermore. Glorious Edward!

XVIII. Isn't it curious that the generality of even educated people fail to see that the idea of sex as a principle, and in _all_ its implications, runs through everything, even language? In French there's no _it_, as with us, but everything is _il_ or _elle_,--her or she. We all know that human speech is the result of the gradual development of the race through ages of time; its different forms being determined by the differences of latitude, soil, climate, physical and other concomitant surroundings. Letters are but external symbols of human thought; and in them all two basic predominate--i.e., the thought; and in them all two basic ideas predomin- ate--i.e., the male and female. The letter D and its equivalents, the Egyptian hieroglyph and hieratic figure, and the Phoenician one likewise, is but the feminine symbol, more or less perfectly drawn, according to the ability of the scribes or sculptors who made them. Thus also -- and nearer nature -- are their equivalents of the Roman R; while their N, L, and she, are unquestionably suggested by the phallus, or lingam, the opposite idea. And so it is all through the entire list of alphabets, ancient and modern; some letters representing one emblem, others its opposite, and still others the _union_ of the two. Instance the Archaic alphabet, Greek, Phoenician, Italic, as they existed from 1,000 to 600 years before Christ's date--for the Aleph, Beth, Gimel, Daleth, He, Var, Zyin, Cheth, Kaph, Teth, Lamed, Samekh, Ayin, and Tav; and their English, Phenician, Greek and Italic equivalents, as unmistakably emblematize the above three ideas, as that rain tells of growth in field, forest and fen! What is the soft, sweet, flowing circle or ring, but the symbol of Faith, Eternity, Eternal Love, Magnetism,--the YONI,--the female emblem--the letter O? What is the letter I or the figure I, but the symbol of generative power,--the lingam, or male? Ay, all letters are but interchanges, interminglings of the two original forms--the I or male, and the O or female ideas.

For instance, B is two-thirds female, one-third male; C is mainly female; D is both sexes; Q suggests union; and in fact, all letters convey the same meaning in clear, or less clear form.

XIX. The Lingam, Linga or Lingum (male organ-worship), is but the reverse of the discal or oval worship. The dome everywhere is but the female idea; the minaret represents the male; and as said before, actually the colors of all our flags, red, white and blue, green and yellow, are representative of the same, or Garter Idea; the first two meaning the spiritual purity and sacrificial blood of woman; the blue already explained; the green representing the result of the union of male and female --production, fertility, growth; and the yellow typifying ripeness, or the first completion of the destiny ordained to both.

XX. Torches, flambeaux, and fireworks everywhere symbolize sexual, therefore creative passion (and what this last means will be seen hereinafter; for it is _not_ limited to the generation of progeny). They typify vaguely to some, clearer to others, the strange, inner mystic FIRE which, unlike all other forms of flame, has its origin in God, and its flow from _within us,_ _not_ from without; for passion rises in the mind when normal,--in the soul; not the body, save when our natures are in- verted; and even then its fountain is in the unholy soul, before it leaps to the still more unholy body. Desire is _always_ first metaphysical before it is material in human kind; but when the conscience and moral poles are reversed, the spark that explodes the mental flame may be, and often is, sent from the body first to the soul. Thus certain foods or drinks generate an excess of caloric in the nervous ganglia of the reproductive system; a spark--spontaneous combustion--leaps thence to the brain, the soul catches fire, and hurls its masses of lurid flame through the cerebrum, cerebellum, spinal cord, ovaria, prostate gland, testes or vagina--and--draw the curtain o'er the dreadful scene!

XXI. Just as sex runs through all nature so does it obtain of nations, tribes, peoples and ages; some are entirely female or male in their genius, art, literature, and general specialties; and so plainly does this truth manifest itself that I do not care to occupy time in proving it. But this will I say: The most masculine nations tend greatest to feminine worship; and, per contra, the ideal of the feminine peoples is the masculine worship.

Finally, the most masculine man adores at the female shrine, and his god is far more she than he; while the most feminine woman worships the most masculine man. Thus here, there, and everywhere the two universal principles seek each other, blend, fuse, intermingle, and unwittingly obey the mighty dual law!

XXII. Love between human beings of opposite sexes is of two general kinds: 1st, that in which passion is not an integrant, such as the love between parent and child; that which is wholly amicive or purely friendly; that which is platonic or purely spiritual, ethereal, based upon affinities of taste, similitudes of soul; that which is founded upon gratitude; and, lastly, that which is wholly and absolutely mystical--the don't-know-why-but-it-is-so kind of feeling--and which, while it may be a limited extent gratified on earth, yet its full fruition can only be achieved, felt and realized after both shall have become citizens of the country of disembodied souls. Now it often happens that people in whom this sort of love exists mistake its nature and significance; imagine that they were born for each other; and, so they are, but not for the life below. They marry, and, to their first surprise, and subsequent horror, discover that for all the purposes of matrimony one is oil, the other water, without a particle of mental lime to combine and fuse the two together, and thereby form a true kalsomate of soul.

> "I think the pity of this earthly life
> Is love. So sighs a singer of the day
> Whose pensive strain my sympathetic lay
> Sadly prolongs. Alas! the endless strife
> Of Love's sweet law with cold Convention's rules;
> The loving souls unloved; the perfect mate,
> After long years of yearning, found--too late!
>
> "The treason of false friends; the frown of fools;
> The fear that baffles bliss in beauty's arms;
> The weariness of absence; and the dread
> Of lover, or of love, untimely dead, --
> Musing on these, and all the direful harms
> That hapless human hearts are doomed to prove,
> I think the pity of this life is love!"

So do I. But even a greater pity exists where, fired by the most ardent hopes, one or both find out that not a real tie of soul binds the twain together. Then comes the unveiling; and, my God, what an awful, horrible spectre stands frowning where each expected to behold and hold--she an Adonis, he a perfect Hebe!

When the mistake is made such parties marvel and wonder how on earth it can be so; and why the actual marriage produces effects so utterly foreign to their expectations and hopes. In the union of two such there is a compatibility of spirits to a great extent, but none whatever on the amative plane,--the sex of form; for the actual fact of marriage produces utter dissatisfaction to him, horror, pain, mental anguish, disease and lingering death to her. This generates discord and despair, general unhappiness, and is almost sure to drive the man to the house of the strange Woman, and his wife either to insanity, the grave, or the arms of a lover who can affiliate with her to some extent, at least upon the external or mainly senuous plane; and the upshot of the matter is divorce and two wretched lives. Now, in my travels up and down the lanes of Marriage-land, I have seen scores of just such cases; and there are other scores, ay, millions that I have not seen, and of whose terrible secret no one but themselves are aware; and sometimes they do not know what alis them, and attribute their distresses to a thousand causes, not one of which is the real and true one.

When, further on in this New Revelation, I shall analyze the matter, hundreds who read it will see the real point, and, probably, make no effort to better their sad condition. From such unions as these spring a class of children so utterly angular and deficient that the marvel is they ever find peace at all on earth, or enjoy a happy hour.

XXIII. The second general kind of love between the sexes may be numbered ONE and TWO. The first of which is the exact opposite, in nearly all respects, of that just described in Section 22d. It is just as earnest, honest, and deceptive, as the other, but is far more endurable, because there is a better cohesion between them than in the other case; their lives are evener, their marriage satisfactory; their offspring more adapted to life on earth, and in society; their own physical health and that of their children is better; and their union will last longer and produce generally better results, albeit said union is quite as far from being right and proper as anything can well be.

In the first case, to use a meaning metaphor, the first couple only met each other upstairs, in the garret; they only fused in the brain. They could not affiliate downstairs--in the passional rooms of the house marriage; although they were compelled to descend once in a while, it was something to be gotten over as quickly as possible, and to be only remembered with a shudder by her, a smothered malediction by him.

In the other case it was kitchen and cellar life all the time; a monotony endurable certainly, but very unsatisfactory for all that; for it so happens that although some of us overvalue body, its adjuncts, functions and offices, yet, being human, we require a little intellect, soul and emotion with our lives; cannot be contented with body only, and feel the need of a little sour leavening to season the dry bread of earthly being. Such couples grow tired of each other; of the monotony; and either party of such a firm will strangely take to other persons who manifest qualities and powers, which, from their own state of woul-starvation, they know how to appreciate! The origin of such marriages takes its rise in physics purely. He is stout, magnetic, robust, full of fire, and passional auras envelop him round about; and passion always exaggerates both the properties and qualities of the object upon whom its eyes are cast; mentally endows it with what it has not, and never will have; and at the same time revels in an insane dream of fancied joys, destined never to be realized, because his whole being is in such a red-hot fever, that, could he actualize his desire, death would stop him instantly, because nothing human could endure such a poignancy as he hopes to enjoy.

She is young, round-limbed, rosy-cheeked, spirited, vivacious, full of health,

--and from what she has learned through other females--full of curiosity as to the facts of _marriage_. Well, she has passed the rubicon, and they twain lengthen out their honeymoon for about a year; at the end of which time it is an old and flavorless story, and discontent comes in, because each feels the need of a little change. The upshot of such a union is that neither of them see a genuinely happy hour, till that wherein each hopes to be free from the other, and try their chances elsewhere. So much for general division number one. The next division is that which is being, with its mysteries holy and unholy--that is in its normal development, and abnormal or unhealthful one--about to be treated in the pages that follow.

XXIV. Love being much more than a mere sentiment between the sexes, it is plain that neither its ground-work, nature, or cryptic meaning, has hitherto in any land been thoroughly understood. I have for long, weary years studied it in many countries of the globe. Here and there I got--not a new idea of it, but suggestions which led me to investigate and explore. And now, in this, probably the last book but one or two which I shall ever write, I desire, _not_ to make a _confession_, for I am proud of the truths alone I delved for and brought up from the zem-zem of mystery --but to make a statement and explanation. I had struggled so hard to get a fair hearing at the bar of the world, that many a time, in view of the cruel fact that I was met everywhere with suspicion, slander and malignant envy, I have bathed in the dark waters of despair; and but for, as I believe, the protecting care of the dead, whose loving hands either held me up in the bitter strife, or, failing to be able to do that, eased my falls--I should have rushed of my own act into the awful fields of eternity. Early in life I discovered that the fact of my ancestry on one side, being what they were, was an effectual estoppal on my preferment and advancement, usefulness and influence. I became famous, but never popular. I studied Rosicrucianism, found it suggestive, and loved its mysticisms. So I called myself The Rosicrucian, and gave my thought to the world as Rosician thought; and lo! the world greeted with loud applause what it supposed had its origin and birth elsewhere than in the soul of P.B. Randolph.

Very nearly _all_ that I have given as Rosicrucianism originated in my soul; and scarce a single thought, only suggestions, have I borrowed from those who, in ages past, called themselves by that name--one which served me well as a vehicle wherein to take _my_ mental treasures to a market, which gladly opened its doors to that name, but would, and did, slam to its portals in the face of the tawny student of Esoterics.

Precisely so was it with things purporting to be Ansairetic. I had merely read Lydde's book, and got hold of a new name; and again mankind hurrahed for the wonderful Ansaireh, but incontinently turned up its nose at the supposed copyist. In proof of the truth of these statements, and of how I had to struggle, the world is challenged to find a line of my thought in the whole 4,000 books on Rosicrucianism; among the brethren of that Fraternity--and I know many such in various lands, and was, till I resigned the office, Grand Master of the only Temple of the Order on the globe; or in the Ansairetic works, English, German, Syriac or Arabic.

One night--it was in far-off Jerusalem or Bethlehem, I really forget which--I made love to, and was loved by, a dusky maiden of Arabic blood. I of her, and that experience, learned--not directly, but by suggestion--the fundamental principle of the White Magic of Love; subsequently I became affiliated with some dervishes and fakirs of whom, by suggestion still, I found the road to other knowledges; and of these devout practicers of a simple, but sublime and holy magic, I obtained additional clues--little threads of suggestion, which, being persistently followed, led my soul into labyrinths of knowledge themselves did not even suspect the existence of. I became practically, what I was naturally--a mystic, and in time chief of the lofty brethren; taking the clues left by the masters, and pursuing them farther than they had ever been before; actually discovering the ELIXIR OF LIFE; the universal Solvent, or celestial Alkahest; the water of beauty and perpetual youth, and the philosopher's stone,--all of which this book contains; but only findable by him or her who searches well. The thoughts which I gave to the world, that world paid me for, as it always has paid for benefits. But what of that? Justice is sure to be done me by and by.

I am induced to say thus much in order to disabuse the public mind relative to Rosicrucianism, which is but one of our outer doors--and which was not originated by Christian Rosencrux; but merely revived, and replanted in Europe by him subsequent to his return from oriental lands, whither, like myself and hundreds of others, he went for initiation.

The Rosicrucian system is, and never was other else than a door to the ineffable Grand Temple of Eulis. It was the trial chamber wherein men were tested as to their fitness for loftier things. And even Eulis, itself, is a triplicate of body, spirit, soul. There are some in the outer, a few in the inner crypts.

These, the facts concerning Rosicrucia and myself, are out at last. Now let us go on with the book.

Enthusiasts are the ambassadors of God. It is through such only that great truths reach the world, and that world takes exquisite pleasure in crucifying all such; and yet they will arise, proclaim their mission, deliver their message, establish new truths, and then march straight to Calvary or Patmos! In all ages there have been men cut out after a different pattern from their contemporaries, and who, for that reason, had and have a different destiny to fulfil. "To be great, is to be misunderstood," ay, and crucified time and again. Among all who have ever lived, none have worked harder, or accomplished more good for mankind than that class of men known in all time as Mystics, foremost among whom was, and is, that branch of them known as Hermetists,--men of mark; Pythagoreans, Rosicrucians, and lastly, the Brotherhood of Eulis,--all of whom were, and are, students of the same school.

When David G. Brown, of the city of New York, more recently connected with Bennett's "Herald," was, in Montreal, I believe, asked concerning the origin of the Great Society, or rather Fraternity, (the Rosicrucian branch,--but differing essentially from the branch of that august brotherhood represented by adepts in Europe, Asia, and myself and confreres in this country,--yet identical in spirit, so far as the general welfare of universal man is concerned), he responded as follows, save that he disguised certain names, which disguises I now throw off!--As one standing upon the beach by the sea, and gazing far off over the turbulent waters, finds the horizon lowering in the distance, and shutting out the land unseen that lies beyond; so we, standing upon the sands of time, and looking back over the sea of our past history, find there is a boundary beyond which the vision cannot extend, a point where many have written, "No more beyond!"

And, as the ocean casts up from its unfathomable depths wrecks of vessels lost, which float upon its surface, and are lost upon our shores; so sometimes, from the immeasurable gulf that has buried in its depths the secret of our origin, a waif drifting on the bosom of time finds its way to the limits of the historical epoch, and reveals to us something of what was, and is lost. Then let us learn all that we may from these waifs. Let us wander upon these trackless shores of a silent sea, and bring from its drift-wood and wrecks all that may be gathered. Let us add all that may be added of our childhood's glory to our manhood's suffering, and our coming triumph. We will be proud that we are disciples of Hermes Trismegistus, that thrice-sealed Lord of Mind,--the Mystical Mal-Kizadek (Melchizadek) of Bible repute; but let us not forget to be proud that we are disciples of the viewless God. . . Twine the laurel wreath for the victor, but add the cypress for the victim. . . . . Let us go, then, to the land of romance and of dream,--the land of the Holy Byblus, and the Sacred Ganges. Standing upon their shores, our minds will revert back in the dim ages, to the days of our childhood, and the birth of the mystical reign of Ahrimanes. We will behold in our mind's eye a succession of kingdoms, like the succession of seasons, a rise and fall of dynasties, like the sowing and reaping of grain. We will count the number of patricians who live in idleness and luxury, and shudder at the multitude of plebeians who die in agony and want. Behold those monsters of selfishness and cruelty, whose insatiable appetite of ambition and pride, wealth and power, could not appease, and for whose maw the quivering flesh and trickling blood of a people became food. Here and there, we will find men struggling against oppression as we have struggled; people teaching virtue and charity oppression as we have struggled; people teaching virtue and charity as we have taught,--reviled and scorned as we have been. We will discover that others have borne our burdens who had no hope of receiving our reward; that knowledge is universal, and has no royal road; and that they were as wise in the wisdom of their generation, as we are in ours.

And now tread softly. We are entering the dark realm of the slumbering ages. The dust of a million years has gathered here, and no voice has awakened its echoes since the days when the Indian Bacchus consorted with the daughters of men.

We have left the land of the probable, and are journeying in the regions of the possible. The footprints here and there are of mortals, but of those who have beheld the hidden mysteries of Eulis, who are familiars of the Cabbala, who have raised the veil of Isis, and revealed the Chrishna, the--YAE or the A.A.

Behold in the distance, shining from the east as the sun from the sea, the unquenchable torch of her who is nameless; observe the stars that circle round her, as she kneels to write upon the sand. See the sheen of her golden hair, and the spotless white of her robes; catch the first strains of that wondrous philosophy, classic and pure; as they fall in wordless music from her lips; and remember how its infinite truth and marvellous beauty, have, in all the ages that are past, bound us together by an indissoluble bond of brotherhood, and leavened with our faith in the innate kindness of the human heart, taught us to sacrifice ourselves, that the peoples may advance.

They were fragments of this philosophy which we wore as a crown of glory on our natal morn, that were disseminated by our Master and his innumerable followers, and cast hither and thither upon the stream of time, were finally washed by successive waves of war and pilgrimage, to the shores of Egypt. It is of these the author of the "History of Civilization in England" speaks as "forming one of the elements in the school of Alexandria, and whose subtle speculations, carried on in their own exquisite language, anticipated all the efforts of modern European metaphysics."

They were fragments of this philosophy which, perverted by the strong individualities of Plato, Aristotle and Pythagoras, became alike the systems of their schools, the Portico, the Grove, and the Garden.

Melchizadek, or Hermes, was our first great master; but like many masters before and since, he lived when the "times were out of joint," and the age was not attuned to symphonies of thought and feeling. He taught his rich philosophy to all, opened great hidden depths of thought to the public eye, explained the most subtle truths to barbarian ears, and--threw pearls to swine. And his success. He gathered round him his disciples, and looked beyond at their followers; they extended in every direction, as far as eye could reach, surging like the waves of the sea, when tossed by tempests,--and with all the deep undertones and matterings of the ocean. Were all these his pupils? All these versed in the shoals and depths of reasoning? No. They were families, some member of whom believed an abstract philosophical truth, and all the rest believed the man.

They reduced the laws of nature to form a creed, and they made a golden calf of some special physical force, and fell down to worship it. They resolved, themselves, after their agitation, into their own natural element. That was all.

As a rustic, uninstructed in the principles, might with open-mouthed wonder watch the burning of coal, and endeavor to associate it with the inflation of a balloon, so Hermes, expecting only the preconceived consequences of his teaching, was awed by the immense bubble he had formed. As he comprehended the magnitude of his creation, and its now evident consequences, perhaps there arose in his mind that inevitable conclusion that from all his teachings and all his labor little would be accomplished. The great minds among his followers would be philosophers, but they would have been philosophers without him. The mass would be fanatics, as they had been fanatics before him. He had done only this--given a direction to their studies and speculations, given a name and method to their ignorance and madness. And all this scholasticism and philosophy, all this ignorance and madness, would be the new religion of India, would take the place forever of her first idolatry. Hold! It is not yet too late to retrieve, and by one of those rapid and eccentric movements in literature, which the great genius of Bonaparte was wont to receive in war, to change the whole features of the campaigne. And I am so changing it!--I, the last Grand Master of the Order, prior to its final absorption into regnant, peerless EULIS!

So we received our heritage, and the soul of philosophy vanished from India and the world as a dream. The kernel was hidden, and the shell alone permitted to remain to excite the awe of past generations, and the wonder of ours. Ah! most noble Master, you have long since, like Her who came before you, passed forever among the shadows of the invisible, and the dark, but deathless realms, where our fathers have gone before us. But as the material form was indestructible, and lives forever in that land of blossom and of flowers, so that spiritual and ideal emanation shall, through all coming time, live in the minds of men, and never cease to be born anew, for Eulis' nature is infinite and eternal!

How safely our secrets have been guarded, let each answer according to the progress he has made in mastering them. How little was abstracted by the Essenes, Gnostics and Batiniyeh, you all know.

For ten thousand years after Hermes, we lost no more, in our contact with all the various peoples of the world, than the electric elements we threw off in grasping their hands!

Though few in numbers, we guarded the great trust committed to our care with a never-ceasing vigilance. Every member realized that the flowers gathered from the graves of dead years must be preserved as a wreath to crown the age to come. Amid the swarm of sects and societies that sprang to life in the East, surrounded by all the schools that flourished in the Golden Age of Greece, that little band of souls preserved their purity.

Secretly and silently they moved over the sands of time to the coming of the Nazarene. . . . . . . In the twilight that succeeds the crucifixion of Calvary we we can see indistinctly the movements of individuals, and the banding of men. They seem to move with an uncertain purpose, and to have lost their old effectiveness. One, two, three, five hundred years roll by as one would count the hours to midnight. Then there is a bustle. Work is at hand. Into those dark ages that succeed, pass the mustering bands, and for a thousand years death at the stake, persecution and despair on the one hand, and the retribution of the Vehmgerichte and kindred associations, alone point out the position of the contestants, and the progress of the fight.

Then from his cradle in the Alps looms up Christian Rosencrux. Seizing all at a glance, the society is reorganized; no more to dream, but to work; no more to wait for the human race to accomplish its destiny, but to assist in its accomplishment; to offer her bosom to the unfortunate; to raise the fallen; to succor the oppressed; to interpose her form between the tyrant and the slave; to lead the van in the great fight. She has the gathered knowledge of her ages of student-life. She has the patience taught by centuries of adversity. She has the courage of the true and the beautiful; and, above all, she loves the peoples, and Paschal Beverly Randolph succeeded Rosencrux, as the legitimate Grand Master of Rosicrucia, and Hierarch of Eulis.

And now I would say one word in regard to contemporary societies. Many of them were organized with meritorious objects in the days gone by, but the state of things that gave them being has long since passed away. They presented a sad spectacle of having outlived their usefulness, and drag out a fitful existence of senseless ceremonies and abstract forms, from which the soul has long departed. A few should receive the tribute of respect due to that which is venerable and good, and Freemasonry should ever be associated with the broad mantle of its charity.

In the superstructures which have been erected at different periods, upon these foundations, one will often observe a pillar, here or there, called the <u>Rose Croix</u>, or occasionally hear the mystic name Eulis, softly pronounced.

I was conversing with a gentleman whom I supposed to be a member of one of these "Chapters," and he said, "The Rosy Cross is dead. We have, it is true, galvanized its skeleton into a transitory life, but the Rosy Cross of history is dead." Dead! I cried. She lives!--lives with the rich blood of the South in her veins; with the vigor of the North in her constitution; with the clear brains of the temperate zone, the depth of thought of the Orient, the versatility of France, and earnestness of purpose, and boldness of resolution of the New World; lives these three hundred years that you think her dead, as she lived the countless centuries before you thought her born; and may she never cease to have a fitting casket for her jewels, and remain a reflex of the glorious truth and beauty of the superlative wisdom, power and goodness.

So far well; but at last the world wants to know more of that wonderful fraternity, which, nameless at times for long centuries, blossomed a few centuries ago as Rosicrucia, but now has leaped to the fore-front of all the zeal reform movements of this wonderful age, and lo! the banner of peerless Eulis floats proudly--rock-founded--on the breeze. We, the people of Eulis, be it known, are students of nature in her interior departments, and rejecting alike the coarse materialization of the ages, and the sham "philosophies" of the ages past and current, accept only that which forces conviction by its irresistible logic. Men who <u>realize</u> the existence of other worlds than this are not apt to give loose rein to passion; nor be content with fraud in any shape. We cannot take so-sos for facts, and therefore we reject much that appeals to others with the force of truth. We are ambitious to solve all possible mystery; we prefer one method to all other hyper-human agencies, knowing it to be infinitely preferable to all other modes of rapporting the occult

and mysterious; and this book, and all others from the same pen, is but a very imperfect sketch or outline of the sublime philosophy of the Templars of EULIS. We
know the enormous importance of the sexive principle; that a menstruating woman is
an immense power if she but knew it! that a pregnant one holds the keys of eternal
mystery in her hand, and that while thus she can make or mar any human fortune! We
know the mystic act is one unhinging the gates alike of heaven and of hell; and we
know two semi-brainless people may, by an application of esoteric principles, stock
the world with mental giants. But where shall we find students? Are not all the
people, nearly, the slaves of lust, place, gold? Well, we find one now and then;
and we hail him or her as the Greeks hailed the sea--with excessive joy! Thalatta!
Thalatta! They are not multitudinous now, but will be in the good time coming.

   XXV. Unquestionably while we occupy flesh and blood bodies, and probably after
we wear our electric or ethereal ones subsequent to death, Love, other than amicive
and filial, will depend upon the magnetic congeniality existing between the two concerned; although even the most perfect state of magnetic fusion and reciprocation
is liable to be disturbed by any one of quite a numerous list of causes.

   We are all of us, more or less, counterparts and embodiments of nature; and
nature has her ups and downs, fogs and sleets, storms and heats, ice and fire,
volcanoes and wintry blasts; and so do, so must we, just as long as the earth and
nature are as at present; when they change, so will we, and very likely not much
before. If between a couple there be a full and mutual play of magnetism, if neither
draws from the other, except to replace with his or her own, there is a good chance
of general harmony, joy and content for them. If not, then not. If one party over-
flows with magnetism, and the other has but a scanty supply, strong love may exist
between them, all other things being equal; and the weak one will depend almost for
life itself upon the strong; and the strong be firmly drawn toward the weak. But
there must be an assimilation between, and blending of, the two magnetisms, else
they will assuredly antagonize and repel each other! One party may be very glowing
and loving and magnetic, say, for instance, on plane A,--a solid, physical, muscular,
needless, jolly, devil-me-care-sort of individual--say a man; such an aone could make
a perfect heaven--on his plane--with a woman of the same grade; but how would it be
were he conjoined with a joyous, rich-souled, healthy, magnificent, intellectual,
refined, delicate and spiritual woman,--equally magnetic as himself, but the grade
of whose magnetism was as satin compared to his own--tow-cloth? Now just such
couples, or those as naturally and organically incompatible, somehow or other, manage to get together, and the consequence is a life removed from happiness by a great,
yawning, impassable gulf, whose black and sullen waters cannot be bridged.

   Some day, in the future, there will be honorable methods whereby the present
general mixed-upness will be made straight, and people having unfortunately made
the wrong choice, and gotten some one's else wife or husband, will be able to--yes--
in some cases actually "swap." Why not, if themselves are rendered happier by it;
society is satisfied, the prior families duly provided for, and no sin committed, no
harm done?

   Woman faces heaven when she gives herself to Love and man!--willingly or
victimly. The rule is universal, the exceptions monstrous; for there are, there can
be none save in three cases--utter human depravity; certain physical malformations;
and third, in those mysterious forms of prayer in vogue before Nineveh the first
was founded, and whose tremendous importance and vital sacredness compel me to allude
to no further herein. The first fact above is not only her nature, but I hold is
an especial sign of her celestial nature, and of heaven's mystical favor. She receives both the human and the divine in her demise of affection,--if even by force!
But coarser man looks toward the world's face, for then he is almost entirely of the

earth earthy. Woman never is; she may be indifferent; horrified--but she looks toward the empyrean, and from it--however degraded--receives a measure of life divine; for low as she may be, but touch the right chord, and she can mother heroes,
and give gladsome Marys to the world.

Now here comes in a mooted point; of one unfaithful wife, and one unfaithful
husband, which commits the greater sin?--or is it an equal grade of offence before
God? To this I reply: In the act, right or wrong, man gives of himself, whether
good or evil; and woman receives. The malign influence is external with and to
him; internal with and to her. It is easy for him to rid himself of the bad effects, compared with her ability to do the same; for the foreign influence imparted to,--remains with her, and becomes an integrant of her very being; and, as she
naturally stands nearer heaven, the greater is her fall--far greater than his who
is already a great deal too near the earth. Hence I hold her sin greatest, just
as I would tell an angel who had sinned, "Be thy punishment severe," but would bid
a half imbecile to "Clear out and not bother the court."

XXVI. But there is another thought arising right here: It sometimes, and in
this age and country, very frequently, happens, that one or both the parties to a
marital compact, from a variety of causes, some of which I will state, manage to
lose this magnetic attraction toward the other party; and ten to one each will at
once conclude that all love between them is wholly lost or dead, when the fact is
that each has quite as much as ever, but the bridge is broken down--that mystic
bridge, which, resting on the abutments of both souls, spans the gulf of eternity.
But, although often broken, this bridge is seldom utterly destroyed. The statis-
tics of divorce prove the position here affirmed; for a large percentage of divorced couples after enjoying a brief period of "Freedom", begin to think about it;
conclude they had not been wise enough, and were altogether too hasty; that, after
all, there's no home like the old one; no love like the old one; and they marry
each other over again, and, having cut their eye-teeth, steer clear of former
faults, and lead happy lives thereafter.

Why? Because they have a little more care; a greater amount of give and take,
without being mad about it, and make more strenuous endeavors to please each other
--and that's just it! for as soon as people do that, they cease fretting, scold-
ing, fuming, worrying, complaining and borrowing trouble; and therefore cease to
waste their magnetisms, consequently the honey bubbles up again and life's vinegar leaks out! Now, owing to these causes, married people are not as they should
be,--the happiest beings on earth; far from it; the youths and maidens discount
them largely on the general average; and you can almost always tell a married
pair wherever you clap eyes on them; for it's heads up! and a smirk or smile to
every one else but each other. Not so with unwedded lovers. The former lean away
from each other, and gaze askant; the latter lean to each other and drink in delicious draughts of ecstasy from each other's eyes. Now the man who accounts for
his state of things on the hypothesis that the one is passion appeased, the other
only anticipatory, is a fool, besides being a selfish knave. The true reading is:
Magnetic exhaustion in one case--magnetic reciprocity in the other. What magnetism is I will tell you presently; suffice it at this stage to record its existence, and to note such facts as above adduced.

I have already, in a previous paragraph of this section, indicated, generally,
by suggestion, the cure for this state of affairs. Briefly, they are to utterly
put a stop to all sources of magnetic depletion. Keep cool everywhere, under all
provocations and circumstances. Eat, drink, sleep well, and whatever you do,
make a business of it. When you work, with hands or brain, do it with a will, but
don't work all the time. When the day's labor is done, forget all about it, and

devote at least two hours of the evening to social talk, chat, visiting, or receiving visitors; walk out; read, listen to music, and persistently have your two, or even one hour a day, free from sordid strife and worldly care. Hard to do it at first in thes grab-all days, wherein, as the sailor said, "People eat hard, work hard, fare hard, sleep hard, have a hard time generally through this life, at length dying hard, and going to perdition at last," which the sceptical old salt said was "particularly derned hard"!

A pint of water contains latent force enough to blow a town to flinders; an equal amount of magnetism contains active force enough to incarnate a new being, and launch an immortal soul upon the limitless sea of eternity! and yet in five minutes of growling, stewing, fretting, anger, or in a wanton's or libertine;s arms thrice that amount of imperial life is lost--and it means, also, the shortening of at least ten good days on earth!

XXVII. Of course excessive venery is an effective nail in any one's coffin; and so is excessive child-bearing, seeing that both are broad rivers, discharging magnetism from the human body and soul. And this reminds me to say something in reference, not to the fetid and unclean subject of conception-preventives, for I hold nearly all of them as utter abominations; but on the culture of the will directly , and the use of that will, and it alone, in determining for and against excessive progeny; for a couple had better have three really fine children, than thirty half-formed and delicate ones.

Escessive connubial pleasures invariably produce dyspepsia, not only of the body, but of the mind, intellect and soul; and when off-spring results from such conditions, what wonder that they are lacking in all the grand essentials of a genuine and perfect man and womanhood. Absolute and prolonged continence is but a less evil, though its penalty is inflicted upon the transgressor alone. The human will, next to love, is the most powerful attribute of immortal mankind. In most people it is splurgy, occasional, paroxysmal, and, as a steady power, practically of no account. I have told some persons to "will", and straightway they screwed up their faces, clenched their teeth, and looked most absurdly and amusingly awful --or ridiculous. They strained and fumed as if trying to life a ton. Now will is no such thing, to be exerted in no such way. It is simply a quiet power, and requires no muscular or nervous, but simply a still, mental force, to urge it into play, when it is feeble, as in most it is; it should be cultivated by thinking determinedly, at intervals, of one thing only. ataa time, to the total exclusion of everything, topic or subject besides. Thus one can will--after practice--tears to the eyes, blushes to the cheeks, pallor to the face, as thousands of ministers and other actors constantly do. We can will to close our hands or eyes; and just so we close or open the sphincter ani, or that of the bowels, bladder, lips, and close them at pleasure. The Oneida Perfectionists declare, and with undoubted truth, that any man can, at will, after a little practice, effectually control the ejective action of the seminal vessels; but he is an unwise and suicidal man who attempts a thing so unnatural and injurious.

But how is it with woman? Can she control corresponding uterine muscles? I answer, most assuredly. All mothers and obstetricians know the enormous expulsive power of the uterus; and that contractile and expansive power, like that of any other sphincter, is measurably under her will. When she sees fit to keep it closed, no other power but her own can defeat her purpose; and she ought to know when to exert that power; and there is no necessity to use it, save when she believes an ovum is then present, and undesirable maternity threatened. In the will she has the only natural agent and means, justified of nature and God, of controlling the number of her children; but she is only thus justified, when disease, excessive maternal weariness, a sickly, disordered, depraved or drunken husband, or one whom she hates, or is hated by, or insanity, gloom or malformation, tell her in thunder tones she ought not to give to the world what she cannot give well, and with safety to her own life. By simply willing, and without much strain, the os uteri will close, and remain thus for days together; hence all washes and preventives can be consigned forever to the bad limbo whence they originated.

But this is only one of the silent energies of the human will, It is said, and I believe, that whom a woman blesses or curses when her moon is on her, stays cursed or blessed till that same woman removes it; well, if she curses, she hurts herself, hence cannot afford to do it; but she can, and ought to bless, all the time. This will-power, once started, grows apace; and with it, you, O wife of the troubled heart! can powerfully, silently, resistlessly, use it to direct the mighty magnetic power of your own soul upon him you love, would retain and wear, and wean too, from bad habits, and the malign influence of those who, claiming to be his friends, are really your foes, and, by their bad power over him, are practically enemies to both.

Fail you cannot. NOTHING GOOD CAN EVER FAIL! True it may, to quote Poe, be trodden down; but it will rise again to the life everlasting. But to its present application. In far-off Oriental lands I was the guest of some Arab brethren, of a certain mystic tie; and one day, in a boat, we sailed away from Boolak, the port of grand Cairo, up the stately and solemn Nile. How far we went, whither, or what for, matters not; but then and there I ascertained that the women of that brotherhood, and some others in that distant sunny land, knew some natural secrets, which their fairer sisters of the West are totally ignorant of. When one of those wives is per- fectly assured that, by reason of illness, age or weakness, she cannot safely bear more children without hazarding both lives, she shrinks with unutterable horror from what our American women contemplate with a "pish." At the house of one Mrs. L--ds, in Boston, I once heard a "woman," then on the point of marriage, declare she never would bear a child; but would kill them just as if they were "so many puppy dogs!" --the worse than female demon! The Oriental wife, I repeat, shrinks with superlative loathing from the idea of murdering, or conniving at the murder of the fruit of her womb, as all true women do, and ever will, knowing she were a murderess if she; and that she is just as certain to suffer for it subsequent to death, as that death it- self is sure to come. She knows that the nature of the ties that bind her in marriage will, time and again, subject her to the chances of maternity. Refuse those risks she never dreams of doing, well knowing she would be either laughed at, abused or divorced, or even, if not, that such denials failt to generate quietude in the tent, or peace in the family. What then? Why, she either times her meeting with her husband, with reference to her periods, so as to avoid distasteful chances; or, if accident prevents that, she merely places the ball of her thumb in her mouth, breaths hard upon it, strains and "bears down," and is instantly out of danger, for both ovum and zoosperm are forthwith expelled by the forceful contractions of the uterine and abdominal muscles. In these respects the law of God rules in the Arab tent, instead of the abortional devils which haunt the boudoirs of civilized and Christian mankind.

It is indeed very seldom that an Eastern woman resorts to that sinless method, and then only when age, disease, or malformations render it imperative. On the contrary, offspring are rightly considered as special blessings from the Supreme God; hence, the first lesson a bride receives from her mother are those that favor such a result. She is told to wholly, fully, freely, prayerfully abandon her entire faculties and being to the one grand end of woman-life--the sacred mission of the wifely mother. Hence it happens that the Oriental wife is always pure; there are not a hundred adulteresses or child-killers in all Islam, with its 200,000,000 votaries! There is not as many of those fearful crimes committed among all the

Moslms, in ten years, as disgrace Boston, New York, or Philadelphia every month we live. The Oriental wife, with all her glowing soul, wills--save in very rare instances--to be fruitful, as all women should; and becomes so. There are rare cases in which a wife cannot, without imperilling her life, undergo the ordeal of maternity, and then, and then only, the timely exercise of the will alone forestalls death, prevents crime, and obviates all suffering.

XXVIII. Love, I have stated, is magnetic, and subject to magnetic law. It is a force also, capable, as all know, of exerting very strange effects both upon human souls and bodies. But how? that's the question! Tell us that! I will, listen:--

Matter and mind, in some mysterious way, are not only both alike and unlike, and conjoin to form the thing called man, but they act together directly and indirectly, fully or partially, and yet are not of the same nature, albeit they act and react upon each other in myriad ways, a fact which every one's experience demonstrates beyond cavil. One thing is absolutely certain; that the mind resides in the brain; that in it inheres what constitutes as human; and that the conscious point resides in the centre of the encephalon, at that spot where all three brains meet, viz., cerebrum, cerebellum and medulla, or spinal marrow, which is an elongated brain, is a clear fact, the proof of which can be found by consulting any good anatomical and physiological atlas. In this central point, as through and around the corpus callosum, there is, in death, a nervous and spheral waste; in life a brilliant SUN varying in size from that of a large pea to a perfectly gorgeous sun-shining diamond three inches in diameter.--A ball of dazzling WHITE FIRE!--and this is the SOUL-- the being par excellence, the tremendous human mystery. It has a double consciousness one facing time and its accidents and incidents; the other gazing square and straight right into eternity. For its hither use it fashions material eyes; for its thither use every one of a myriad rays darting from it is an eye whose powers laugh Rosse's Telescope to scorn! But there arises a fog from the body which mainly so envelops this central point that the EYES are veiled; sometimes in magnetic or other sleep the clouds shift, and then one or more eyes glance over infinite fields, and momentarily glimpse the actualities of space, time, possibility and eternity. (Were I, at this point to reveal what I know of soul, its destiny, nature, and the realities of the ultimate spaces, this world would stand agape! but I resist the temptation, and go on with this book.)

This central ball draws its supplies from space, air, ether, and being mystic and divine, directly from the Lord of the universe,--the Imperial Mystery,--Infinite and Eternal God. (About which mystery the Savans are as greatly at fault as they are concerning the facts of GROWTH.) It breathes; has its tides, its diastole, systole, flux and ebbs; and, being compelled to gaze on the outer world through opaque glasses, diseased bodies, it takes but distorted views of things, and scarce ever can rely upon the absolute truth of what the SENSES tell it; from which results mistakes, confusion, misapprehensions, crime, and whatever else of evil betides its fortunes here.

The breath of the body is atmospheric air, which air is more or less penetrated with the ether of space, the breath of God, and the magnetism of the heavens surrounding the entire material universe. On these it subsists; and when it means a thing it discharges a portion of its own sphere, its divine nerval life toward the object of its desire and attention; and the vehicle is magnetism, and magnetism is that specific vif or fluid life manufactured by the sexual apparatus of either gender, as said before. The thing conveyed by it is the purpose of a soul; the result, a certain yielding of any other force on earth--for nothing can withstand the absolute decree of the waked-up human soul. Illustration:

XXIX. The soul of a woman non couvert sends its fires all over her form, because she loves the man. The atmosphere surrounding her bulges at the equator of her body--the pelvic region--across the hips; and she draws all males to her then with a very powerful attraction.

But after couverture, and before impregnation, if she be disappointed in her dream of bliss she sends the same sphere out to any one else but him; and for all affectional purposes thereafter, so far as she is concerned, he might as well be dead; for the sphere flattens up when he is near her, and although he may compel her obedience, he can never reach her soul. Then comes Hades; if not openly, then assuredly behind the scenes! For there's no more warmth, verve, elan, or passion in her for him, because he has lost the power to evoke them; and while he may, by right of human law, and her sufferance, possess her form, her soul in its secure citadel grimly laughs him to scorn, and dispises him with perfect unction, because it knows that every time he profanes her he stabs himself to the heart; for he outrages her soul, and outrage invites, curses, and whomsoever on God's broad earth a WOMAN CURSES then and there stays accursed, and horror and defeat follows in his footsteps wherever he may be! What d'ye think of that, my lady? What d'ye think of that, my man?

But take a woman couverture, to the point of pregnancy; no sooner is the monad, seed or germ lodged within the sacred and most transcendently holy and mystical chamber of the womb, and the filamental door has closed the aperture thereof, shutting out and in its treasure, and from all eyes concealing the divine workshop of the Eternal, than her soul withdraws its attentions from the womb direct and alone, and begins to concentrate it and its magnetism upon that womb's contents; and from that instant she begins to love the man no less, but the unborn baby more. Why? Because, up to that point, her soul depended on the man; but now a new soul depends almost wholly upon IT. She must search out all the best particles of her blood, brain, food, drink, air, light, nervaura, muscle, bone, lymph, cartilage, carbon, and a million chemicals wherewith to build up a new body, from original materials, wherein this new soul is to dwell for a time and times and half a time,--if the abortionists, quacks, and fashions don't kill it. The soul sends lime, iron, silver, gold, calcium, nearly all the earths and salts to make the body stout and strong. Then she stores up fire in the body,--phosphor,--manufactures canals, pumps, reservoirs, telescopes, drums, cylinders, flutes, columns, domes, cellars, chemical laboratories, and mechanical contrivances of the most marvelous kind. After which she goes aloft and brings down fire from heaven, metaphysical flame, and lodges angels all over the little mansion; music here, science there, mathematics and memory, ambition, hope, joy, sorrow, love and aspiration. After which she takes a lower flight, and calls up tempters from the deeps of being to offset the angels, among whom are avarice, anger, lying, robbery, lust, and a fearful host beside; well knowing that if her new charge reach heaven it must do so alone; must toil, and sweat, and tread upon and over red-hot sands; wade through a million hells on its own feet; fight its way with its own strong hand, alone; while God looks on and smiles, he knowing that the goal is sweet, though the road be bitter, and that victory may be won at last.

Now, what time has a woman got for the frivolities of love when she is doing so grand a work as that?

Well, is it any wonder her love changes from her uterus to her bosom? Not any; and yet there are fools called men who cannot, will not, see all this, but think and insist that she who was so then shall be so now, when in fact a whole universe rolls between the two states. She is queer, short, snappish, soft, cranky then, and no wonder, for she has an undoubted right to raise the very Satan then if she choose; and most of them do it, for the simple reason that they can't help it! Why? Reader, I have already told you that the human being is all nature incarnated. Nature is changeable in her moods, sunny, tempestuous, coarse, foul, mean, genial, calm, blustery; and all these things and states she is _forced_ to incarnate in the soul, spirit, and body of the new pilgrim about starting on its way from the valley of earth to the eternal land of paradise, the splendid city of the Ineffable God.

XXX. I have said that,--pregnant states aside, and even to a great degree _then_, for the mother is aided in all her mystic work by the husband and father if he be a _man_, and loving, gentle, kind and forbearing as he should be, and not fly at her in fury and anger, because she fails in some essential things,--the ethereal, magnetic vehicle, with its load of soul-born love, can be by the persistent will projected upon, and made to effectively operate on, _almost_ any though not _every_ human being. There are those that a given person's magnetic effluence will no more touch than water will a duck's back; it rolls off, and never contacts at all. In such hard cases the attempt had better be abandoned, for two reasons: first, it _cannot_ succeed, owing to organic differences of constitution; and second, if it could it would be effort thrown away. But the same power and force can be directed upon ourselves by ourselves, either upon an afflicted member of the body,--from brain to heel,--or upon the internal viscera, as in cases of dyspepsia, liver trouble, kidney diffi- culty, heart disease, cancer of stomach; above all, the pelvic viscera of either gender when disordered, as most are; gravid uterus, ulcerated, originating frequently in lacerated, vagina; ovarian disease, vulvular congestions; inflamed prostate, or febrile testes and vaginitis,--all these are reachable by the force named, exerted in the manner specified in a preceding section, but which are worth repetition. Direct the attention toward the cause of anxiety,--a person, sick or well, generally, or to a specific point of body, mind, morals,--and strongly, yet calmly, desire, wish, will, the love-cure to be effective; but a few trials will be needed to ensure absolute, if qualified, success; an assuagement will assuredly follow, nor is the genuine cure far off. It is a scientific application of the mother's power over her babe, exerted on a wider scale.

XXXI. But what's the use of anything unless used and enjoyed? There are thousands of married couples living in a very bad and unhappy state, simply because they won't fairly try for any other; and so magnetic will-force is of no account, whatever, as a force _per se_. It must be exerted to be available. Then, and not till then, it, and the love borne on it, is one of the most powerful instrumentalities on earth. Witness the many undoubted cures of disease effected by those who go about laying on of hands; for although some of them ar charlatans, yet others are not, in proof of which behold the results following their practice. But wives and husbands neglect this matter, and suffer in consequence. People find one another growing cool--from causes already set forth herein,--and instead of checking that coolness, by _trying to_, they fly off at a tangent, set up a domestic growlery, create in- numerable excuses for a fuss; grow sullen, morose; and contrive, by every earthly means, to render matters _ten_ _times_ _worse_ _than_ _ever_; when a timely and persistent resort to the aid of the great magnetic law would speedily correct all the trouble, which, in married life, nine times in ten, originates either in outside or inside magnetic exhaustion; or in domestic passional satiety, and excessive nervous waste, which creates disgust on one side, antipathy on the other, with a grilling fire of discontent between the two. Now this, to some, may be an unpalatable truth, yet _true_ nevertheless. And here, as well as anywhere else, let me say further, that a fair share of obedience to the supreme law of cleanliness, sunshine and ventilation, will go a great way toward preventing magnetic exhaustion, and put a stop to that same satiety and disgust, with all their attendant and over crowning horripilances. Some people bathe too often, and I have seen those whom I did not believe had bathed five times in sixty years.

If a wife finds her husband growing cool, let her attend to her dress, manner; smiles instead of frowns; sugar, not salt; honey, not vinegar; and place her will steadily, strongly, persistently, upon him, at the same time sending forth her woman's love, sympathy, and magnetic force of magnetic love. The man don't live who can resist it! His love will revive just as surely as that heaven exists. But she cannot work this magic charm in anger, jealousy or indifference. Let her remember this, for it is the grand true secret of fascination--was learned from the birds, and has worked miracles in human life. The same principle obtains among unwedded lovers!

When wives dress up and put their best food forward to please their own households, as they do for outsiders; when the husband dons his best coat and pantaloons, boots and hat, cane and gloves as often and readily, to walk out with his own wife, as--when away--he does to do the same for somebody else's, the world will be a good deal better off than it is to-day.

Men's lives will be happy and pleasant when they learn: 1st. That a woman is a woman--not a softer sort of man. 2d. That wives appreciate forbearance. 3d. That occasionally a woman's organization becomes so deranged that she needs sympathy, love, tenderness and great patience on his part, for she cannot help her vagaries. Bread thus thown upon the waters will return a harvest of love ere many days. 4th. A wife is a truer friend, even if homely, than the most beautiful outsider that ever lived. 5th. Take your wife into your counsels; the place of amusement; walk, talk, and be pleasant with her. Attentions pay large interest. 6th. Never bring all your troubles home to saddle them on her; and 7th, and last, Study your wife, and adapt yourself to her; let her really be your other half; for lo! ye twain are one flesh. No matter what mothers-in-law, or any relation, may say or do. Remember that ye are one, and "For this cause shall a man be such in soul and spirit, as well as in law, gospel, and appearances.

Any mother, can, if she will, produce offspring that shall be superior to either parent, by avoiding all disagreeable of whatever kind of nature. By believing she shall and will produce a superior specimen of the race, and by firmly resisting discontent, anger, jealousy, hatred, and all evil--dwelling only on that which is true, beautiful and good.

Women suffering from affectional perversions, resulting in the trains of evils known as "female complaints," have a positive means of rejuvenation in the will, in the cultivation of the purer attributes of their nature; observance of the law of soap and water, and a firm determination to be no longer slaves to drugs, anger, selfishness, the doctors, envy, or anything else calculated to unbalance them. Thus mentally they can heal themselves, become healthy, and gain the new life, energy, and power.

We now pass to the consideration of one of the most strange and aberant phases of love--if love be not a misnomer as applied to it--with which the mind has to grapple during its search into the mazy labyrinths concealed beneath the human form.

XXXII. If it was possible for me to look upon this broad world and broader universe with the jaundiced eyes of some zealot, full of bile, gloom, bitterness and bigotry; if I were capable of believing that God is not all good; if I could imagine a yawning gulf, and it peopled with tortured souls, whose agonizing shrieks for sudden death were answered back by the exultant shouts of jubilant fiends, with a KING DEVIL at their head,--which I can't--but if I could, then would I believe that from that pit, clean back of the shadow of God, came trooping forth a score of superlatively horrible gorgons, destined by the mandate of the chief fiend to desolate the earth, and torment mankind, among which, one, always clad in rays of light, yet sweltering with venom at its heart, stands among the foremost. I mean that awful thing for which/English there is no name, but which ever and always assumes the garb

-38-

and mien and office of the bright, heaven-born angel, LOVE. In other of my books I have named this pestilent thing Vampyrism.

Now the name is familiar to everybody, because, in the first place it pertains to a monstrous leech which inhabits tropical waters; fastens on to whatever has sentient life, and never lets go until the last drop of blood is sucked out, and the victim topples into the arms of death. Secondly, the same name is applied to a huge bat inhabiting dark caverns in Oriental and other lands, darkness and gloom being its natural habitat; and when man or beasts travelling along that way chance to fall asleep, this bat of Hades stealthily approaches, and gently, soothingly, flaps its huge wings, croning and droning its weird sing-song the while; thus fanning its victims, until a deep, comatic sleep falls upon them, so hard and strong, that not a stir is made while the bat opens a vein, and drinks its fill of living gore!

When the awaking comes, the eyes open in another world than this, for mankind, never at all for beasts. The name in the third use is attached to certain peculiar, fantastic beings,—half human, half demon, of Oriental and German story. These beings emerge from deep darkness in the middle of the night; open new-made graves, take out the bodies therein, eat the flesh, and then , the horrid banquet over, stealthily return whence they came, surfeited to plethora with the dreadful repast. But it sometimes happens--so goes the legend--that no new-made graves offer their temptations, and still the ghouls must live; wherefore they gain access to houses and drain the veins of whomsoever they possibly can. These harpies are, however, vulnerable to shot and death; but if you kill one, be sure to bury him five feet or a fathom, beneath the solid earth; and be sure you run a stake through his breast, with a cross on top; and if possible, at a cross-roads; for if you neglect to do this, and the vampyre's body remains above ground, just as soon, and as surely as the moon's beams shine upon it, just so surely will its life return and it go scot free to continue its ravages through successive lives and deaths. All these horrid things, whether creative of nature in some of her dark moods, or whether some of them are the offspring of perverted imagination, the reality, if of life or of legend, alike are all bad enough, and we turn from the bare contemplation of each with a shudder, begotten of horror on the body of disgust; and yet, fearful as they are, not one of them, or all combined, can equal the horrible reality--the absolutely unmistakable genuine, living human ghouls, right in our very midst; devouring gorgons, who are everywhere about us; who go up and down our streets, and in and out before us, clad in fine raiment; faces decked with smiles; and who only enter our houses, and partake of our hospitality, to betray our trust, and fatten on the lives of us and ours--for where of the male gender their sole aim is to gratify their own infernal morbidity of passion at anybody's expense whatever; and the wives and daughters of our friends become the prey of wretches, for whom no punishment is too severe;--doubly-dyed vampires, from whom conscience has forever taken its flight, and to whom gratitude is unknown. The ghoul originates in such marriages as have no love to cement the union. The father is a coarse, selfish, material surface man, without tenderness, affection,--anything wholly human; and his wife, if not as cold as himself, is probably just the opposite, and from the altar to the grave never realizes the least love;--nothing but selfish passion,--is a woman who yearns, and mainly, for what she cannot get,--true love; and the consequence is that her child comes to earth with yearnings never to be gratified; love-hungry from eternity to time, and through time all the way back to eternity again! Now, when he or she thus born, encounters those of opposite gender, who are full of love, they cling to such with the tenacity of death itself, until they sap out the full soul, and fill their empty ones. What care they even though desolation, despair and death follow in their footsteps, and all their tracks are blood spots from hearts that they have broken? For so long as these leeches get their fill, no matter what evil betides those upon whom they feed,--and whom they ruin. These ghouls have no principle, declare love with like fervor to every one they meet; and having ruined them, blasted their happiness, destroyed their peace of mind, shipwrecked families, violated daughters, debauched honest men's wives, they brag of it, and send fiery clouds of remorse and shame, to crown the victims of their rapacity, and coarsely brutal lust. Their crime is fiendish. I conclude this section by briefly recapitulating the res gestae of it, which may be thus summarized:--

Many people of both sexes often experience a terrible attraction toward another, that resembles, but is not, love. On the contrary, it is a fearful, monstrous passion, and they almost vainly struggle to escape it. Such persons are vampyrized; and a vampyre is a person born love-hungry, who have none themselves, who are empty of it, but who fascinate and literally suck others dry who do have love in their natures. Detect it thus: the vampyre is selfish, is never content but in handling, fondling its object, which process leaves the victim utterly exhausted, and they don't know why. Break off at once. Baffle it by steady refusal; allow not even hands to touch, and remember that the vampyre seeks to prolong his or her own existence, life and pleasure, at the expense of your own. Women when thus assailed should treat the assailant with perfect coldness and horror. Thus they can baffle this pestiferous thing--which is more common than people even suspect; in fact, an everyday affair. Many a man and wife have parted, many still live unhappily together, some aware, but many unconscious, that the prime cause of all their bickerings and discontent is vampyrism on the part of one or the other. It causes fretfulness, moodiness, irritability; a feeling of repugnance arises toward the one who should be most dear; and eventually positive dislike takes the place of that tender affection which should ever grow more and more endearing between those who have given themselves to each other. This dislike becomes in many cases so strong that the parties cannot endure each other's presence; and separation becomes inevitable, neither, perhaps, conscious of the true cause. This is sometimes owing to an inferior development of amativeness, sometimes to debility, lack of vitality, the consequence of a feeble or shattered nervous system; and in either case the cure is to be found in less frequent contact, separate rooms, health, and mutual endeavor to correct the fault.

XXXIII. What vast hosts, what tremendous throngs of what are called husbands, and notoriously what almost infinite numbers of married women find home a real hell on a small scale instead, and all for want of mutuality, domesticity, sympathy, and, above all, reciprocity, that is the impartation and reception each by, to, and from the other, of the mysterious thing known as magnetism! And many such there be, who, realizing nothing but the worst kind of blanks in their lottery of life, actually long for death, or anything else, to mitigate or change the current horror of their lives. People, too, make great mistakes about this self-same mystic magnetism. They imagine it to be either all physical, or all mental, when, in fact, it is both; and this subtle fluid, or emanation, is the absolute connecting link between soul and body, matter and mind, and, ultimately, between man the Deity. Thus in a few lines is solved a mystery which has puzzled the world for centuries, --that of the subtle something which was, and is, the connecting link between the two. There is a magnetism or effluence of soul, arising in, and flowing forth from, the persons of either sex, who are, by nature, endowed with large, open, free, sensitive, generous souls; and this sphere is deeply charged with mind, love, and all else that distinguishes noble from ignoble souls. Nor does this magnetism depend at all upon size of brain, or mere physique; for it abounds as much among the small people, intuitive and physically weak, as it does among those who are materially opposite in construction. Hence a man or woman of this sort, if the partner be loved, will be able to parent offspring every way perfect, and, physically speaking, better than themselves. There is but little danger of such persons going to the bad, because all their natural tendencies are upward and advancive, not retrogressive, barbaric, or descensive; for their soul-magnetism charges their physical, and it is full of life, energy, emotion and goodness; hence, whoever comes within the area of its action is benefited, not injured; and this is an imperative, universal rule.

XXXIV. But there is another, and to some extent, more powerful magnetism than this. And I may here remark that it is a generally conceded fact that illegitimate children are nearly always _smartest_, as compared with the fruits of honest marriage; but are they the _best_? Doubted, as a general thing. They are smarter, fuller of nerve, dash, _elan_, because struck into being at passion's highest tide; but their moral natures and principles are almost universally, wofully deficient; and of all the famous bastards of hisoty not one was ever noted for _goodness_! True, they all have a very large measure of personal magnetism, and mental force; but let it never be forgotten that goodness alone is absolute power, and, therefore, the _best_ is always greatest, even though the good man make less show than the more volatile and estimably gifted son of earth; wherefore, he who would beget the noblest sons and daughters must do so under the dominance of a calm and steady love, within the pales of those barriers which society has erected to protect itself from barbaric savage principles and peoples, individual as well as aggregative.

XXXV. There is another sort of magnetism, rich, full, voluptuous, Websterian, which originates in _body_, not in soul; and it flows in copious streams from the persons of such as have it, suffusing everything and everybody with its warm and vivifying power. It is charged with passion, enthusiasm, volcanic fire; and while it warms others is very apt to _burn_. It comes of full veins, large lungs, livers, good digestion, steady nerves, fulness of habit, appetite and spirit, and always more or less wins influence and marked distinction for its possessor. Aaron Burr was a good example of its nature, character, and power. Now mark this: The ghoul wins and ruins, because affectionally and in love he is a perfect vacuum; and silly, female butterfly women rush to him, and get their wings scorched like any miller at a candle, because the empty gorgon draws upon their fulness. They think to find reciprocation, but attain utter exhaustion and ruin instead. On the other hand, the physically magnetic man suffuses the bodies and souls of _his_ victims with his own magnetic fulness; the woman, or man, as the case may be, is drawn to him or her, and while he or she is there to keep up the incessant play of aromal forces, both are happy; but when the parting time comes, and the lesser person no longer has the full one to draw, drain, or feed upon magnetically, then heart-aches and excruciating pangs follow upon one side, and, generally, a magnificent indifference and don't-care-much-about-it-ness on the other.

People with debts of gratitude to pay name towns, countries, lakes, rivers, ships, inns, horses, and boats after their benefactors and friends. I never exactly follow precedents, yet have a little bill to pay, and do it by christening a hither-to nameless crime. I allude to the horrible one committed by a species of human ghoul differing from either of the others just described. The Dentonite,--for such is the name I give the awful sin--is soulless, and altogether void of human feeling; I mean he is not immortal any more than a mongrel cur-dog is, and his lack of soul impels him to seek to supply the dreadful want from young girls, whom he will re-morsely violate and ruin, even if cool deliberate knife-butchery aids him in his fiendish crime--as is often the case; and terrible, awful, outright murder ends the dreadful tragedy. I can conceive no worse horror than that, nor give it a more befitting name.

XXXVI. My investigations into the mysteries, philosophy, and rationale of the human being, and its loves and passions, has led me to the inevitable and irrestible conclusion that Force is of body, nerves, and muscular organization mainly; and that real POWER lies in the soul alone. Now, by the term power I do not mean, as some have misunderstood me in the past to mean, the mere genital powers common alike to man and brutes; but I do mean that irresistible energy latent in all souls, and developed but in an exceedingly limited few. I hold that no power, such as is here intended to be understood, ever comes to man through the intellect. I affirm that the Baconian adage, "Knowledge is power," is not wholly, but only partially true; for I here repeat, Goodness alone is power, and goodness inheres not in brain, but in heart, metaphysically speaking, or on the emotional side or department of man's intricate and involute nature; wherefore, I lay down as an axiom, that power can only come to, and be developed in, the soul through Love; not passion or lust, look you, but Love; the underlying, primal fire-life of the immaterial soul; the invisible being that constitutes us man or woman; the fire-energy subtending the very basis of our being and, indeed, of all else that exists outside the Eternal Flame itself, the unimaginable Lord God of the Infinite Universe, that most mystical Heat which fuses all things, subtends all existence, and which is the formative floor of the worlds now rolling in silent majesty through space, cushioned upon the AEther, the very breasts of the mother side of ! Now, the true sensing of that higher, deeper, inner love is the beginning of the road which leads the soul into, and invests it with, real power in the loftier degrees; for Love, I maintain, lieth at the foundation. And it is the very synonym of life and strength, and lordly will, and clingingness, and truth, and real development; wherefore, I lay it down as another immutable truth that the true=love conjugation of man and wife is the loftiest and most sacred prayer to, and imitation of, God, possible to any creature in the whole vast realm of matter and mind, spirit and thought. Thus, in proof: how often it happens that a loving couple continually grow more youthful in soul, fruitful in happiness, and joyous in habitude, instead of servile, decrepit, warped and prematurely wrinkled, as in the cases of those to whom the wondrous realities of love are as thrice-sealed books! Why? Because they who thus truly love, in their sacred, spiritual passion, strike out this divine spark; partake of that celestial fire; replenish themselves with the quintessence of life itself; grow better, and spiritually stronger, and more beautiful, ripe, morally wealthy, calm, hopeful, attuned to this upper music; pass the brutal lands untouched; walk unharmed amidst moral malarias, and draw down to their souls, as copper-rods the lightning, the divine fervor and fire of the aerial spaces, the far-off heavens, and become baptized of the Holy Spirit, and earthly proteges of the supreme Lord of Glory,--our God.

Now once in a while couples do love each other, and from the product of such unions, what few civilized people there are take their rise and departure; and thus the world is saved by God's fiat, just as one honest man, and good, was declared sufficient to prevent the overthrow of Sodom.

The world owes its salvation to the accidents of Love; but by and by, what are now exceptional cases will become the universal rule, and then farewell human Boyhood, and welcome Manhood.

Couples not loving each other are mutually exhaustive, and, as a consequence, fret and fume, worry the life out of one another, and wear their very souls threadbear and to shreds, so that here on earth they amount to but little, and after death enter the ethereal realms in a state of immortal leanness, wizzenness, scranniness, requiring, perhaps, ages of time, or, at least, a long lapse of years, before they can ever reach a condition of soul-fatness, or celestial plumptitude. We can gain much by truly loving!

XXXVII. LIGHT is the shadow of God! Deity is never to be seen, for He ever recedes from telescopic or visual scrutingy. But He is always to be FELT; and whosoever feels for God is sure to touch and find him! for when we feel for him, he invariably comes forth and whispers to the soul: HERE AM I! But the inscrutable

BEING dwells within the Everlasting SHADOW,--behind the the Everlasting Flame; for HE IS THE ETERNAL FIRE! and the quintessence of All HEAT: not the heat of combustion, but its opposites, like unto that which is evolved from within our souls when we truly LOVE. Men gazing upon solar light have been struck dumb with the tremendous conception that God was concentrated Light, and that to find him they must rush into the intolerable effulgence, the awful brillance of all the focal spaces! But they erred. The amazing glories they beheld and conceived, and which they confounded with, or to be the very God, was but the dark shadow shielding him from view in the penetralia os mystery! Man, not God, is concentrated, focalized fire,--a condensation and crystallization of God's Nervous Fluid; and everything, especially the human soul, is a form of that fire. But man, as we know him here, is not the only self-consciousness in being; nor is this the best or worst of worlds. There are, and the AErial spaces abound with, multiform intelligences, having their conscious origin in AEthereal realms, as we have ours in matter. But as the divine Fire is the base of all alike; and as love and interfusion is the destiny of all, it follows that there is one common point where the sub-human, human, and ultra-human can contact each other and meet; and this point is that of interblending, for that one point everywhere, and in all things, is the only one thing common to all which exist as living entities anywhere.

It follows again that the higher the motives urging us when that universal duty is accomplished, the more powerful is the prayer it really is; the higher it reaches; the more it brings us en rapport with the blessed ones of the purer AETH, and the greater rain of goodness, power, health, life, mystic enjoyment, and all possible good it calls down upon our heads to saturate our souls. But there are grades of these ultra-human orders, towering away from our place and position in the eternal scale, in series vast, inconceivable Eterne; and other series descending to an equally unimaginable deep of the opposites of what we call goodness; and these, too, meet us on one common ground as the others; and can and do, when we give lust the rein, instead of love, ascend from the depths to us, and infuse us with strange ills and evils. The White Magic, which I here reveal, teaches how to rapport the good. The Black Magic of Africa and America (Voudooism) rapports us with the denizens of hell; and crime and wretchedness as surely flow out from the one affiliation, as the good flows forth from the other. I have made this revelation here, because it will do good, and afford a new field for the explorations of such as are interested in solving the tremendous problem of evil, its nature and origin.

XXXVIII. I have already told the world herein and elsewhere--(in "Soul, the Soul-world, and Homes of the Dead;" reprint and enlargement of the original volume "Dealings with the Dead")--that the seat of human consciousness is in the brain,--that it is a polar world or globe of white diamondesque fire in the human head. It is subject to two states, a positive and negative, masculine or electric; and a feminine, magnetic, or womanesque state. In its intellectual or male mood, it thunders forth its edicts from its throne in the brain, the central point of the head. But in its most awe-inspiring, creative and mystic moods, its fiats are given forth from another seat within the body. The brain is its throne of Force; the pelvis its seat of POWER! In sleep, especially that which is healthful, therefore dreamless, the soul sends a fibril of fire--an incandescent railway, from the corpus calossum to the medulla oblongata, down the spinal marrow to right back of the stomach; to the solar plexus,--the great storehouse where the servants of the body bring all the treasures they have gathered during the wakeful day, from the various laboratories,--stomach, intestines, ovaria, nerve-ganglia, lungs, liver, testes, arteries; and there the soul charges the fine aroma with its own life, and sends them back to become parts and portions of the living being; it imparts life-fire to every section of the human frame. After this the soul sometimes sends a filamental cord out into the air, above the earth, and on that ladder of light mounts the azure, and scans and contemplates distant scenes, and occasionally unfathomable mystery itself! Hence all dreams, could we translate them, have a fixed and determinate meaning.

But there is a farther revelation to be made right here. If human interblending occurs while weary, half asleep, vexed, anxious, distrustful, suspicious, thinking of money, or in an excited, passionate or mental state, two things are likely to occur, i.e., pregnancy,--in which case the child is sure to come here and stay here, die here, and go to the other world, and remain _there_, for centuries perhaps--half asleep, vexed, anxious, distrustful, suspicious, and mentally or otherwise excited all the livelong years; for although the woman builds up the child, the father invariably imparts the bias, because:--

XXXIX. In the beginning of the _marriage_ every fibre of his body sends a spiritual--material portion of itself to the _left_ half of the prostate gland, and his spiritual, emotional, soul and mind send corresponding portions of _themselves_ to the _right_ half of the prostate, and at the exact instant that these all meet at that point, the nervo-vital muscles spasmodically contact, and the procreative fluid passing through, takes with it the prostatic exudations, and the immortal being is thus charged with a joyous load of heaven, or a grievous burden of intolerable horrors. _But_ impregnation may _not_ occur; yet the fluids thus charged, and discharged, are absorbed in great measure by the innumerable mouths and ducts of the vaginal parietes, and she absorbs his physical, mental and moral poisons as surely as if the husband was freighted down with syphilitic virus;--only that the one eats away and cankers her flesh; while the other corrodes her soul!

Men are proverbially, in these matters, careless of possible consequences, and this is a source of terrible dread to their wives; to such a degree, that fear paralyzes their passional nature; and on their side there is, and can be, no response; finding which to be the case, the average husband grows crisp and cranky, offish, petulant, downright angry; all of which she feels, and discord and misery reign beneath that roof.

Well? Reply: By an effort of the will the male can prevent the prostatic flow; and, secondly, the wife by becoming mentally positive at the crisis, and _willing_ that she _ought not_, _must not_, _will_ not conceive, _cannot_; or that she will _not_ absorb that which will impair her mental or physical health--cannot so absorb it. Hence she is safe, whenever she _wills_ to be!

XL. Power, true power, can only descend from heaven to true loving souls, because power is feminine, and woman represents it, albeit she is practically ignorant of the fact; and a man has yet to learn that the _seeds_ of power descend either through the feminine channels of _his_ soul, or to him through woman. All great men have been made so through women, either by their mothers, or by some woman whose love made her will and wish him to be good, great and happy, during the sacred prayer of holy, loving wifehood. I have already alluded to the ability of a woman to utterly ruin any man her soul loathes and hates, under precisely the same circumstances; for it lies within her power to make or mar the best man living. I _have_ seen it tried, in both the make and the mar, and with results magnificent in the one case, and insufferably poignant in the other. Thus man, by love _all_ the time, but especially _then_, can wholly modify woman's character, and _kindle_ her ice to a gentle, constant and invigorant flame. But carelessness and ignorance on the part of many millions of wives, in some sense, make them responsible for their own miseries; for they all have the ability to resist the depleting effects of pestilent vampyrism, and avoid all the diseases, disasters and ailments, mental, moral, physical and emotional, thus engendered; and also to wholly transform the nature and character of almost any man, no matter how coarse, inconsiderate, careless, indifferent or mean.

In declaring these new and weighty truths I victoriously plant the white banner over the frowning ramparts of the social world. Why? How? Attend:--

XLI. Because almost everywhere in this broad land marriage practically exists as a repressive system; it is all head, and the man is that head, while the wife is but an appendage, and by no means either partner or equal; and, so long as such is the case, things will not grow better, because happiness is what every one seeks for, and if not found at the fireside at home will be searched for elsewhere. Now I want to stop all that by showing the law underlying human weal as it has never been shown before on earth. The system of marriage should be one of absolute equality and partnership between couples. I want to help along that system; for the one now in vogue practically drives enormous hosts of people to heaven across lots, over steep-down gulfs of social and domestic horror. I am teaching all to avoid such. On the marriage question, as mainly discussed at present, there is too much everlasting gabble on the horrors of deformity in all parts of the social machine; but I seek to make people purer, nobler, truer, and draw, not _drive_, them heavenward by appeals to the good, the true, and the beautiful latent within them, and which, when active, brings bliss to every beating heart.

XLII. Too many marriages concern themselves about mourning; I wish them to be deeply, continually interested about joy. They think mainly concerning how to make the best of a bad bargain; bearing life's crosses; abiding with befitting patience to the end, and all that; while I am teaching them how to make a bad bargain an exceedingly good one; how to neutralize the social poisons by wholesale--and the worst of them are generated at home; and all through the triple white magic of Love, will, and persistent trying; that is, to cure their ills by the constant exercise of common sense, which, it seems, after all, is a very uncommon thing, judging by the stupid way in which nine married couples out of every ten totally ignore its clear and plain behests; for common sense is the genius of the average mind, and is an excellent guide to go by.

XLIII. I have said, and it is true, that the other, the feminine, magnetic, and, therefore, superior pole, or polar dwelling, of the viewless soul of human kind, is in the genital system of each sex respectively; whence it follows that in all nuptial unions, where true love reigns and rules, governs and controls, the entire beings of each party, the _entire_ _soul_ of each officiates at the banquet, and the celebration; wherefore, both the positive and negative powers and forces of each party assist at the--in the--incarnation of the new soul, _if_ a new soul is then and there called into outer being, to run the gauntlet of time in its race to the fields of eternity; and all such generation is holy; and, it being a genuine _marriage_, none but truly human children are called into the world.

But where no love inspires the parents, only _one_ of the two grand forces of their souls officiate either in, or at, the generation of their mutual offspring; and such children are death-sure to be deficient in some quality, and to pay through lives more or less angular, limited and bitter, for the sins of their parents, and their profanation of the holiest of all human sanctities, and violation of the grand- est and deepest law of the human world--that of Love; from such conditions it happens that the lands are teeming with half-men, half-women, and abound in human weaklings. "Illegitimates" are exceptional in brilliance, because at least some tolerable measure of Love, and a great deal of Passion, obtained when they were called into earthly existence.

Apply the principle herein laid down, and it is not hard to see the reason why inferior-brained, but strongly loving and loved women, become mothers of mental-moral millionaires, while brainy mothers give us children born to intellectual penury. Men with comparatively small cerebral capital and calibre, but whose love-nature is large, full, open, generous, almost invariably become fathers to their mental superiors; while per contra we all know that great talent, and actual genius seldom produces anything higher than a very low grade of mediocrity. Their children are notoriously below par--and PA also. These truths may be new and novel, as are many of those to follow herein, but they are assuredly destined and commissioned to revolutionize the world of thought on these subjects, nevertheless and nothwith-standing.

XLIV. The negative or brain pole of the soul, so to speak, is Thoughtful. Its mission is to scan, search, explore, investigate, reason, understand, know. It is en rapport more or less perfectly, with the intellectual and knowing universe; that is to say, it is masculine and electric. Now an electric man "progresses," stores up, advances toward, and captures knowledge, facts, things, ideas and principles; and only give him time, and he will become an encyclopedia on legs, for all that's knowable he feels bound to find out. But the positive pole or sphere of the soul being feminine or magnetic, is in direct contact or rapport with the very soul of being itself;--the foundation fires of the universe--with all that vast domain underlying increase, growth, generation, evolution, emotion, heat, expan-sion, energy, power--the sole and base of being, the arterial blood of God Himself --measureless LOVE--the primal fire-flow of the whole vast realm of universal existence, whence the female is nearer God than the male, and God is far more female than its opposite; for it is in him, as in the human, a far less labor to create than it is to gestate and bring forth. God struck the universe into being a single fiat of his Imperial Will; but it took even him billions of centuries to gestate and bring forth man; just as a man occupies one second of time only, to plant a monad in the uterine soil, but it takes woman forty odd weeks to prepare it for its uses on the earth; or it takes man one second to begin to work, which occupies all the energies of woman's soul and body about twenty-six million seconds to complete what he began! Hence one good mother is worth at least fifty millions of male drones, without love to guide them heavenwards; and her influence for good in the universe, bears the same ratio to his worthlessness, as a general rule; and right here I desire to impress upon my readers, not only the tremendous value and im-portance of any human soul, and the awful consequences of destroying human life at any stage; but to enforce upon them the absolute necessity of marriage and parentage, --for every child, no matter how imperfect, is eventually a positive gain to the universe; and every female who goes to the grave childless; every man who fails in his duty to himself, God and nature, and dies without prolonging his human line, commits a grave offence,--so grave as not to be easily forgiven.

Thus it is readily seen that through Love man seizes directly on all that is, and is in actual contact and rapport with all and singular every being that FEELS and Loves within the confines of the habitable universe. But any amount of brain or learning he may have affiliates him to a very few at most, because all sentient creatures love and feel, while comparatively few can think and know. LOVE FOREVER against THE WORLD! The positive throne or seat of the soul, in the male, is in near, and about the prostatic gland, with three radii extending to the connected viscera, whence it happens that emasculation injures the very soul itself.

In the female, the major force of the soul resides in the uterus, with three radii extending to the right and left ovaria and the connected viscera, whence it happens that illness or injuries there have the most baleful, injurious and debilitat-ing effect upon every portion and department of her being and nature. We often hear the phrase "A fine specimen of a woman!" "A magnificent woman!" but such terms are _never_ applied to any mere bundle of brains, but always of those of fine physical presence, geniality of demeanor, and magnetic fulness, indicating Love within the soul, whether it be well and highly cultured or not. Now it is possible for a man to grow fat who is lean, or lean who is fat, by pursuing steadily Bantingism-- I _believe_ they call it--or its opposite, as the case may demand; and I _know_ that a lean soul can also grow fat, and non-magnetic people reverse their states. The mode I have already herein pointed out, hence need not again recur to.

XLV. Do not forget that herein and elsewhere I have declared the great truth that true manhood and woman hood are more or less en rapport with one or more of the upper hierarchies of Intelligent Potentialities, earth-born and _not_ earth-born. I believe there are means whereby a person may become associated with, and receive instruction from, them. More than that, I believe in what I may call will-magnets, or talismans; that it is possible to construct and wear them, and that they emit a peculiar light, discernible across the gulfs of space by those intelligent powers, just as we discern a diamond across a play-house; that such are signals to the beholders; and that they will, and do, cross the chasmal steeps to save, succor, and assist the wearers, just as a good brother here flies to the relief of him who shall give the grand hailing-signs of distress. _This_ _is_ _provable._

This grand mystery of the will, properly cultured, is the highest aid to _man_, for it is a divine Energos, white, pure magic, the miracle-working potentiality which cometh only to the free and wholly unshackled human soul; while to woman it is the only salvation from marital vampyrism, the shield and buckler of her power, and the groundwork upon which must be builded the real rule of her influence in the world and at home. The reasons _why_ will be readily seen by recurring to the basic propositions of the divine science, which declares that God, the _soul_ of the universe if POSITIVE HEAT, CELESTIAL FIRE; that the aura of Deity (God-od) is LOVE, the prime element of all power, the external fire-sphere, the informing and formative pulse of matter. The deduction is crystalline; for it follows that whoso hath most love--whether its _expression_ be coarse or fine, cultured or rude--hath, therefore, most of God in him or her; the element of time being competent to the perfecting of all refining influences, over the ocean of Death, if not upon the hither side. Conversely put, the statement stands thus: whoso most resembleth God, therefore, hath most of love, goodness, and the elements of power. God is not a _libertine_! Now these latent energies I claim to here give the true knowledge of, that all may understand the laws of love, will, and ethereal force, and the principles and modes of their evolution, and crystallization in the homos; the result aimed at being the elimination of the gross, and their orderly consolidation into personal power. I hold that LOVE is, ever was, and eternally will be, absolutely pure. Paste is not diamond, though they resemble somewhat, nor is LOVE ever anything but its own transcendant self; yet normal passion is divine, because through it alone God gives TRUE MEN to the great man-wanting world. There can be no such thing as unholy _Love_; nor good badness, nor bad goodness.

XLVI. Silence is strength, and the silent lip and steady head alone are worthy. I do not believe in the, to _me_, absurd dogma of human equality; it is the demonstrable negation of all human reason and experience; is a hypocritical, cruel, and delusive falsehood; puts people out of their element, and into wrong positions; it never was, will, nor can be, true; for "aristocracy" of some kind always rules, is always a unit in interests, while "democracy" is always _ruled_, and is eternally at war with itself, and clashing about its own interests, which interests it perpetually injures and destroys. But it _is_ true that some souls are nobler, better, higher, finer, richer, riper, rounder,--these SEVEN,--than some other souls, and are worth immeasurably more, whether weighed or plumbed in God's scales or man's. For some souls are young, green, acid, acrid, bitter, imperfect, and non-poised,--_these_

-47-

seven,--and such stand for aeons of ages gaping, on the highways, at regal souls rushing across the deeps toward Achievement; here, there, now, then, up the streets of the worlds, and down the corridors of heaven. Splendid, "aristocratic" souls, who will circumnavigate eternity while the others are wondering,"What next?" and, "Did you ever!"--new souls, just created, requiring a thousand or two of ages to get their eternal sea-legs on, before being able to steadily walk the decks of the eviternal ship of centuries and power, or compete with those who, living now, yet have passed their ordeals long before this civilization had taken root in the mouldy soil of scores that had preceded it.--Men who make and govern circumstances instead of allowing circumstances to govern them.

XLVII. True Passion is but one, and a minor mode of Love's expression; its offices are triplicate; and when people understand that one grand secret, farewell to social, domestic, and all other ills; and it is this grand secret I have, for long years, been teaching, somewhat, not fully, in all my books, on both shores of the oceans that girdle the world. I know that brains and intellects differ, but hearts and affection are ever the same; that through these last man can attain unto Godness, and woman reign queen and equal, where she now serves as drudge, toy, and legal and illegal--something worse; that woman, as such, has most of love crystallized within her, and for that reason is entitled to stand the peer of the best man breathing God's free air; not by reason of her beauty, accomplishments, wealth, or any other accident, but because she hath the womb,--the perfected laboratory wherein she fashioneth, and alone completes, what it took God, Nature, and Man, singly and combined, to only begin; and that, too, so badly, that the wonder is, that swarming hordes of murderers do not throng the world's highways where civilized man now walks. But so infinitely great an artiste is she, that from the worst of seed she has raised many a splendid human tree; redeemed the race from savagery; fostered and cultured art, science, religion, and all that renders earth habitable, and that, too, under all sorts of repressions and bad conditions; assuredly entitling her now to a chance of trying what she can do, under favorable circumstances, who did so well under the bad; and I hold this to be the strongest argument for woman ever made since the world began; and I advance it only as one of the external reasons I entertain, holding in reserve others as much stronger and more cogent than these, as a chain-cable is superior to a child's slender whip-cord.

XLVIII. I further hold that there are AEthereal (spacial) centres of Love, Power, Force, Energy, Goodness, and for, and of, every kind, grade, species, and order of knowledge known to man, and whereof he knows not anything; and that it is not only possible to reach those centres, and obtain those knowledges, but that it is achievable by a vast number, who now drone and doze away life, die half ripe, and wake up, when too late, to find out what fools they have been, necessitating what it is not the present purpose to reveal. In the present instance it only remains for the purposes of this Declaration of Principles, to draw a brief comparison between my system and the very best that can possibly, truthfully be said of any single one of all the others now extant anywhere. They are divided into two parts, one of which proceeds to totally ignore the body, mortifies the flesh, and renders life truly a semi-graveyard operation from birth to baptism, from that to death. The other allows the utmost limit to lust and license to the elect, and roundly berates all others outside. Vide Mormonism, Perfectionism, and Islamism, and contrast them with their opposites in belief, as the Shakers. But current systems, as a general thing, bend all their energies toward the salvation of men's souls, and, in spending time in trying to get souls into heaven, lose sight of the bodies, which, practically, may go to the other place, of so little account are they. They believe in crucifying the flesh altogether, and generally effect that very thing for the soul. They wholly lose sight of a fundamental principle of human nature, which is to take delight in doing the very thing it is sternly forbidden to.

The people of a town might not, if let alone, leave its boundaries once in ten years; but you just make a law that they shall not leave it, and that town will be empty in less than a single day. Again: Said landlord Boniface, "Traveller, you must go further to pass the night, for my house is full, and I have no place to put you." Says weary traveller, "DON'T say so; don't say no; poor me!. How can you serve me so? I'm so fagged out I can't walk another step. I'll put up with any-thing rather than go on." Says Boniface, "Poor, weary man, I pity you, and on one condition you can stay; there is one room with two beds. The one nearest the door you can sleep in; the other--at the far corner--is occupied by a lady, who must not be disturbed in any way. You must enter it on tiptoe, without a light on, go quiet-ly to bed, and at daybreak quit it in the same manner. Do you agree to these condi-tions?"--"I do;" and he was shown the door, and again strictly cautioned. But, by and by, there was a sound of devilry by night, and that weary, wayworn traveller lifted up his voice and yelled aloud; and his voice went flying the descending stairs, and his body, with protruding eyes, and hair erect, cam speedily following down, down, reaching the lower floor just one second after his voice. "O Lord!" said the traveller. "What's the matter?" asked Boniface. "Why, that woman's dead!" --"I knew that before," said landlord; "but how did you find it out?" Just so. Human nature is strongly perverse, and this incident suggests the query that were social life and marriage based upon CONSENT and ATTRACTION instead of what they are based on, there wouldn't be a hell on earth or anywhere else, in less than one hundred brief years --brief to God, and to immortal man.

Finally, to conclude this section, I admit, and triumphantly, too, that in the cultured, or magic, because magnetic, will, I find a remedy for very many of the ills besetting us on the earth, especially in our marriage matters of the false of to-day; and furthermore, that by obedience to law, herein set forth, the ELIXIR of life may be found, and the human stay on earth be prolonged a great deal beyond the storied threescore years and ten.

Let us now proceed to the consideration of a phase of the matter in hand, never before fairly treated upon, or even touched by those who assumed to discuss it, by reason of its recondite nature. It being my highest ambition to do good while the frame lasts, I possibly may achieve it better in essaying the unravelling of the knot alluded to, than in any other way.

Men are often seen whose actione currente is wholly feminine; but a far greater number of females are found who have all the yearnings proper only to the opposite gender. Understand me. It is the proper function of man to impart, to give, to en-force, to generate, to beget his kind; and of course the impelling sensations are peculiar. It is the proper function of woman to reverse all this--to receive, respond, provoke passion, accept, exude, gestate, and to have all the sensations proper thereto. But thousands have the characteristics of their proper sex, physiologically, with their normal sensations, impellant or nervo-vital action, and instead have all the latter characteristics of the reverse gender. This abnormal state, so very common, results from their mothers wishing and hoping that the unborn may be of one sex, while nature determines to, and does produce its opposite; where-fore such girls will love like a man; such boys love like a woman, and of course can never be satisfied in this life on that very account. The upshot of it all is, that urged on by an irresistible impulse, such persons resort to unnatural methods to appease the quenchless thirst; assuage the yearning appetite,--hence we have onanists, masturbationists, pederasts; those who associate with four-footed beasts, and in t other respects sink to very infamous levels--even to those horrible ones, to name which I fairly shudder, and therefore will not.

When a woman is pregnant, her whole desire should be that of giving to the world a perfect specimen of her maternal work, allowing nature to determine the sex; and then we shall behold no more such improperly constructed human beings on this fair earth of ours; wherefore we shall be rid of agitators of the "Sexual Question."

XLIX. In announcing the law and fact that the subtle element called magnetism is the connecting link between mind and body, the flesh, sinew, bone and muscle, and the incorporeal viewless soul of man, I declared a new truth, or rather one newly discovered. True, it has been suspected that electricity, in some of its subtler forms, was that link, but I am not aware that the subtler element, magnetism, was ever even suspected to be such link. Body is the seat of the senses; soul is the seat of the deeper faculties; for Emotion, Love, Sympathy, Memory, Fancy, Judgment, and a hundred other human attributes belong to the region and domain of soul, spirit, mind,--the invisible man within,--and the vehicle of their display and action upon, and in the outer world, is magnetism. Proof: When we are in perfect magnetic rapport with an individual, that person can be made to imitate our action, think our thoughts, do as we do, and be for the time our exact counterparts; but we may be in absolute electric contact, and not one of these strange results will follow. Observe these facts: cohabitation, love not being the spur, is a magnetic halfness; with love, it is a magnetic circulation, that is to say, pleasure results from a nervous current rushing along the nerves of each, and mingling in chemico-magnetic union in and at the termination of the nervous filaments radiating from every portion of the two beings, and converging to a point at the respective vital centres of each.

There can be no mutual joy unless such nervous currents do flash along the nervo-telegraphic system; nor can we experience any pleasure, whatever, either nerval, gustatory, or in any other manner, unless such currents do thus pass; and, moreover, every true, or even false human joy, must first be in the soul, before the body can participate. We cannot lift a board till we bend to it, and brace the muscles to the task. This is the principle of POSISM: i.e., placing ourselves to do the work, receive a blow, shock or impression. We hate, and all our external features array themselves--involuntarily--ever to materially express the metaphysical emotion. Now for the application of this principle to the subject under consideration.

L. It would look foolish for one to verbally protest burning love, while the face betokened its deadly opposite, or actual, stupid indifference! If the heart means love, and the lips assert it, the voice, manner, eyes, and genial glow, must express it also, if one expects to be believed. Yet in spite of the notoriously plain truth, there are thousands who talk love, while face, feature, voice and conduct give the lie direct to all the lips have spoken; and yet the speakers marvel because their story is not credited. Such persons, too, may honestly mean just what and all they say, yet, failing to pose themselves to the requirements of the case, fail also both in winning credence, and retaining what of love they have already won. Counsel: If your lips speak love, always pose your features to the natural language of the passion or sentiment. For the expression of feature, the soft and flowing modulations of tone, the mellow cadence and inflection of the voice, tells the immortal story of the heart quite as plainly, and far more eloquently, than can possibly any collocation of mere words, which any one can marshal to his or her aid; and soft and gentle tones will do more for errant, faulty husbands and wives than all the protestations or verbal storms that one could utter in a century!

We have societies for the protection of beasts; and need a larger one for the protection of human beings in certain vital respects. It ought to be just ground for instant divorce wherever and whenever a human male forces unwelcome embraces upon any female, whatever. The beasts of the field don't do so. Why should men? More than that; it ought to be a criminal offence in the eye of the law; and as such, punishable, for any human male, under any circumstances, whatever, to force the inclinations of any woman, whatever, or to exact or seek wifely offices or concessions, except when <u>she</u> wills and ordains that such may be. Make this a law, and we shall have less work for sextons in digging graves for "Mrs. so and so," at any age between sixteen and thirty-five. The common sense of mankind knows full well that he is no man, but only a satyr, who demands what cannot be granted, save with a shudder of unutterable horror and disgust; pangs past endurance, or at the risk of health and life.

The action of the muscles is as clear an expression of a passion, and the mental states behind it, as are the tones which utter it; for"Actions speak louder than words" is not only a truism, but an absolute and unqualified truth itself. Wherefore if you mean love, look love from top to toe, and all over!

LI. You never saw a sick man, really, desperately sick, whoever denied the existence of a God. It requires a fine stomach, keen appetite, and excellent digestion to make a first-class sceptic. Why? Because conditions of body effect changes in the soul's feelings; and the play between the outer and the inner being is mutual, fot the soul affects the body for good or ill quite as much as the body affects the invisible soul. Married people are either not aware of this double-acting law of the homos, or else wilfully ignore its heavy meanings. They live a cat-and-dog life, because neither reasons that some physical disturbance unhinges the soul, or that some metaphysical derangement unfits the body to express what the soul itself may be completely full of. Thus, a woman suffering catamenial pains, or some other ill, is apt to be <u>rather</u> Novemberish externally, even while July really reigns deep down in her sweet, but ruffled, soul; and a man, worried to death with worldly cares, is not always either in mood or condition to lavish tenderness even upon the children of his loins, or the wife of his bosom, all of whom he loves beyond his then-capacity of expression. A person in certain physical states is insane for the time being; is fully willing to curse God, and die; yet a dose of opening medicine would unbar the gates of his soul, and within two hours that self-same man would bless God, and live.

And a wife in certain magnetic and mental states, the result of physiological causes, would fly at a man and scratch his eyes out, when, next day, after a good dose of senna, she would love and caress him half to death.

At this writing I am suffering from partial paralysis, partly the result of a severe fall,--a mere matter of twenty-five feet through the trestle-work of a bridge, upon a not very soft pile of rocks at the bottom, sent down there by the savage threats of two converging locomotives, one behind and on before. But <u>that</u> injury I could have recovered from, by reason of the strong resilient energies of my constitution, had it not happened that for months before, <u>then</u>, and months afterward, I was continually laboring with brain, hands, and pen,--bad enough,--but was also subjected daily to violent and continued affectional and mental emotion; cause: 'A woman at the bottom of it;" and that sort of excitement is quite sufficient to bring on paralysis, without the help of any locomotive that ever screeched over the 'Middle Ground," --a place in Toledo, where more ghosts of mangled dead walk than upon any surface of equal area in the entire universe.

As physician, I have treated many cases of disease which the patients attributed to scores of causes other than the right one,--affectional trouble. Merchants, bankers, men of large business, are almost invariably, and inevitably, stricken down in the midst of life and hope, by apoplexy, paralysis, chronic dyspepsia, stone, gravel, or embolism; not alone by reason of their business activity, or even nervous exhaustion, but because they do not loosen up, change their modes of motion, and devote more time to the homeside, social life, and "fun." Business, the infernal demon-god, is all in all; passion but a spasm; love, a myth, an unrealized dream, its joys still more unreal, vague, phantomesque, until at length nature wears out, God insulted, and he send the Angel of Midnight to drop the curtain, and change the scene.

Aphrodisiacs are certain preparations--most of them outright infernal--which excite the amorous or passional appetites of the human being. There are long lists of them; and many years before this book was written, its author discovered the best six tonics the world had ever seen, or has yet. I refer to the Protozonic Remedials. And I have known hundreds upon hundreds of people, who lived so close to the dollar-counter, that nature withdrew her smiles from them, and impotence, dead, sterile, <u>horrible</u>, became their lot, and for years they had never known love in its physical aspects unless under the forcing power of some disastrous stimulant. To these the protozones were blessings, indeed, and once more the mad-house and a-poplexy were left behind,--not because they were remedials, but civilizers; humaniz-ers; fitting the wasted nerve, balancing the tottering brain, restoring the primal conditions upon which human happiness in the social are depends, not being mere chemicals, but alchymics or conveyers of spirit: soul. But what a state of things is that wherein men, otherwise sensible, so far forget their duties to self, home, wife, society, and God, as, in the mad chase for wealth, to sacrifice Manhood, Love and Paternity. Paternity! just think of it! what a glory, and what a joy, compared to which all the wealth and honor earth can give were but hollow shams and empty mockery! while Parentage, Fatherhood,--above all Imperial Motherhood, is a diadem which even gods might well aspire to. I have seen women pass along the streets who gave token of their coming pain and glory; and I have seen things shaped like unto men laugh and giggle as they passed along; these doers of God's finest and greatest work; the incarnators of regal soul; these unappreciated martyrs of love, and victims of man too often beside,--and I have felt like rushing upon, and tear-ing the heartless scoundrels to pieces; for if there be a transcendantly glorious thing on earth it is a mother. And I, Paschal, the writer, here say that I took off my hat, and did homage to every pregnant woman I ever saw; and I would do it, were that woman no higher than a common troll, so highly and devoutly did I, do I, adore and worship MOTHERHOOD. There, that's my soul!

But if these laughers, these careless husbands, knew the truth I now reveal in the next few lines, they too,, like myself, would laugh, but with royal joy, instead of coarse derision. It is this: 1st, most seekers after domestic bliss, like him who builds from the roof groundward, begin at the wrong end. It is to be found in soul, not sense; spirit, not form; heart, not dress; and love, not passion. 2d. A pregnant woman, judiciously loved and treated,--not spoiled and pampered, or kept at a dead level of life, love, temper, feeling, passion, ardor, fervor, labor, rest, but made to develop her womanhood,--will, in every ten days, add more soul, strength, fervor, beauty, compactness, energy, power, and force of character and genius to her baby than she could in all the forty weeks of gestation if neglected in the above respects; for she will knot more greatness in it every hour she lives; and each step or stage of gestation will be carried one or more degrees toward perfection. The only difference between a genius and a human ninny is, that one is finished up as the work goes on. He is well kneaded, and <u>needed</u>, too; will keep well; give excellent satisfaction all around, and will be longed for, and wept over when gone, just as children mourn the good things that have passed away forever.

LII. Paralysis, caused other than by physical injury, is the result of over-emotion; too acrid states of the blood and fluids--(often removable by continued catharsis) and by nerve-embolism, as well as that of the blood-vessels, consequently the system is not supplied with a proper amount of vitalized pabulum. Paralysis more often results from affectional troubles than anything else, and the only cure is their re-arrangement, accompanied with phosphorized cordials, and phosphoric food, to which may be added the daily pouring over the head and backbone of at least two pailfuls of hot water, as hot as can be borne, alternating with ice-rubbing of the spine, or rhigolene-spray baths; this will cure it nine times in ten, when mentally caused; and would have saved Napoleon III., and perhaps a disastrous war, had his physicians been wise; but they were not, and suffered him to eat, drink, smoke, and libertinize to excess, until at last his constitution, enfeebled by amatory outrage in his early life, refused to respond to desire; his embolism increased; fistula attacked the perinaeum, involving the entire pelvic system, necessitating castration at the knife of the surgeon, and ending at Chiselhurst, in fever and death, but a few months after,--and the crisis hastened swiftly by the keen anguish resulting from the consciousness that he, the great emperor, was no longer a man, but only a eunuch or human stag. This fact of his loss occasioned the "Decheance" act of the French Senate;--for they would not be ruled by either a woman--or a castrato.

Barrenness of woman results from similar causes; and so also does the four kinds of male impotence, now abounding everywhere to a frightful extent. These are, 1st. Lack of muscular force; 2d. Inability to elaborate the vital fluid; 3d. Inability to retain it at all; or to retain it if, and when, elaborated; 4th. Inability to vitalize it by reason of trouble in the prostate gland. Hitherto the medical people have recognized but one form of impotence, whereas there are no less than four, each, of course, requiring quite dissimilar methods of curative treatment.

LIII. Nothing goes on either in soul or body without some sort of expenditure. We have a mental, moral, and affectional digestion as well as a physical one; and we all know that unless we excrete the superfluous matter of the food and drinks we take, dyspepsia comes in, and finally we grow dull, sleepy, and stupid from the accumulated phosphates, acid or alkaline, lime, carbon, etc., urea, uric acid, etc., and death soon comes tapping at the door; but who ever suspected that it is just as necessary to void mental, moral, and affectional wastes, and thus prevent soul-dyspepsia, or cure it if established? Yet such is the case. The mind that would be healthy must cast out of it all it cannot appropriate, assimilate, and transmute, else mental, moral, and affectional diseases set in, and psychal debility is the result, terminating in a complete deadening of all these higher qualities which par excellence make us truly human.

LIV. Now he or she who dwells mainly in the brain is subject to enormous nervous waste; and the blood, charged with refuse brain and nerve-rust, rushes to the kidneys, and there unloads its bad freight; but all servants get tired, and so do the organs named; so that after a while they cease to drain and sift so perfectly as of yore; consequently the alkaline phosphates and urea are not all discharged, but a portion is poured back into the circulation, until finally every inch of the physical body is poisoned; and a healthy soul cannot healthfully act through poisoned nerves and tainted fluids. The kidneys begin to suffer and give out; the suprarenal capsules change their fibre, and no longer act as storehouses for the kidney-life placed there daily by the watchful soul. The bladder goes next, then the testes, prostate, ovaries, or uterus follow; and before you know it, the man or woman is a splendid wreck. Wherefore follow Solomon's advice, and remember two things: 1st, that there's a time for work and rest and sleep, and amusements and converse and amorous diversion; next, that all work, and no play, makes Jack a dull boy; meals, sleep, love-seasons, all should be as nearly as possible orbital or periodic in their motions, just as the day, night, winter, spring, and autumn in the world without. In a little while nature will assist, and each season will come in full force at its proper time, just as eclipses occur, and green fields smile again.

Surely married people will understand this delicate, but very important suggestion. Hundreds of people, consulting me as physician, have benefited by that advice, and by resolutely sleeping apart, as a custom, have begun to realize a domestic felicity they never before imagined to be possible. Nay, it is _absolutely_ necessary in all cases where perfect restoration does not follow every night's slumber.

Reader, you have one hundred and sixty bones, and five hundred muscles; your blood weighs twenty-five pounds; your heart is five inches in length and three inches in diameter; it beats seventy times a minute, four thousand two hundred times per hour, one hundred thousand eight hundred times a day, and twenty-six millions seven hundred and twenty-five thousand two hundred times per year. At each beat a little over two ounces of blood is thrown out of it; and each day it receives and discharges seven tons of that wonderful fluid. Your lungs will contain a gallon of air, and you inhale twenty-three thousand gallons a day. The average surface of the air-cells of your lungs, supposing them to be spread out, exceeds twenty thousand square inches. The weight of your brain is three pounds. In the average American man it will weigh about eight ounces more. Your nerves exceed ten millions in number. Your skin is composed of three layers, and varied from one-fourth to one-eighth of an inch in thickness. The area of your skin is about one thousand seven hundred square inches, and you are subjected to an atmospheric pressure of fifteen pounds to the square inch. Each square inch of your skin contains three thousand sweating tubes, or respiratory pores, each of which may be likened to a little drain-tile one-fourth of an inch long, making the aggregate length of the entire surface of your body of two hundred and one thousand three hundred and sixty-five feet, or a tile-ditch for draining the body almost forty miles long.

Now in any act which requires more than a normal drain, every atom of this magnificent machine is injured, and its life jeoparded. But in sexism, true and normal, and false and perverted ones also, yield up a portion of the life of every particle of the being; also when we sleep with nervous or organic incompatibles. In righteous conjugation what one gives out is instantly replaced by the other, and perfect rest and equilibrium follow the natural shock. But in the false rites, what of life goes out, _stays_ out. There is no return in kind; no change given for the golden coin of life recklessly thrown on the counters of lust!

LV. The bitterest matrimonial discontents arise from the half-unconscious misconception that happiness, not growth, is the end of marriage, and the forgetfulness that human nature is universal. It is impossible for two people thoroughly to know each other until they have been tested by the exigencies of a united life. If then a radical antagonism of temperament is developed, which makes the union oppressive, why should the discordant souls be kept together? What is to be gained by holding them in the bonds of hatred? The remedy cannot be found in the abolition of the civil contract of marriage, leaving them free to repeat again and again the disastrous experiment, because _that_ has been tried and failed. Now it seems to me that there should be schools of marriage; that is, institutions with professorships, expressly to teach the laws which alike, everywhere, underlie human happiness. As it is to-day, pretty faces win male stupidity, and disaster invariably follows. Above all, our system of nervous life, the good food poorly cooked, the way we eat, drink, sleep,—all are axes laid at the roots of the tree of domestic life!

There's not one sound man in five hundred; nor a woman in a thousand, who does not have the doctor's care for ills resulting from this false life. The food we eat, and what we drink, act upon our souls, our emotions, and our loves, quite as much as upon our mere bodies; and I had rather have one meal cooked by a good, loving old mother, than all the hotels of earth, with golden plate, could furnish; because such food is seasoned with goodness.

LVI. I am satisfied that sleeping together, and too frequent yielding to the impulses incident to the chemically fevered state we are in, produces a peculiar nervous exhaustion which, if long continued, always results in a chronic morbidity closely verging upon actual insanity,--indeed, in most cases, upon some points, it is insanity itself; for what else can that state be called which sees nothing at all but ill, dark-omened shadows continually floating over the sky of life; and which beholds, in the wife or husband, nothing but demons or gorgons; chatters about him, or her; exposes faults, magnified mole-hills into rocky mountains; and only breathes venom, spite, and malignant hate, upon one sworn at the altar to be loved and cherished till death did them part. This is sheer madness; downright insanity; and in that mood what worlds of wrong are daily done, and that, too, by people in whose hearts angels slumber, and long to be awakened, that their wings might fan the fevered brow, and lull the weary souls to rest. This insanity has its rise in satiety, and non-reciprocity in the more intimate relations of husband and wife; and is akin to that which falls like a leaden pall sooner or later upon the onanist and debauchee.

Owing to the imperfect marriages of to-day, and the few past decades, millions of half-children, or unsound ones, have been born: crooked, angular, violent, un-reliable, impulsive, vagarious, and constitutionally morbid, with a powerful bias toward unquestionable insanity. Passing along the streets it is easy to pick out people thus born; their faces and heads betray the unmistakable brand of incipient lunacy; and it requires but little provocation to fan the latent embers into a glow-ing and terrible flame. The average insane head is smaller in all its dimensions than the sane. The latter shows, also, less irregularity of outline. The left anterior quarter of the sane head is usually larger than the right, while the right anterior quarter of the insane head is almost always larger than the left. Many in-sane people show a decided projection in the right frontal region. Now mark the conduct of your friends thus organized.

LVIII. But why are they insane? What's the actual--not theoretic--but purely scientific facts of such cases? Reply: Magnetic and amative depletion act upon some people precisely as starvation acts upon everybody. When the stomach can no longer get food, the body begins to consume and feed upon itself; first it absorbs the fat, and we grow lean; then it attacks the muscles, and we become skeletons; next the liver goes, and we become cadaverous; then the mucous surfaces are called upon; and at last the serous plates are attacked, and the grave closes over a bunch of bones only. In the case of the sexual pederastic, Dentonian debauchee, when his lust alone drives him to either excess or sexive horrors, there is no return, and his passion consumes his body. First, the nerves become strained and tensioned beyond endurance, and one after another gives way; then the muscular cords are slackened; then the testicular glands decrease; then the prostate; then the marrow of the back-bone softens and yields its fat to feed the fearful fire, creeping up till it reach-es the brain; then the substance of the brain goes down to death's hot furnace; the soul shuts itself up, moodily waiting its time of flight, and when it acts at all is compelled to do so through diseased organs and perverted channels; hence, all it does is distorted, outre, queer, abnormal. The man is mad--and --let the curtain fall; the tragedy is ended.

LVIII. When teaching those who were desirous of mastering the principles per-vading the books, and constituting the soul of the system evoked and elaborated by him whose pen scores these lines, it was the custom for him to address them in these following words, or their equivalents: First, the mystery of Life, and Power, Seership,--in its loftier, not merely its lesser meanings,--forecast, endurance, insight, far-sight, longevity, silent energy, mental force, magnetic presence, and impressive capacity, lie in, flow out of, pertain to, and accord with, the SHE or mother-side of Deity, the love-principle of human-kind, and the sexive natures of the complicate homos. Outside of its sphere of operations all is cold and deathful; within its mystic and magic circle dwells all there is of fire, latent and active, actual and metaphysical; all there is of energy, procreant power, physical, mental, spiritual, and all other; and it--Love--is the master-key unlicking every barred door in the realms that are. Remember, O Neophyte (and reader of this book), that I am not dealing in mere philosophical formulae, "recipes," or trashy "directions," but in, and with fundamental principles, underlying all being. Fix this first principle firmly in your memory, and roll it under the tongue of your clearest understanding; take it in the stomach of your spirit; digest it well, and assimilate its quintessence to, and with, your own soul. That principle is formulated thus: LOVE LIETH AT THE FOUNDATION (of all that is); and Love is convertibly passion; enthusiasm; affection; heat; fire; SOUL; God. Master that. Second, the nuptive moment, the instant wherein the germs of a possible new being are lodged, or a portion of man's essential self is planted within the matrix, is the most solemn, serious, powerful, and energetic moment he can ever know on earth; and only to be excelled by correspondent instants after he shall have ascended to realms beyond the starry spaces.

LIX. If a man actualizes that moment while under the dominion of animal instinct, or human lust alone, then the effect is losing, unmanning, degrading, to both himself and her; murderous toward the recipient, and suicidal to himself. It means hatred, disease, and magnetic ruin to both; its influence for evil spreads over a wide area on earth; feeds and sustains barbarism; nourishes the monstrous Larvae of the middle kingdoms of the aered habitats of disembodied beings, even when no progeny results. But if there shall, then he and she generate misery, crime, and possible murder as the heritage of that child. If, on the other hand, love be the prompting angel at the hearth-nuptial, then strength, goodness, truth, harmony and sweet melodies of life ensue to the twain, and are insured to the offspring God shall give them. Third, at the very instant his seminal glands contract to expel their treasures, at such instant his interior nostrils open, and minute ducts, which are sealed at all other times, then expand, and as the lightning from his soul darts from the brain, rushes down the spinal-cord, leaps the solar plexus, plunges along the nerval filaments to the prostate gland to immortalize the germal human being; and while the vivific pulse is leaping to the dark chamber wherein soul is clothed in flesh and blood, at that instant he breathes in through the inner nostrils one of two atmospheres underlying, inter-penetrating--as the spirit does the body--the outer air which sentient things inhale. One of these auras is deeply charged with, because it is the effluvium of, the unpleasant sphere of the border spaces, where is congregated the quintessence of evil from every inhabited human world in the entire congeries of soul-bearing galaxies of the broad universe; else he draws in the pellucid aroma of divinity from the far-off multiple heavens. It follows that as are the people at that moment so will be that which enters into them from the regions above, beneath, and round about; wherefore, whatsoever male or female shall truly will for, hopefully pray for, and earnestly yearn for, when love, pure and holy, is in the nuptive ascendant, in form, passional, affectional, divine and volitional, that prayer will be granted, and the boon be given. But the prayer must precede.

Discord reigns in marriage-land to-day, and one principal cause is, that while the magnetic tide is at its height, and before the soul withdraws its power from the pelvis back to the brain-seat, they part company, and the spiritual auras and vital air escapes into the external world, instead of being stored up and absorbed by the woman's spirit and soul.

XL. The consequence is that the evil forces take hold, with deadly grip, upon the very roots of their triplicate being, because in acting as they do, they defy, annul, prostitute, violate and disobey, the very primary law of human existence, and voluntarily seek to defeat God Almighty's great purpose, underlying their creation.

LXI. Balzac says: "He who begins with his wife by a rape is a lost man!" I say, it is next to impossible that she ever can love him after, as before! and I say this after a large medical practice of not less than thirty years. But most "Men" (?) not only begin thus, but keep it up--the fools!--and their name is legion! --till hatred, horror and disgust either kills her outright, or suggests an evil from which every true human shrinks.

LXII. Abortion at any stage from conception to birth is--MURDER in the first degree. It effectually kills the child, demoralizes the mother, destroys her moral and physical health, while living, and after death dooms, irrevocably DOOMS, her and her assistants to the perpetual society of MURDERERS beyond the grave, from which doom there is no appeal. So beware of the crime.

LXIII. Circumstances may demand non-increase of family; therefore, avoid all risk forty-eight hours before, and one hundred after the Catamenail period. Avoid all risk after a return from a journey or temporary absence; and

LXIV. After the make-up following an unpleasantness, tiff, spat or downright family quarrel, because the reaction creates not only increased affectional and procreative energy, but also a peculiar liability to the risk of unwished-for parentage, then especially.

LXV. Mental, moral, physical and domestic trouble, mutual magneto-vital exhaustion are easily preventable between couples if they will but sleep apart, have hard beds, good ventilation, never sleeping in day-worn under-clothes, and each magnetizing the other at the seven magnetic points of the human frame--sides, spine, throat, head, breast, and over the stomach.

LXVI. Superior men, whatever their rank or calling, are very attractive to women, as a general thing; therefore such men--as they are almost always very licentious--have great need of watchfulness and prayer; considerable prayer--but more watch!

LXVII. The true nature of any wife is quickly changed for the worse by the pigness and private brutalisms of their husbands; and "can't a man do as he likes with his own?" requires a universal No, even if ownership of the wife is conceded, which it isn't.

LXVIII. When a husband's private conduct, unreasonable demands, etc., has estranged the dear love, so precious to every genuine man, there is but one way to change it back, and that is forbearance, self-restraint, care, gnetleness reciprocity, LOVE. It is best to eat only when one is hungry. But why force an unwelcome feast_ to you, horror to her, except she be ahungered as well? If she be not in sympathy with her husband in all respectw, it means death to her affection for him, in time, if not at once; and he is a poor bird who foolishly ruins his own nest, and how many human birds do it!

We are triplicate beings--soul, spirit, body. Our loves and passions may be of either one, two or all three of these. If our love be only of soul it is too fine and ethereal for this lower world, and for all practical purposes is useless.

If it be of spirit only, it is too vague, unsubstantial, unthoughtful, and physically unsatisfactory. If it be of body only, then lust is regnant, with hell all around, and crime swelters in the air. If our loves be of SOUL and SPIRIT only, then we are bereft of the power to become Energies in the world, because we lack the material force to either make our mark on each other, the world, or to give good physioco-vital constitutions to our offspring. If our loves be of soul and body, we are isolated from the rest of mankind, and are lone pilgrims all the way along. If they be spirit and body only, we are extreme--either all transcendental affection, or downright animal passionists. It is only when our loves are triplicate that we fulfill our true mission, and realize the supreme joys of existence.

The marital office and function is therefore material, spiritual and MYSTIC. The Christian world knows much about the two first, but nothing whatever of the last. This book of my doctrine only contains it, for it alone declares and establishes the fact that the marital function if unquestionably the highest, holiest, most important, and most wretchedly abused of all that pertains to the human being. Its offices are so vital that I hold as cardinal, indisputable axioms, that

LXIX. He who is diseased or unsound, pelvically, is not a true man while thus; that his soul is barred out from the heavens whither all souls repair during sound sleep, and that his immortality is not certain till he does become sound. Woman everywhere is subject to the same law and penalty.

LXX. We hold that any over-assional, inconsiderate male human is no man, and that such a husband must necessarily destroy the best wife ever given by God to the son of man; and

LXXI. An over-passional woman can easily destroy and ruin any husband on the earth, and totally unfit him for combat with the world.

LXXII. Children are the gifts of God. They will not come unless the message is sent from them during the wife's lunar season; hence any artifice to prevent conception, save such as are based upon time, will, and her moon's changes, are diabolic, inhuman and dangerous to both the man and the woman, souls as well as bodies.

LXXVII. Giours and fools think to avoid all disaster through the murderous habit of incompletion of the conjugal rite. But they are mistaken, both the wife and husband, for such folly begets hatred, disease ef bladder and brain, nerves and soul in him, and a corresponding host of evils in the wife. Why?

LXXIV. Because it is not merely suicidal and unnatural, but is also a conjugal fraud, among whose results may be reckoned dyspepsia, insanity, paralysis, and impotence on his side, and uterine, vaginal, and ovarian inflammations, ulcers, leucorrhae, and prolapsus on her side, physically, and hatred, disgust and ruin on both sides.

LXXV. Too few husbands respect the modesty of their wives; forget that drapery, perfumes, beautiful trifles, are powerful adjuncts; do not know that it is impossible for a wife to love him unless she is WON, not forced, to compliance; that he can never hold her soul, and she be made to realize the natural God-intended joy of conjugal association, except by those affectional and magnetical caresses and endearments which to the wise husband suggest themselves. ABOVE all let none be careless of modesty; for WHOEVER CANNOT BLUSH IS LOST!

LXXVI. Too frequent exercise of any power, quality, or faculty is ruinous.

This is especially true of marriage matters, which are only productive of two re-
sults--hell or heaven. For the true and holy rits is ascensive, and leads to health,
happiness, delight, longevity, gracious, celestial and glorious joy; or descensive,
leading to the lowest depths of social, moral and domestic horror, on which sad
rocks too many souls are wrecked.

LXXVII. Love between husband and wife should last to the brink of the grave;
but it don't. With careful obedience to these rules, and judicious foo, drink, and
occasional baths, it WILL. Doctors, clergymen, merchants, lawyers, people of
letters, all whose minds are constantly on the stretch; also, women of like mental
culture, are all more or less deficient in vital energy, and all will speedily
reach primitive vigor, endurance, and elasticity of spirit and body, only through
the natural methods herein set forth.

LXXVIII. Conjugal love never stands still. It either increases or diminishes,
and husbands and wives both injure and mar it by heedlessness.

LXXIX. She who yields to a libertine is sure to be despised by him. He who
patronizes a harlot is worse than a beast, and either are unworthy of the forms
they bear, for no beast sins against beast-morals, as humans do against theirs. .
. . Whoever yields to passion not love-founded is not only a fool but a suicide;
for love-passion builds up the human soul, but mere lust absolutely wastes soul,
and every one guilty of the folly knows this from experience, for a debauch lessens
the entire volume of power. Whoever is false to a true wife or husband contracts
the malaria os the SHADES, and is sure to bring home the subtle poison, and lay the
broad foundation to domestic RUIN. Sexual faith and purity is the price of power;
just as LOVE is the sole base of immortality. ALL PEOPLE DO NOT HAVE SOULS.

LXXX. Both husbands and wives will grant as a boon, when either would refuse
to accord a rite claimed as a right. Nothing is lost, but everything is gained by
the persuasive mood. He comes too near who comes to be denied. Insistence is
brutalism. Ask in love--be sure to show it; if you're true, she's sure to know it.
Slow paces last the longer. Unless there's mutually, a little, but growing pande-
monium is kindled.

LXXXI. Govern yourself, then you may rule a kingdom, and then your mate.

LXXXII. Nothing but love can keep a man faithful, and not that always, unless
he finds greater solace at home than abroad; and that's just it. They too often do,
and that's her fault; for unless he does she's never sure of him.

LXXXIII. A woman must have love--must love and be loved--in all its true
meanings; ought, of course, to have and exercise it at home, but if she don't have
it there she will elsewhere; and he who imagines he can keep her true, in heart,
at least, without loving her right along, and right straight from his to her soul,
is an egotist, a fool, and dolt! Lost love seldom returns. It can only be won by
truth, assiduity, and genuine manhood.

LXXXIV. An idle wife may be successfully tempted; so may a dressy one, or
one subject to flattery. For such to be tempted is to fall. She will forget everything but a slight to her love--not passion; but a man will forget a slight to
his love, but never forgive a sin against his conjugal rights. Ought he?

LXXXV. No power can tempt a woman against the man she loves, and whom she
knows loves her in return.

LXXXVI. No rite of marriage gives ownership, but equality. Proprietorship means despair to her, dishonor to him.

LXXXVII. A woman in love can be wholly trusted, but not so with a man.

LXXXVIII. One sheep-killing dog will ruin all the other dogs he comes across, if you grant him time; and one loose woman will corrupt five hundred innocent girls or wives in six months if you but give her the chance to do so. It is their chief delight.

Finally I commend these twenty-eight points to the study of mankind, as also that portion of knowledge which is yet to be taught you here (in) after.

LXXXIX. The entire social, conjugal and domestic worlds today, are in an up-roar, chaos and revolution.

It is deplorable that such much ill-will, sickness, discontent, hatred, sadness, insanity and wretchedness exists among the married of _today_. But it is true, and domestic happiness is the exception to an almost universal rule, at least among the people of every sort and section of this nation, and scarcely anywhere else, in such frightful forms upon the globe. Husbands neglect their wives and practically hate them; wives the same, and universal domestic chaos reigns supreme. The worst of the matter is, that both wives, husbands, and society at large attribute the bad state of thing to _wrong_ causes, for the fact is, that the _real_ one lays right before their very eyes, yet they _will_ _not_ see. Such a state of things cannot exist among Oriental nations, or the dark-skinned people of the world. Were it not so serious a matter, one would laugh at the absurd and puerile folly that permits the reign of such social non-concord for a single day, when its causes are so palpable, and its cure so easy. As things exist, wives are defrauded, husbands do not love them, and wives fail to hold their lords in affectional duress. How few, indeed, know how, or even care to accomplish health and happiness at home; and yet, it is in every man's power to make his wife love him, and in every wife's to make her husband wor-ship God through her. On my soul, I truly believe, that if my rules were followed, the social millennium would be close at hand. No strictly good human power can dwell in, or be developed by any man who is sexually unsound, imbecile, puerile, weak or impotent; nor in any woman with fallen womb, leucorrhea, ulcerated vagina or passional frigidity. How, let me ask, in God's Holy Name, can you expect home, happiness or heaven in a family where the wife never, from the altar, where she swore her life away, to the grave that closes over her fretted corpse, never realizes the slightest _marriage joy_, or anything else than utter and profound disgust? How can a man be constant, faithful, good or great, who is in a sense, compelled to run after harlots because his wife is concentrated ice? You can't expect perfection from condi-tions themselves imperfect! But there is a clear passage and open water out of this Polar sea of marriage land.

XC. There cannot be a doubt but that the "Philosopher's Stone" of ancient and mediaeval lore, and the "Elixir Vitae" Water of Life and Perpetual Youth, so vaguely hinted at by old writers, and which constitutes the burden of the celebrated book "Hermipus Redivivus" OR THE SAGE'S TRIUMPH OVER DECREPITUDE AND DEATH, means this identical triple mystery, which scarce any one practically knows, but which all should learn, and which every physician and divine in the land ought to be _compelled_ to teach their subjects under heavy penalties of neglect, because it is the secret of sustained youth, grace and beauty; it is the gate of power, and the crown and signet of ineffable human glory; it unveils the throne of Will, and taps the fountains of excessive joy; it is the Jemschidgenie of Persian story; and he or she who knows, appreciates diviner and celestial bearings of life and its meanings, becoming indeed a child of the Infinite, and no longer a stranger to the Father's face; and they alone who have it, are able to reach that magnificent sweep of clairvoyant vision, which, leaping from earth at a bound, scans the unutterable glories of apace, and beholds the rain of starry systems as we view a gentle summer shower.

XCI. The great source of crime, illness, wretchedness, and suffering has been traced to its one single source, and that is, the abuse, improper use, and mismatching of people in their loves, conjugal relations, and sexual imcompatibilities.

It is proven that these bad conditions are frequently the result of organization, and sometimes spring from incompatible, electric, magnetic and chemical relations between couples. That absolute separation is the only cure for some who are wretched in their married state, or inter-relationship; while attention to health, and a fair amount of TRY is a certain cure for other cases.

XCII. The body of man is a mere conglomerate of earths and metals, gases and fluids wholly material, but penetrated and permeated in every atom by imponderable elements essentially electric in their nature. Thus beneath, and liming our eyes are ethereal organs corresponding thereto; beneath our limbs, heart, lungs, brain, in short, all our parts are corresponding electric organs, and the totality of these constitutes the ethereal, spiritual, death-proof man or woman, and when dissolution occurs this inner man or woman oozes out of the material structure, becomes self-conscious again, and takes its place among the countless armies of the departed, but neither lost or dead; and this internal, ethereal man, woman or child, can be contracted by us in the flesh, by conforming to the laws governing such contact, and the observance of a few simple rules.

XCIII. A passionless man or woman is a human nonentity. It is only when we are wholly man or woman in the higher, holier, and also physical sense, that we can reach the loftier and more significant heights of any sort of power whatever; therefore, those who would cultivate those loftier instincts, and gain mental wings where-with to sclae the heavens, should at once attend to the business of regaining perfect health, mental, physical, emotional and passional. Presently great-hearted love and blessed compassion will nestle in all our hearts, and in this glad, prophetic hope we may all be happy yet. We are none of us ever wise except when merciful. Let us all be so, for only then can we be perfectly human--only then become vessels for the influence and effect of GOD-NESS. Never yet did man come to the absolute conviction of SOUL and Immortality, but he also came to that of God and Prayer; for, say what you will, both are and ever will be positive realities in the universe.

IN LOVE alone lies the boon of IMMORTALITY! INJUSTICE reigns to-day.

> Sad are the times when wedded wives decay,
> And brothels flourish, and Cyprians bear the sway;
> These are the times! their scarlet banner waves,
> And honest wives, neglected, fill up a million graves!

> "When woman's eye grows dull,
>   And her cheek paleth,
> When fades the beautiful,
>   Then man's love faileth;
> He sits not beside her chair,
>   Clasps not her fingers,
> Twines not the damp hair
>   That o'er her brow lingers.

"He comes but a moment in,
  Though her eye lightens,
Though her cheek, pale and thin,
  Feverishly brightens.

He stays but a moment near,
  When that flush fadeth,
Though true affection's tear
  Her soft eyelid shadeth.

"He goes from her chamber straight
  Into life's jostle;
He meets at the very gate
  Business and bustle;
He thinks not of her within,
  Silently sighing;
He forgets, in that noisy din,
  That she is dying.

"And when her heart is still,
  What though he mourneth,
Soon from his sorrow chill
  Wearied he turneth.
Soon o'er her buried head
  Memory's lights setteth,
And the true-hearted dead
  Thus man forgetteth."

But it won't be so when both sides have fount out, as a rule and law, that no
happiness is direct, although joy may be--but always reflected; in other words, that
to be happy, and loved, we must first love and render happy some other soul. This
is the eternal law of Love's equation, and is as absolute, rigid, and unalterable,
as are the laws of number, reflection and gravitation.

We all need, at times, a little, and occasionally a good deal of, coaxing. We
are a perverse set, and often times refuse to do the very identical thing others
want, and we ourselves are aching, dying, to do, simply because some witling has not
sense enough to coax us; and many a good man, and better woman, has been suffered
to gallop straight into the jaws of death, right into the mouth of hell, for want of
a little, gentle persuasion, even of the blarney sort; especially is true of men,
even quite as much as of the other sections of the human being.

I believe the only physician who has been known to condemn exercise was
Cardenus, a physician of Milan. He exclaims against using any exercise that can
fatigue a man in the smallest degree, or throw him into a sweat, or accelerate his
respiration. He gravely observes that trees live longer than animals, because they
do not stir from their places. About the same time Asgill, a French writer, under-
took to prove that man is literally immortal, or rather that any given living man
might probably never die, if he used sufficient prudence, and a forcible exercise of
the will. He complains of the <u>cowardly practice of dying</u>, considering it a mere
trick, or unnecessary habit.

XCV. I copy from my manuscript of the Ansairetic Mystery, a medico-religio,
and mystic composition of mine upon the same general subject as this book, but which,
as it expounds certain very delicate facts and principles, adapted only to the mature,
and therefore for private study--the following paragraph--stating, before I do so,

-62-

that while alive and able, such of my patrons and patients as need that now widely
famous letter, can write for it; but in no case will/be sent save under seal, as a
private message from physician and teacher to patient and pupil; and genuine
candidates for full, true,noble Man and Womanhood:--

"Wherever you see a rich, jouissant, beauty, spirit or power in a boy or girl;
wherever you behold force of genius, you may rest assured that the conception of
which they are the result, occurred when their parents both loved and were impas-
sioned. Au contrarie:--whenever you come across genuine meanness, lean, weazelish,
deceitful, slanderous, lying scrawny, white-livered people, grab-allish, selfish,
and accursed, generally, you may safely wager your very life that such beings were
begotten of force, and were mothered by passionless, sickly, used-up sives, without
the slightest danger of perilling your stake!"

XCVI. The best people on earth see the most trouble; while the heartless,
dry and mean go on to success swimmingly, and never feel a soul-pang from the cradle
to the grave; yet, nevertheless, true men and women are never failures! Sham ones
always are! because the good influence survives, the bad dies out. The good, when
they enjoy, do so intensely; but the bad, coarse being's life, in all its phases
must be on a par with--him or herself; and there's as much difference between the
joys of such as betwixt the Dundreary skip of a fop and fool, a ninny, or idiot,
and the joyous romp of a gushing-hearted, brainful girl.

It has been my lot to encounter a great deal more of human pinchbeck than the
solid soul-ful gold; not that I have not known some noble and glorious people among
the radical classes, I for years associated with; yet, as a general rule, I found
it unsafe to trust to the honor of those who were extreme in the business of world-
bettering; they are a bad breed; and Diogenes' lantern is still needed by whomsoever
travels among them.

A happy man never writes a book! This is my twentieth! But I might have been
happy and I kept away from the world-saving "Philosophers." Here and there I have
met a real lady or gentleman, such as that king of nature's nobleman, Jesse B.
Furgusion, of Tennessee--God bless his green and pleasant memory!--and latterly a
few others of the same State; but among professional reformers--and I speak only of
such as I personally know, I found a few golden ingots, and a plentiful surplusage
of brass ones--born malcontents who take to world-saving, themselves needing it
most by far. Such people as preach divine charity and all that, yet constantly
yelp and howl down to the bitter depths of death, slander or disgrace, and every
human being whom they cannot use at will, or who disagree with them. They are
magnificent demonstrations of the sublime truth of the philosophy I teach, viz.,
that as was a person's anti-natal circumstances, so will his or her subsequent life
be. If begotten in lust, alone, then that will be their bias from the breast to
the grave; if of "authority" backed by brute force, on the body of half-dead compliance, then such will go through life, biting, barking, snarling, growling, making all sorts of trouble; incapable either of generosity or appreciation, and
scattering discord wherever their scandal-scattering footsteps fall;--generally,
long, lean, lank, slab-sided human halfness, one or more of whom infests nearly
every neighborhood. Thus in close juxtaposition with nature's noblemen, I have
never failed to meet men of souls so contemptibly small as to make one ashamed of
the form one wore. Who would naturally have dreamed, surmised, or indeed have ever
suspected there was the slightest connection between Love and Slander? yet there is.
Read this scrap, which I cut from a paper many years ago, and then to the proof:--

"The slanderer is a pest; an incubus to society, that should be subjected to a
slow cauterization, and then be lopped off like a disagreeable excrescence. Like the

viper, he leaves a shining trail in his wake. Like a tarantula, he weaves a thread of candor with a web of wiles, or, with all the mendicity of hints, whispers forth his tale, that, like the fabling Nile, no fountain knows. The dead--ay, even the dead--over whose pale, sheeted corpse sleeps the dark sleep no venomed tongue can wake, and whose pale lips have then no voice to plead, are subjected to the scandalous attacks of the slanderer--

> "'Who wears a mask the Gorgon would disown,
> A Cheek of parchment, and an eye of stone!'

"I think it is Pollock who says the slanderer is the foulest whelp of sin, whose tongue was set on fire in hell, and whose legs were faint with haste to circulate the lie his soul had framed.

> "'He has a lip of lies, a face formed to conceal,
> That, without feeling, mocks at those who feel.'

"There is no animal I despise more than these moths and scraps of society, the malicious censurers--

> "'These ravenous fishes who follow only the wake
> Of great ships, because perchance they're great.'

"Oh, who would disarrange all society with their false lapwing cries! The slanderer makes few direct charges and assertions. His long, envious finger points to no certain locality. He has an inimitable shrug of the shoulders, can give peculiar glances--

> "'Or convey a libel to a frown,
> Or wink a reputation down!'

"He seems to glory in the misery he entails. The innocent wear the foulest impress of his smutty palm, and a soul pure as 'arctic snow twice bolted by the northern blast,' through his warped and discolored glasses, wear a mottled hue.

> "'A whisper broke the air--
> A soft, light tone, and low,
> Yet barbed with shame and woe!
> Nor might it only perish there,
> No farther go!

> "'Ah, me! a quick and eager ear
> Caught up the little meaning sound;
> Another voice then wreathed it clear,
> And so it wandered round,
> Fron ear to lip, from lip to ear,
> Until it reached a gentle heart,
> And that--it broke!'"

Now observe that it is inflexibly true that every slanderer, of whatever gender, is nearly always a long, lank, little, lilly-livered, tucked-up, wizenish being, without the slightest love save that of self; and when modern spiritualism came along thousands of such rushed into its ranks, disgraced the cause and themselves, and foisted their miserable twaddle upon the world as true supernalism, when, in fact, spiritualism really had nothing to do with it whatever. As at present constituted that ism contains, within its ranks, three, nay, four, sorts of people. 1st. Those who hail it as the demonstration of human continuance beyond the grave, and the

-64-

celestial harbinger of the good time coming. These people are true supernalists; and among them have I ever found sympathizers, and people fit for the heaven they seek. 2d. A large class of social revolutionists under various leaderships, who, accepting the facts, are eager to push on toward the realization of the promised good time. These two comprise the army whose iconoclastic blows right and left are demolishing some of the idols of the Past; but they are builders yet, and it remains to be seen what sort of edifice they will give us in lieu of those now crumbling before their fierce artillery. 3d. A smaller class who cling to old traditions; insist upon tying this century to the old dead ones, and fastening their faith about equally on the Bible and the manifestations. The fourth class is made up of malcontents; always making trouble, never satisfied; having, here and there, an able leader who has his hands full all the time. The rank and file of this trouble-making army wouldn't pass muster at the gates of heaven; for a more ungenerous, malignant, back-biting set was never developed by any civilization earth ever saw. Born of loveless parents, they rush through life striking alike, hap-hazard, at friend or foe; discontented from the nipple to eternity; full of malice; steeped to the lips with cruel, cool, cobra-like venom, they are never happy save when slandering their betters, picking flaws in others' characters, and in stabbing in the back those whom they dare not face. Beware of such! They abound, and like some snakes, not on legs, are dangerous. I have already described them physically, so that they will be known when met. I owed this duty to mankind; and I now proceed to pay my little Bill.

XCVII. Reduced from competence to nothing, by the terrible Boston fire of Nov. 1872, I went to Ohio from necessity, and finding materials at hand, in great abundance, made it my especial business to study the workings of the organic law of sex, as displayed in the product of marriages, accomplished at periods varying from fifteen to sixty-five years anterior to 1873. One remarkable case was that of a man in Ohio, a long, lank abortion, whose nature constantly impelled him to find fault with everything and everybody—even himself, or rather _Itself_; nor was it ever happy, except when going up and down retailing slanderous tales and scandal concerning whoever failed to suit it, come or go at its beck and call, and do humble homage at its feet. Now the fault is not altogether theirs—these unhappy ones,—for they had no hand in their own make-up (save in that they usually make no effort to correct their shortcomings), but is that of their progenitors. We have no right to run the risk, —of being guilty of the insensate folly of parenting such monstrosities,—for such they are, and moral abortions beside- nor to parentage at all unless mutual love, esteem and respect be the prompting spur.

People of that grade are usually one-sided, angular, not to be depended on, and generally passion-driven; or rather you may set it down as incontrovertibly true, that wherever you find one of the class alluded to, there also will you find a devout disciple of Onan. I once lost the "friendship" of a male human being of a slightly different type from the above, yet still a monstrosity. He had fed me for months in exchange for information marketable at far higher prices than he paid— still I was grateful; and one day he proposed that I should aid him a cruel scheme; but I preferred to go hungry, ay, starve outright, rather than comply with his demands; because I well knew that to do so would be conniving at an outrage against an innocent child, in the first place, and at his own destruction and probable death, in the second; hence my pity for her made me foil him; and my friendship for him caused me to defeat his well-cherished plans. I knew I should transform him, and his household, too, into bitter enemies of mine; yet still I determined to do right, no matter at what sacrifice or pain to me; and at once decided to protect a young thing, and save him from himself, by in no manner leading either knowledge, power or influence, to do an evil deed. Magic powers, too, he wanted,—he, an old man, of eight and sixty!—to enable him to compass the ruin, or "marry"—just think of it!—a mere child, of but a few months over fifteen summers,—fair to look

-65-

on; a hundred weight of beauty and glee; simple, heedless, joyous as a morning bird, carolling its sun-greeting roundelay; and he coarse as rag-carpet; brutal as a Kaffir on the war-path; lecherous as a satyr; one-third human, two-thirds goat; nearly two hundred pounds of rough, uncouth, unwashed feculence, whose presence anywhere was a sign hung out, warning passers-by to "keep to the windward." And yet this man had a great, rich jewel of goodness, away down in the inner deeps, and that it was which, as will be hereinafter seen, urged him to sacrifice all things in the vague hope of achieving one certain, but tremendous guerdon,--the salvation of his own soul; yet he knew not what he was striving after. I did; and so instead of helping him wed her, I cautioned the child against it, because I knew such a step meant inevitable death to her within a few brief, lust-harried, agonizing months; for the gentle Adonis had confidentially boasted to me of his intentions, yet he said that, passionally a moderate man was he, and that, save under extraordinary circumstances, he would be content with--what may God protect even a woman of the wilderness from! Finding some Power working against him--for I had taken a woman and a man into my confidence, to enable me to save the girl from the horrible fate threatened her, the old "man" desired me to use certain magic spells, common among the people down South, and other lands I wot of, to enable him to gain control of her, to be used for awhile, as only a human beast can use God's image in female form--and then, utterly ruined, to be cast aside as a loathed and loathsome thing forever, with a bagnio close by, and a darkly rolling, sullen river, in the near distance! For the life of me I was so stone blind as to be wholly unable to view the matter as he did, and so--well, he lost the game; for a young man honorably wooed and won her.

XCVIII. I missed many a good meal by doing as I did, but I kept my manhood unsullied, by defeating a wrong. To this day I hold his own written letter requesting me to disgrace myself, and tarnish my soul, by an infamous deed in furtherance of his abominable and abnormal passion, said letter being written that I might clearly and distinctly comprehend his meaning. That man thereafter hated me with fifty thousand horse-power, in which he was natural, because all animals are rendered furious if their lusts are defeated.

Not only do individuals in their conduct proclaim the cat-and-dog lives led by their immediate progenitors, but it often happens that whole classes in a community do the very same thing; for instance: Once I went to a "Religious Picnic," of the "Reformers," and while taking a drink behind a tree,--it was whiskey, too, a beverage plentifully provided and dispensed by the saints, most oall of whom were excellent judges of the article,--and at the earnest solicitation of a particularly reverend brother, I tried it on; and as it passed along the tube leading to my stomach I experienced a sensation, only comparable to a desperate encounter between two infuriate ironclads, going on simultaneously with an electrical storm, a couple of Vesuvian volcanic eruptions, and four typhoons, all going on in my internal man, until I gasped for breath, and mine eyes resembled a pair of exceedingly large peeled onions, or two burnt holes in a blanket; which experience satisfied me once for all, and led me to wonder if that was the best brand of Reformer's whiskey, what could be the quality of the article served out down below. I failed to see wherein whiskey was a high moral motor.

While trying to catch my breath, I overheard one saint counsel another to get me to orate, and both spoke of me in such opprobrious terms as would have fired me with indignant anger without the additional damnable stimulus of the rankly poison draught. Ten minutes afterward, against my will, I took the stand and spoke my piece, just as we Randolphs are accustomed to, and dealt out justice to my traducers; for doing which, and differing from them about what constitutes manhood, the leading saints proposed to silence me, demonstrate their sainthood, and end the dispute by cool, calm, deliberate, premeditated MURDER, by drowning me in the river hard by.

They did not attempt it, because when they proposed it my hand slid round to my hip-pocket, and cowards seldom attack a well-armed man. This experience satisfied me that, until people are really spiritual, it is best to be always prepared with carnal logic to withstand their material arguments. I have alluded to these things to make a point in my book, and not because the savages who proposed to murder me are worth the slightest notice, but solely, only and for the express purpose of making two remarks; the first is this: that the world needs something better than it has now before Reform will be a thing of heart and conduct, instead of empty words as at present; and second, to point out the characteristics of certain salacious and other self-assumed "Reformers." Of course, your pseudo-philosopher is never a full, round, genial, or generous man; but will invariably be found, on close examination, to partake largely of the hang-dog, sneak-thief, and lecherous look. They are generally moderately tall, thin, and angular, heads, than either large, fat, or little-bodied men. The same holds true of females--such as delight in breaking up families, creating scandal, and ruining other people by slanderous tongues or innuendo. Husbands, wives, be very chary of entertaining guests of either sex thus made up; else you may expect moral poison and ruin to remain after themselves have departed. Theirs is the vampire build, and that sort of influence is theirs, seven times in every eight, where they have taken to the business of world-saving. In thirty years I have conversed with scores of such and found, exceptionless, that their ideal of love was that which better men stigmatize as unhallowed lust and fiery passion, unredeemed by the faintest spark of manhood, womanhood, or genuine goodness. They all declare for a "central, solar, or pivotal love, with planetary loves revolving round it;" that is to say, a main one with "outside" indulgencies to keep the cosmos in order; which means, in plain Saxon, that man is but a featherless rooster, entitled to one queen-hen with a flock of lesser chic-a-biddies to relieve her during incubation. I should not like to lionize, but would assuredly glory in caponizing that species of foul fowl; such people can see no higher use for certain organic functions than to fill their own places after death, or to gratify their morbid natures.

They cannot imagine anything else, nor even dream that through the offices of monogamal, conjugal life, the soul itself may be enormously intensified and expanded, and the evolution of mighty thought itself go on at a more rapid rate, taking higher flights, skimming deeper oceans, and, consequently, the mental, psychal, emotional, and creative powers of the human spirit be enhanced a million fold. This is all Greek to these harpers on a single string, and that a base one. Some of these people call themselves physicians, and pass their time in inventing "preventives," embracing "shields," "pellets," "plugs," exoriating and tanning "washes," and a hundred other infamous abominations to entrap the suffering, and enrich themselves. Let all henceforth know, not only what is set forth on this point elsewhere herein, but that the man who wishes to spare the partner of his joys, who, poor soul, always runs the risk of death every time she yields, not to please herself, but to bless the man she has called husband, can, by will, restraint, and firmly holding his breath, when so disposed, prevent the inhalation of the monad or germ, and its descent to the prostate, and, also, by will, the flash of fire from his central soul, which alone, and only, can render fruitfulness possible. They never dreamed of that, yet it is as certainly true as truth itself! They cannot see these splendid things, because their visual range is groundy, while these lofty truths are at their base anchored in the substance of the human soul, and held there by a cable, Love, whose other end girdles the Infinite God!

Man deals with masses; woman with individuals; and the Great One deals with, protects, comforts, solaces, and, through pure love alone, redeems both. Would that these revealments might reach every human heart, even though mine own is aching and breaking the while.

XCIX. Said Lewis Kirk, "An ounce of heaven, a pound of hell, makes life. Not many ever experience mental pain--mind-suffering--in its keenest sense. Financial trouble!--Pshaw!--is nothing!" and as times go, the first statement is correct; for none but those who are conscious of soul, can experience soul-pangs;--and it is these who turn in any direction for relief, and fall victims to the abominable quackery of the would-be world-reformers,--a class which sprung into notice with Fourier and Graham, and which, since the advent of Spiritualism, has increased to an alarming extent all over this land. Their hobby is "Sexism,"--a thing of whose basic principles they are as ignorant as they are of who built Baalbec. These tramps scour the country, victimize honest men's wives and daughters; and even have the effrontery to enforce their odious embraces upon decent women, on the infamous and filthy plea that they, the lady-victims, require a change of magnetism--forsooth! --which change themselves are the very ones to triumphantly effect. Hoodwinked by psychologic power, deluded by specious sophistry, anxious for relief, ready to make any sacrifice to obtain it, women, by hundreds, fall into the accursed net, and are ruined; for no matter how secret the deed may be, her soul knows the fact, feels the weight, and suffers untold agony in consequence, and all because of salacious wretches who ought to swing by their heels, if not by their necks, at the nearest tree. I can have some pity for those who fall for lack of strength to resist temptation; but none for those who ruin by a "medical theory!" These people find a woman ill with gravid uterus, leucorrhoea, or ulcerated vagina or womb, whereupon they proceed to the most infernal exposures, inspections, and tactual manipulations, conceibavle, and utterly horrent to any sensitive and delicate woman; the upshot of which is she takes his stuff, and grows ten times worse than ever, because wholly bent on symptomology, they are ignorant that all these troubles are physical expressions of internal, mental, emotional, affectional or spiritual states half the time; and that ulcerations proceed from lacerations,--or brutalisms on the part of the he head of the house. They do not realize that disturbances, originating in spiritual commotions, can only be cured by administering spiritual remedies,--that is to say, operating upon the soul as well as upon its physical garment--flesh, blood, bone and nerves. How this is accomplished, has already been set forth therein.

C. It is my intention, if I live, during the years I spend on earth, to devote my time to teaching such as desire more light on the matters which have been the sole study of my life. Ostracized by those for, and with whom I had labored since 1848; met with ingratitude at every step, I gladly accept the ostracism of the many for the good companionship of the few; yet not so few after all, for day by day the ranks of the discontented army, who have been content to follow where impulse led, has grown thinner, and our Brotherhood of Thinkers has increased correspondingly, until at last we, of Eulis, know we have but to let the world know that our doors and hearts are open, to welcome acolytes by thousands. Neglect, slander, vile prejudices, contumely--all have--in this trial of six and twenty years--though ranking millions armed with staves, crying, "Crucify him! crucify him! --proved signally unequal to the task of defeating a single solitary man, and that man the penman of this book,--PASCHAL BEVERLY RANDOLPH!--the sang melee!--Proud of his descent from the kings and queens, not of Nigritia, but of Madagascar, to say nothing,--to say nothing of the Randolphs, nor their rise from Warwick, the king-maker! Listen to one of our wild melodies, and then say if such blood should bow and bend before the ignoble crowd whose only patient is that they boast the line-age of the seashore sorcerers:--

MADAGASCAR SONG.

Translated by Sir John Bowring.

Trust not--trust not to the seashore sorcerers!

-68-

In the times of old the sorcerers came
To our island and were thus accosted:
"Land is here, so tarry with your women;
Be ye good and just, and be our brothers!"
Thus the sorcerers promised--we believed them.
Soon they overturned our walls--erected
Threatening fortresses, which poured forth thunder
In their fury; and their priests would give us
Other unknown gods than ours to worship;
And they spoke of services and obedience.
Better die! The fight was long and bloody.
They were masters of the murderous lightnings,
And our multitudinous hosts they scattered;
All were scattered--all--our people perished.
Trust not--trust not to the seashore sorcerers!
More invaders came, yet bolder--stronger.
On the seashore they their banners planted;
But Heaven fought with us, and they were conquered!
Heavy torrents fell; and mighty tempests,
Storms and poisonous winds o'erwhelmed the stranger.
They are gone--are dead; and we, the living,
Live to know that we are free and happy.
Trust not--trust not to the seashore sorcerers!

I did not follow the counsel thus given; and lo, the terrible penalty I paid.
My crime was rete mucosmal, and for that scarce a lecturer or paper devoted to
"Reform" but had its fling at me, even to the extent of abusing my dead mother, who
went to heaven nearly fifty years ago. But I bided my time! VENI! VIDI! VICI!
Hundreds of "Lecturers" and thousands of "The faithful and unco-Godly," most of whom
I never saw, considered their labor incomplete, and their speech imperfect, unless
they could soundly abuse my mother's only son. But what did it avail--in the end?
They were compelled to borrow, or rather steal, my thought, and pass it off as their
own; and I have cut out of their articles and speeches thousands of lines, and
hundreds of thoughts, which I had first given to the world! It is a terrible crime
to be by God constituted differently from those who see light in the same thought
you do, yet feel the pulses of manhood throbbing in your veins;--and sure to be
hated on that account. I am a SANG MELEE; and not less than twelve strains of
blood rush through my veins, yet have I ever met insult all the way along of life,
because I dared to be myself! But triumphantly have I done that same thing, "and
all despite my good Lords Cardinal," from the early days till now,--Selah! For the
fault of the Infinite, if fault it was, to make me of an unfashionable cast, have
I been almost crucified, and have suffered, as it were, a thousand deaths. For the
Madagascan tinge on my cheek, not its volcanic fires in my soul--Fires which held
the cowards at bay for five and thirty years--have I been doubly wronged, by these
and them and those, who, when help was needed, gladly availed them of my brain and
speech and pen, to devoutly damn me when the fights were won! Driven by the flam-
ing sword of mean prejudice from all noble occupation and employment, by those
whose pallor, alone, not Soul, or Honor or Manhood, or nobility of character, made
them strong, and gave them warrant to invade my rights, and darkly slander me,--and
invariably behind my back! lacking manly courage to do it to my face,--cowards, all,
whom I felt and feel were, and are, as far beneath me as the floor of space is below
the loftiest Turret of the Immeasurable Temple wherein God resides! Attacked with
bitter and envious malignity, ever without the chance of reply,--by tongue and pen,
--still I survived; and--despite them all. Treated more like a beast of the jungle

than a human being; they exhausted all logic trying to prove me a nobody,--themselves the only real thinkers; and in seeking to justify their own outrage, really vindicated me! They thought it better to denounce and slay me, than to afford me a fair, free field to contest in the matter of Mind!--and heaping abuse and contumely on me all the while, yet what availed it all? I became a power in the world! What are they? I took to Mirrorology, and they did not like it, because it enabled me to laugh their isms and practice to utter scorn!--just where and as, I hold them to and in this hour! But their hostilities--in all these years --drove me back upon God and my own soul; and I prefer being called all the names the discontented could or can apply, to being counted among their malign confraternity, because my Philosophy taught me to forbear retaliation, seeing they could not help doing as they did, being aborts, badly begotten and worse brought forth--constitutionally mean,-- physico-worshipping fathers, half-murdered victims for mothers. My science told me just what to expect of them; while my vision disclosed images of pool-haunting newts, when seeking for figures to represent their souls; and, en passant, it was partly because I advocated Oriental Magic, in preference to their mesmeric and similar revelative methods, that I was hated. I could not help it, for I believe in God, and even so do I believe and know that those dark ovoids, in proper hands, are capable of enabling a true soul to scan more mysteries in a week than they can in a lifetime, with all their fantastic methods combined--Mysteries forever and ever beyond their reach; for we know where we go after death; they but guess at it.

Oh, how I have yearned for everlasting death, in view of the pitiless, remorseless persecutions, insults, wrongs, heaped on my head by thousands whom I never either harmed or even met--envious, jealous, sordid! I pitied them, and longed for lasting rest. It is not so now, for the victory is mine, and I pity and forgive them all,--in the same spirit in which an elephant pities and forgives--a bed-bug! --for I regard all slanderers as most people do that delicate and deliciously odoriferous insect.

During the year 1874 I propose to give the world a test of the powers of Vision of the soul when under the sleep of Sialam,--that upper clairvoyance which comes never by mesmeric roads, nor drugs, fumes, ethers or spiritual circles, but ever by the three principles, through the aid of the Vast Ovoid elsewhere treated of herein. (If I die there is another--a selected chief of Eulis--who, in time, will finish what I leave undone--at least, such is my hope.) Because I know well that weak and impatient ones or mere wonder-seekers, fail with them, as would an Ashantee with a transit instrument; but others, a goodly band of royal seers! succeed, and are able to accomplish loftiest things of seership, not alone by visions, in the oval, but from the point d'appui of mental crystallic, ascensive, penetrative, and comprehensive grasp, reached by steadily gazing on their dark and glorious faces. It is only unripe ones who fail; malignant quacks and folly-driven fanatics who, too low in the sensual scale, too gross in mental and physical tastes and habitudes to appreciate aught of pure spirit, unsullied thought, and the vision that flights immensity, and laughs at towering mountains, and roaring, intervening oceans, of either water or space, denounce through malignant envy and the spiteful jealousy of the Naga, what is forever beyond and above them. These are beneath notice, and their spite and hatred, as their regard and praise, are of equal weight and value,--less than that of the shadow of an atom!

Mesmerism and other methods of reaching psycho vision were but the guide-boards pointing to this, the surer, purer, better, than all others on the globe beside. Many a man has become a libertine, and many a woman fallen low, low, low, from the temptations and facilities afforded by animal magnetism; but in all the broad world no soul has been degraded, but all uplifted, through this Old-new, New-old Sight of the Soul. I expect to produce the Sequel to "AFTER DEATH," and "DEALINGS WITH THE

DEAD," in a volume concerning "BEYOND THE SPACES." Through the SIALAM SLUMBER have I been educated; and I honor and paenize the glorious bridge that enabled me to keep the human bloodhounds at bay, and to span the unfathomable ocean of Eternity!

CI. The saying, that to the pure all things are pure, is not tue, for filth to everybody, and you can't dress it up, or sugar it to deed, suggestion, or thought, be right, no matter what subterfuges of sophistry or false logic are brought to bear to prove it so; wherefore, the slang of these pseudo reformers, stripped of its glitter, is insufferably offensive to any health-loving soul in all the lands. It can never be right to defile the bed of a husband or wife, even though their lives be cat-and-doggish; nor can it ever be right for any one to love one and hold another in unloving, legal duress. Let them fairly, squarely, part company before either hangs out the Sign, TO LET. Be off with the old in honest style before going on with the new!

We people of the world are born to trade in equivalents. If we give love we want it in return. If we labor for and protect even where there's no love whatever in the case, yet still we have the right of being respected, and you shall not live on my earnings yet respect me not, and have dalliance elsewhere. For if you yield to another, you and that other must abide the consequences. That other must care for, feed, clothe, labor for, and protect you; for I am not bound by any law, human or divine, to keep a corner in that I work for, for others' uses!--and, by Heaven, I won't do it! If you do the bad thing then let's part, for you no longer command my respect, nor are entitled to the results of my labor, or deserving of my homage or esteem in any degree whatever. Equivalents is the Eternal law! Remember and abide by it!

Now here is another new revelation: Pleasure, like light, has two modes and motions; 1st, wave; 2d, linear; one in rays, the other in billowy undulations; one like beams from a candle or star; the other like the swelling of the ocean waters. The pleasures of Lust or passion alone, as in unloving union, or the sin of the Onanite, is always Electric, non-responsive-aloneness, non-mutual; therefore, like lightning, destructive. It is keen, sharp, cutting, incisive, and shocks the body and soul to the verge of death. It is wholly selfish, and results from the rush and escape of just so much nervo-vital life, wherefore, of course, is self-murderous, because the electric loss is not compensated by a magnetic inflow from a loving opposite. It is linear. But when pleasure results from a meeting of the electric currents of the male with the magnetic flow of the female, in the nerves of each, as in the touch of loving lips, the two currents spread out into waves, which flow all over the vast nervous network of both, until they die out as they roll upon the foot of the throne whereon each soul sits in voluptuous expectancy. In the one case all joy is local; in the other, it is diffused over both beings, and each is bathed in the celestial and divine aura--the breath of God; suffusing both bodies, refreshing both souls! But this holy experiance cannot be had where habit has blunted the nerves of each; excess has destroyed impressibility. Rest, Repose, Slumber and Activity, Wakefulness, impressionableness, are the equations of the eternal sexive law,--and all others as well.

Let me restate the law in clearer terms: 1st. The joys of Love are consequent upon the rush of nervous fluid along the nerval fibrils, filamental cords, or wires of the system, centring in the vital ganglia of either sex. When it flows alone it is electric. When it contacts on both sides it is magnetic. 2d. The fulness of Love-joy depends upon the plethora of vital life and nerve-aura stored up in the ganglia of the system, but especially upon the greater or less stock magazined within the mystic cripts appointed of Nature for that purpose. 3d. The conditions essential to the maintenance of any special power of either soul or body, especially of Love and its offices, which involves both, are: Regular remission, voluntary cessation of its activities for a period more or less protracted, and whose term depends upon, 1st, the amount of force expended in other directions; and, 2d, upon the recuperative energies of the individual. 4th. In order to reach the highest possible affectional life, there must be lengthened terms of inaction, during which period the forces accumulate; the nervous magazines expand; the filaments grow stronger, more conductive, and sensitive at the same time; while morbid inflammations cease and normal appetite succeeds to insane physico-passional burnings,-- which latter are unnatural, while the former is healthful. 5th. The intimate relations between soul and body render each at times the tormented victim of, and martyr to, the other; hence Love-offices are never in order save when each mind and each body agrees with the other, and, the four combine and unite to one common purpose. Otherwise disastrous results inevitably follow; for loveless union is like a money-lender,--it serves you in the present tense, lends you in the conditional mood; keeps you in the present tense, lends you in the conditional mood; keeps you in the subjective; rules you in the future, and puts a period to you in the end; whereas Loving union wafts you up to Godness; ripens you; increases the bulk of soul and adds immeasurable joys to the sum total of life. THEREFORE TAKE CARE YOUR LOVE DON'T PERISH IN THE USING OF IT! 6th. Remember that the human soul is a musical instrument played on by the fingers and the breath of God, wherefore see to it that it be kept in tune so that none but finest symphonies are evoked; for it is only then that you can realize either the true stress or strain of being. Forget not that the soul is a Republic; that each organ and faculty is one of the States; and that to insure the common weal each should conspire to one common purpose--the happiness of all.

7th. Life without love is perpetual death! To be truly human and purely good, we must love. To be strong, something must lean upon us; and they who live apart, isolated lives, are dwelling in the midst of viewless horrors, ready at any moment to take form and lash their souls to frenzy. We were born to love; to beget our kind to bear children to the world and God; and failing therein, we defeat the very purposes for which Deity launched us into being.

CII. Ever since I began to write on this prolific and most vital theme, I have persistently, constantly endeavored to prove that the overstocked condition of the female labor market, and the preponderance of the female over the male element in society were fruitful causes that led to the increase of the Social Evil; and I now write to show that there are operating, right here in our very midst, the most wicked practices, tending not only to an increase of this evil, but sapping the very foundations of the morals of society.

It is/startling fact that the number of marriages is diminishing; the number of divorce cases increasing, there being forty-four on the docket of the Supreme Court for one term in a single county in Connecticut, the State of "blue laws" and "steady habits." Another starling fact is, that among the native element of society the number of births is less than the number of deaths in many sections of all the States.

A wicked and fearful extravagance in the mode of living, rendering marriage and housekeeping so difficult, is one cause of the decline of marriage. The poorer class must ape the style of the rich, and they make a great display when they marry. Being unable to come up to the standard, they remain single, and plunge into sensuality and vice. It is estimated that in New York City, and the surrounding suburbs, there are more than two hundred thousand females, and quite as many men, living, openly or in private, lives of shame and sensuality. The same causes are operating in New York to-day that led the citizens of San Francisco, years ago, to form vigilance committees, and for the same purpose, viz., to correct intolerable evils, and to purify the political and social atmosphere. Marriage and employment would have a tendency to check this fearfully growing evil. The better portion of society must look to it, or this element in their midst will rush by a pathway of ruin to restore the equilibrium, for they cannot wholly escape the dread influences and effects.

There is the revolting sin of foeticide, or infanticide, the tendency of which is to ruin both soul and body, sunder the bonds of pure love between the sexes, and send our most promising young women and wives into premature graves, spreading a gloom dark as night over hearts and homes that should be bright with health, joy and happiness. It is trying to checkmate the Infinite God.

There is a plan whereby much of this evil may be obviated. I am aware that it has been tried, but never in right-down earnest in these States; or under municipal surveillance. I refer to the establishment of Matrimonial Bureaus, under sworn commissioners, and direct care of Public authorities. So far all such affairs have been in the interests of money-seeking panders and procuresses, and to afford better facilities for supplying men with victims and mistresses, and bagnio-keepers with ruined girls. There are scores of thousands of both sexes without any chance of finding mates, and they are rushed to ruin through "Personals" and blind advertisements; and in trying to sail toward honorable marriage, run straight upon the reefs of social vice, and are forever lost. No one wants to be bad; no one sighs for harlotry or libertinism; and no one prefers a life of shame to one of honor and respect; hence it is the duty of the State to take measures to prevent all such steps, and establish bureaus wherein women, and men, too, may find suitable mates, and establish decent, comfortable homes, instead of filling bagnios, gaming-hells, jails, prisons, syphilitic hospitals, and premature graves. All of us have human hearts and human feelings, and we were created duo-sexed expressly that we might commingle our natures. The soul needs love just as much as the body requires food. Love-starvation--the nostalgia, or homesickness of the soul--is the most terrible evil that can oppress the human spirit. Reader, think how dreadful must have been the suffering that inspired these lines--the requiem of a breaking heart:--

"Out from his palace home
    He came to my cottage door;
Few were his looks and words,
    But they linger for evermore.
The smile of his sad, blue eyes
    Was tender as smile could be;
Yet I was nothing to him,
    Though he was the world to me!

"Fair was the bride he won,
    Yet her heart was never his own;
Her beauty he had and held,
    But his spirit was ever alone.
I would have been his slave,
    With a kiss for my life-long fee;
But I was nothing to him,
    While he was the world to me!

"To-day, in his stately home,
    On a flower-strewn bier he lies,
With the drooping lids fast closed
    O'er the beautiful, sad blue eyes.
And among the mourners who mourn
    I may not a mourner be;
For I was nothing to him,

-73-

                    Though he was the world to me!

            "How will it be with our souls
                When they meet in the better land?
            What the mortal could never know,
                Will the spirit yet understand?

            Or, in some celestial form,
                Must the sorrow repeated be,
            And I be nothing to him,
                While he dims heaven for me?"

     And yet just such wails arise heavenward every day in the year from literally
thousands of bleeding spirits.

     CIII. I do not envy the feelings of those guilty of breaking up love-matches,
or tyrannically ordering what shall or shall not be. If there is a hell, hereafter,
it seems to me that all such ought to go there, at least for a summering, if no
longer; yet there are those who ruthlessly destroy others' happiness, because they
have the power.

     "My wife was _not_ my wife, but always her mother's daughter!" has been the story
ever since mothers-in-law came in fashion; and it is my opinion that more families
have been "smashed into smithereens," to quote a Hibernicism, by that awful power,
than perhaps any other single cause in the list, yet they think they do no harm;
forcibly reminding one of the "Moral man" of the Russian poet, NEKRASOF:--

            "A strictly moral man have I been ever,
            And never injured anybody--never.

            "I lent my friend a sum of money he could not pay,
            I jogged his memory in a friendly way,--
            Then took the law of him the affair to end;
            The law to prison sent my worthy friend.
            He died there--not a farthing for poor me!
            I am not angry, though I've cause to be.
            His debt that very moment I forgave,
            And shed sad tears of sorrow o'er his grave.
            A strictly moral man have I been ever,
            And never injured naybody--never.

            "I sent my slave to learn the art of dressing
            Meat--he succeeded--a good cook's a blessing;
            But he, too, oft would leave his occupation,
            And gained a taste not suited to his station.
            He liked to read, to reason, and discuss;
            I, tired of scolding, without further fuss,
            Had the rogue flogged--all for the love of him;
            He went and drowned himself--t'was a strange whim.
            A strictly moral man have I been ever,
            And never injured anybody--never.

            "My silly daughter fell in love one day,
            And with her tutor wished to run away;
            I threatened curses, and pronounced my ban;
            She yielded, and espoused a rich, old man.

Their house was splendid, brimming o'er with wealth;
But suddenly poor Mary lost her health,
And in a year consumption wrought her doom;
She left us mourning o'er her early tomb.
A strictly moral man have I been ever,
And never injured anybody--never."

CIV. Probably when animal loves die out, and spiritual Loves succeed them, as a general rule, the true civilization we hope for will come along. Society must outgrow the possibilities of evil, and change its impudicities; its scabrous practices its practical polygamy and polyandry; its infernal saturnalias of Lust, for their exact opposites, and then, but not till then, will all the sexive horrors take their departure from the world. We, who ourselves, MEN OF EULIS, beholding the curses and contrasts of the present civilization--this thing that shines so bright, yet nurses Murder at its breasts,--this thing that glitters with the Beaute du Diable, --strive by lifting the veil to show the concealed horror; and to warn mankind against it. We believe not in any form of concubinage or libertinism, but we do not use the same weapons against them that others are accustomed to. We propose to make every man and woman master and mistress of themselves, and enable them to detect the paste from the diamond!

CV. Of late years there has run a chain of peculiar crime the whole length and breath of the United States, from Maine to Texas, Boston to San Francisco. It appears as if the arch-fiend of Lust, himself, had invented this new enormity. I allude to the systematic rapes, by terrible violence, or by drugging, of young children,--girls of from five to fifteen years of age, and generally by hoary-headed, scoundrel lechers, rheumy-eyed, filthy, wholly disgusting in every conceivable sense. Many of these awful crimes are the work of demonized men, acting from sudden impulse upon their own responsibility; but there is every reason to believe that an atrocious gang, with its head-quarters in New York City, and having its laws, rules, countersigns, and pass-words, with branches here and there all over the vast country, and members in nearly every considerable city, town, and village in the land. There are papers which advertise their regular meetings; albeit in a blind way, so that none but the initiate can understand. The principal idea that forms the soul of this infamous band is this: Young girls are by them supposed, while pure, and preceding, and just subsequent to puberty, or their natural advance into womanhood, to be endowed with the power of prolonging the life of him who shall first, by means foul or fair,--if it be possible that such an horror could--which it cannot, never can be, fair,--succeed in debauching her. It is supposed that two-fifths of her allotted term of life will, by the deed, be transferred from her to him; and that the life-stock thus obtained, can be, and is, shared by all others of the band, on the principle of magneto-vital transfusion, not of blood, but of Nerve-aura. Thus a band of forty would gain an average of one month's continued life beyond the allotted term of each, as the result of one outrage--but which they term by a gentler name. It is to this band that is to be attributed eight tenths of the child-rapes, which, by their ultra horror, so frequently shock the nerves of the people of the world. They are all sworn to secrecy, and the traitor is liable to sudden death by murder, the pistol, knife, or poison, at any moment. Perhaps their secret had never leaked out by for the confession beneath the rope, and in view of the fire that awaited him, of the wretch, whose summary, and I almost said--Righteous,--taking-off a few years ago, by an infuriated mob in the West, is still fresh in the public mind. The crime, like that of Onan and the Pederasts, I regard as worse than murder, because it has none of the terrible motives for, or provocatives of those awful deeds, or ordinary rape; for this latter is seldom aided by the cruel knife, nor the dreadful climax crowned with inhuman butchery, as the latter nearly always

-75-

has been.

Lust seems to be having a Saturnalia in these days; and in 1873 of the Christianic Era, a male human, through the Public Press, boasted that he went about the country seducing men's wives on "Principle"!! declaring he did no wrong! Onanism is mainly a physical disease; but the other crimes, including the boasting libertine's, --meaning, one Moses Hull, the author of a shocking "Personal Experience, --are the deliberate actions of lost and conscienceless human souls! in other words, of human brutes, not yet immortalized.

CVI. In September, 1873, I attended a convention of ultra Radicals in Chicago, led by a noted agitatress, with whose courage and persistence in advocating her views I was particularly pleased, and took my stand on her side, because of her sex, and a persecuted member of it besides; and not because it was, is, or ever could be, possible for me to view the social question from either her standpoint or that of her confreres; I do not, cannot, never did, believe in Promiscuity, as some claimed that woman did, but which I heard her emphatically deny,--a little while before either that convention closed, or some peoples' eyes were opened--as mine certainly were, through an incident that occurred in the hall. However, on the ground of her gender, her championship of Fair play for woman; her splendid attack upon the unjust and unequal Taxation laws, and because of her right to a fair and candid hearing, I maintained in Chicago, as in Boston the year previous, when the same woman was up for office--stout battle in behalf,not of her peculiar doctrines, but of human responsibility, individualism, and the sacred right of Free discussion; and I would have stood by the side of any other human being under similar circumstances, even though, as in this case, nearly every one of her points of doctrine were and are quite dissimilar and antipodal to those I hold upon the same questions. I defended her right to a fair hearing in her bold, iconoclastic attack upon the wrongs of woman, and the injurious marriage system of to-day. I by no means could see it right for one man or woman to share the favors of another's wife or husband,--for I was barbarian enough then to have Sickleized him who should victimize a loved and loving wife of mine; and I would have justified any other man or woman in the same procedure then; I justify them just the same to-day; and hope to till I pass away,--provided always that _she_ was not to blame,--assisted not at her own disgrace.

At that convention I uttered no word either for or against "Social Freedom;" confining my speeches to the three points above named; but I hailed that woman and every one else's declaration of belief and confidence in sanctified monogamic marriage; and their denunciation of unbridled license. A few days before I went to that convention I had heard of, and read, the unqualifiedly infamous and infernal recital of "A Personal Experience;" and I went there expressly to measure swords with the _thing_ in human shape who published it; but the coward and braggart dared not show his polluted front; for Mr. Moses Hull was not there to defend his peculiar views and practice.

My command of language is limited; nor could I find words bitter enough to express my opinion of him, who gloried in profaning the very holiest shrine at which Manhood worships and renders grateful homage--that of the family; and I then, and now, would justify the wronged husband who should kill him. My intentions became known by the injudicious gabble of a confidant; and others came and persuaded me to bottle my lightning against him for the time being, lest it kindle a fire not easily extinguished.

On the same day I learned that the foes of Free discussion were preparing a _coup_ against the female leader. She was a woman; I a man; the duty was plain: I would have a hand in the battle, and stand up for fair play until there was good skating upon ice five feet thick on the lurid lakes of Gehenna! I took my stand, and committing the author of "A Personal Experience" to the care of God and his own conscience, fairly and deftly threw _that_ bone of contention entirely outside of the rather warm arena; but in doing so purposely allowed myself to be misunderstood by many people in the conclave, and throughout the nation. I sought in my speeches to make two points only; they were these: 1st, the individual nature of the human soul; its actual life, its personal responsibility and destiny; and, 2d, I declared my belief, and here repeat it,--that a female adulteress or harlot is no worse than a male libertine or voluptuary; that neither is beyond the range of pardon; and that I could, and do, alike pity her who "falls" from force of circumstances, poverty, presents, opportunity, importunity, and organization; and him who, distracted and rendered passion-mad by a billowy expanse of beautiful, snowy, palpitating bosom, loses his seven senses and follows straight in old Adam's wake.

In the Chicago conclave, as in all my works, I pleaded for the female outcast, and held that she who through misfortune stepped aside and became a mother ere a bride, should not be held in less esteem than him who brought the trouble to her door. That it is but fair to remember our own weakness, and give the helping heart and hand. I think so still; and it was in allusion to what the leading woman of the convention said on _that_ _very_ _point_ that I uttered the memorable sentence: "I will stand by this woman (naming her) in the utterance of such views until there's good skating on ice five feet thick upon the Lakes of Tophet!" and so I would, and whereever or whenever a wrong is to be righted and human justice dealth out as God's eternal is.

CVII. It is impossible for me to denounce as an unmitigated scoundrel and villain, any human being whose misconceptions of Manhood and human duty and obligation lead him to trample upon what most of us regard as holy; for we may not know the hidden causes underlying his actions. He is certainly a strange man who can justify his own or another's proceedings when lust is alone the prompter,--to first seduce every woman, married or single, that he can, and then publicly boast of it! Impregnating other men's wives; compelling men and women too to remain in ignorance as to the paternity of a given child, if such should be the issue of the "Passional attraction;" forcing an honest, hard-working man to support his harlotized wife, and the wandering "Lover's" bastards, and he, the "Wanderer," laughing at the man he has dishonored, and the wife he has degraded!--forgetting the last victims while in search of new ones; repeating the ghastly crime everywhere; encouraging his own wife to play the role of common cyprian; and scattering possible discord and desolation wherever his salacious footsteps fall! Supposing such a being to be sane, then such a thing in human shape, who would deliberately win the favors of any woman, save a _very_ common courtesan, and then brag of it, to _her_ shame and his own dishonor, is too small a specimen of the genus homo to be tolerated in society calling itself civilized. Savagery is his status, and to it should he be relegated. But a civilized man of such views and practice is _not_ sane; for he gives incontestable proof of being the victim of chronic prostatic inflammation, undoubtedly of Onanistic, but more likely of Pederastic origin; and thus being sexually mad, is a semi-responsible cerebro-prostatic maniac, to whom the universe appears as one grand discus or yoni and himself the aspiring priapic-phallic godling!

But there! I have done with him; this thing named Moses Hull, having thus handed him and his ilk down the ages, and that's enough! That crime, and the other, child-rape--which latter I call Dentonism--after the most wretched and contimptible thing that ever wore the semblance of a man,--Hull excepted,--I regard as the worst that ever existed within the confines of civilization, and in calling the attention of the public, but especially legislators, thereto, I amply redeem my promise, and have fully paid my little _Bill_!

I never did, by speech or pen, advocate any of the peculiar social theories broached and ventilated in that, or any similar conclave--for reasons already herein and elsewhere set forth in my various writings; and yet, because I held my peace upon the main questions at issue, and in spite of the fact, I was held to have sanctioned and fully endorsed all the radical utterances there made; to have upheld what I have fought all my life long,--the total abrogation of all marriage; and to have espoused the doctrine of connubial handfastening, or temporary marriages, and I know not what else of absurdity the foes of Fair play and Free discussion chose to invent and fashion in fantastic garb out of whole cloth to suit their own peculiar fancies. As I suffered by distortion, so did others, and yet the sun actually rose next day!

LOVE'S ALCHEMY--THE MARROW; RES GESTAE; SUMMING UP.

CVIII. Human marriage, being triplicate,--material, mental, emotional,--has three offices, clear and distinct. 1st. Its functions are humanizing and perpetuating; 2d. They are refining, elevating, a means of soul-growth; and, 3d. The purpose it serves is a mystic one, for beyond all doubt the ultimate of the human is deific --a fusion mingling, interblending--at-one-ment with the Omnipotent God; what came from, must return to, the centre; and he who would be nearer God is he who loves the purest.

CIX. The test of all Love is its self-sacrificing unselfishness; and all amative love is false, unclean, abnormal, unless it be based upon the non-physical; it must be builded of respect, affection, that which is mental and spiritual; else it lasts not.

CX. Woman loves easier than man, and it is easier broken, unless its roots are grounded in her very soul; then it is next to death to give it up. When a man loves in right down earnest, and from the feminine side of his soul, it, all other things being equal, evermasses, overweighs, any love modern women--Society people, I mean --are capable of. But take the two and probably the loves will balance each other, with this eternal fact in woman's favor; she is self-sacrificing, and her love, when it is love, is untainted with earth; is never external, never merely sensual.

CXI. Woman can conceal, dissemble, pretend love,--not a spark of which she really feels,--to perfection; and hoodwink any man she chooses to play upon; but a woman with her eyes open cannot be served the same way by a man; for live, if it be real, tells its own story. More men love their wives than wives their husbands! He cannot make believe half as well as she; for the lady can coolly kiss a man with the intent of playing upon him at the very first chance; embrace him, with a load of deceit in her heart. But when a man loves he loves all over. Blast it, and you destroy him. But in these days love as true and solid as that is exceedingly rare indeed!

The undetected and unconvicted adulterers exceed the uncaught ones five hundred to one. This result from the non-understanding of the real and radical differences existing between true soul-love and its mere passional and magnetic counterfeits --which are fifty times more abundant than the other.

CXII. No wicked person can truly love and remain wicked. That is the redemptive, salvatory and alchemical power of the divine principle! True-heartedness is the corrective agency of the great human world and human soul. Without it we are ships on the stormy deep, with a wild rush of angry waters threatening to submerge us at any instant! With it, we are life-boated into fair havens and secure anchor-

-78-

age! With it, we arise into bliss and blessedness; without it, misery is our lot; for it is the telegraphic System wherewith God engirdles the worlds! From Him it goes; to Him it returns, bringing up from the deeps the poor forlorn ones it finds there, and stringing them like beads to hand round the neck of the ineffable and viewless Lord of infinite and superlative glory!

CXIII. At first Love springs up and surges in our wouls, a newborn and strange power, which rules us with a rod of iron. At the start it is vague, general, diffusive; and we are glad without knowing the reasons why, like unto the babe quickened en utero; and we are irresistibly urged to centre it on some one, some reciprocating soul; and unless we do, wretched are we! If we fail so to do, but expend its forces here, there, everywhere, anywhere, we speedily cease to be truly human; but sink till we are the bond slaves of pernicious, debasing, demoralizing habit, from which there may be deliverance, but a very troublous one. We must love one; for unless we do the measure of our life on earth is unfilled.

CXIV. The new soul descends to man; by him is bequeathed and entrusted to the dear mother's care, during those mysterious forty weeks. By her it is robed in flesh and blood, and during the wonderful and thrice holy process she needs all the vital life that he can spare; and it is his bounden duty to impart it in every possible form, from the gentle caress to the kind word and act of tender gallantry. She knows when she requires magnetism, and she is to be sole and supreme judge of when, and where and how that vital power shall be imparted! Do not forget this.

An hour's rest on his loving shoulder at the eventide, just as they sit by the open casement, is sometimes of more value to an unwell woman, than untold gold and diamonds would be at another time, and under different conditions.

Moreover, I have no patience with the puerile jargon of the "Physiologists," to the end that the great climax of connubiality ought always to cease from the conceptive moment till after lactation;--that non-intercourse should be the rule, and rigidly enforced, all of which I regard as stupid nonsense--prefixed with a dash and two d's,--because we are human beings, not mere animals; and both the mother and babe require that magnetic life and vif which only the father and husband can supply.

There is a very curious thing right here: Instances are numerous of a wife descending, subsequent to conception, to other than the father of her child. In such case, the second man determines the shape, quality and calibre of the unborn infant's soul! The woman has no right to wrong any man in that style; for she ranks but as a cyprian, and the child is essentially an illegitimate; because, whereas, the husband has given body to his offspring, the other supplies it with the elements of spirit, and the babe will be more like him than its own father! because spiritual laws are of stronger force than physical! Don't forget this!

But the husband has no more rights in this respect than his wife; because wherever he goes he is sure to bring a non-assimilable, foreign, magneto-vital influence, which neither his wife nor child can appropriate and absorb; and thus he warps the babe's soul, if not its body, and infuses an aura into the very marrow of the being of both his dependents, which is injurious to all, and may crop out in physical disease or mental ailment, in after years, by the hair-graying conduct of his angular child!

When babes and children have trouble, they cry themselves to sleep; when men and women have trouble, slumber flies their weary eyes. Now when men are careless concerning the substance of this paragraph, they indicate a bad state of puerility; for of all human duties, the grandest is that of fathering those who shall be superior to ourselves. "But how? Suppose an inferior woman to be already pregnant, how shall I, her husband, correct the faults of haste, imperfect organization,--in a word, suppose the child to be has been launched into existence under very unfavorable conditions; how shall I correct the bad bias; and what shall I do that it may come to the world a far better and nobler being than if things ended just as they began? Tell me this, O man of Eulis, and I--I will thank you on bended knee!"

Well put, my questioner. Now heed thou well the reply thereto:--1st. Remember that in her condition your marital offices are never in order save when she determines they shall, ought, to, or may be. 2d. That if offered and accepted at any other time, a direct injury results to the mother and her unborn child. 3d. Wherefore Infrequency is the true policy to be pursued, if you hope for good results. 4th. Remember that consummation is threefold:--of body, spirit, SOUL. That then the greatest streams of magnetism flow from husband to wife, and wife to husband. That said Magnetism is a vehicle conveying the states of the soul, body and spirit; and through it, then both the mother and the child may be blessed or cursed; poisoned or purified; filled with divine life, or charged with the quintessence of horror and hell!

Well, do you see the point? do you understand your duty? and do you perceive that, if by restraint you add vigor to your entire being; and when she invites you to share it with her, you do so, wishing, willing, praying that untold good, unnumbered blessings may follow, and result therefrom,--that they will come, just as sure as God reigns? If you do not so perceive it, it is high time you did. Were you an initiate of Eulis, you would find out more on this wonderful point; but as it is, take what I herein give you, and God grant you may profit by it.

CXV. Love, and love only, can secure the devotion and heartfidelity of a woman, and any other sort is not worth having. When a woman loves, even if unreturned, she is a heroine; but if returned, she is happy, which is a great deal better than heroism!

CXVI. Married people ruin their homes, even though loving ones, by unwise and untimely association. It should never be a matter of course, but ever and always a dual inspiration; otherwise it is defective.

CXVII. Woman and man are not equals. They are diverse compatibles; each contrasts and opposites the other,--offsetting in all ways. The two, together, constitute the being called man. Either alone is but an incompleteness,--a halfness. Neither owns the other, but are joint interestants in the social compact. The idea of ownership is what has made marriage as it is to-day,--a jangle, wrangle, tangle, --anything, everything, but what it should be. It were well if we would each of us constantly bear in mind that we conquer oftenest when we stop to do so; and that more is to be gained by graceful sacrifice than stubborn reliance reserved rights.

CXVIII. The second purpose of marriage is the peopling of the Spaces; its essence is spiritual. In true marriage there is a mutual infiltration of soul, whence it happens that nature, in slowly moulding each to resemble the other, proclaims that marriage real and true; but not all the ceremonies on earth could fuse a couple of natural antagonists. If these likenesses are not observed, it is a pretty sure sign that there is but little love coursing round that homeside, and still less flowing through the channel of their lives.

We do not want to find ourselves growing away from each other; but in fusing natures and blending spirits, to coalesce with our opposites, effecting a chemical union, admitting no separation, and the only solvent of which is the grand Alcahest

--Death:--And if the marriage be perfect, even death is unable to change it.

Reader: don't be a fool! don't lavish your love on one who talks, but never acts it. I, the author of this book, tell you that if your heart is overflowing with affection, you are in all the greater danger of first filling some empty, bladder-like being, with your own soul's sphere, then falling desperately in love with it, only to waken from the dreadful sleep to find him or her a diabolic sham, and yourself wrecked, ruined, prostrate, helpless, broken-hearted, deserted, and wretched beyond description. Prove all thing, especially proffered Love, and when you find it real, give rein to your soul:--But not till then!!

CXIX. When a couple are alike, equally choleric, mental, physical, frigid or the reverse; passive, positive, magnetic, electric, tall, slender, fat, active, indolent; then such are constitutionally, temperamentally, and in most other respects non-adapted to each other; and if they are not careful, there will be more down than up, discord than its opposite, in that family. But, where such persons have already cast the die of what passes current in these days as marriage, there's wisdom in seeking to create or build up an artificial harmony, which care and time will render habitual, natural and permanent; because Habit becomes even stronger than nature, as witness the use of narcotics, which all are disgusted with at first. If people will but attempt in thus making a second nature, the barrenness, usual in such cases, will be obviated, as well as the premature senility and impotence resultant; for that both these effects are often owing to such causes is as clearly established as any other medical fact, albeit the sufferers are not always aware of the reason.

CXX. In all males of the human species the personal, physical charms of woman, based upon desire, is the central attractive point, round which all desires cluster. His better, nobler, higher love comes afterward. Reverse the case for woman. Her love never has that rise. She takes to the better side first--his social, mental, moral, spiritual manhood; and only after the lapse of time, frequently a whole year, does she awaken to the ralization of the purely sensuous or passional; and uncounted thousands there are who never awaken to the ralization of the purely sensuous or passional; and uncounted thousands there are who never awaken thereto at all from the altar to the grave. In all such cases he is an unwise man who does not by careful and assiduous attention, by every delicate and tender means, seek to establish the natural equilibrium; by all true human methods arouse the dormant power in the breast of her who shares his lot and life.

CXXI. Prior to the actual marriage the husband loves deepest, most intensely and devotedly. But after that, his ardor cools, and a revulsion of feeling, amount-ing to dislike, is almost sure to follow; in which he is the exact opposite of woman; for it is then only that she begins to cling to him with a depth and fervor surprising to him, astonishing to herself. Wise is he who then gives her reason to make that love permanent, solid, lasting, even to the brink of the grave.

Men, all males in fact, love fiercest before marriage; all females subsequent thereto. It is the Law. But a man must so comport himself at these primal inter-views as not to wound her sensitive spirit, or cloud her life with gloom, dread, fear, suspicion. First impressions last the longest!

CXXII. Man's Love is never a steady stream, or constant force. He, so to speak, packs it away in the presence of other "Business," and gives it an airing now and again; but woman reverses all that, and loves right straight along from the start, every day and all the time, provided she loves at all. Whatever she may be about, no matter what, her love is the sole theme of her life, the only occupation of her mind; and she takes good care to give it air every hour of the day; and a fair return, in kind, amply repays her for many an hour of mortal anguish. If she fails to get it, God help her! for her life is but a lingering, painful, torturous death. It is even so with man. If he loves,--as I have loved, My God!--and after long months of toil awakens to find his idol but a phantom; that he has been embalming a doll in his own heart and loving it, but getting no return, what wonder that madness comes, and the wild beating of his heart and throbbing of his temples drive him to the brink of ruin, until he stands toppling on the cliffs of suicide, doubtful whether to leap or not; and only saved by the Omnipotent hand of the interfering God!

CXXIII. Lust ties man to the outer walls of human life, and keeps him there a prisoner feeding upon the poorest of husks. But Love frees him from many a gyve and thrall; gives him the freedom of God's gardens of joy; feeds him with the bread of life; opens the gates of heaven; and admits him to the companionship of celestial Verities and divinest life and truth. Without love we are, indeed, poor hermits in the world!

CXXIV. People plunge headlong into perdition and social gehenna by rushing into each other's arms too often! Passional excess generates disease; Love cures them; and all the kidney difficulties and nervous disorders extant are but the physical expression of the morbid and unhealthy states of the love-natures of their respective victims.

Those who love can never prostitute themselves or each other, in any way.

It is just as impossible to kindle fire with ice as to long deceive a soul that loves. But, ah, God, how terrible is the awakening to the fact that all this time you have been lavishing your heart's best treasures on a dead stock! Then--in her case, comes leucorrhoea or gravid uterus,--not physical ailments, but the outward sign that there's love trouble in the soul, and love the only remedy. In his case insanity more or less pronounced, and enduring.

CXXV. There are periods when love insists upon passional moods. It is its natural appeasement. If not yielded to, a frightful train of ills are sure to follow, and madness may end the cruel scene.

CXXVI. Jealousy quite as often springs from magnetic incompatibility and impotence as from love-estrayal; and it brings on heart-pain, dyspepsia, liver and Bright's disease, prostatic, urethral, vaginal, ovarian, and other fatal troubles, long before the allotted span of years run out.

CXXVII. Doctors tell us that actual marriage will cure some diseases of women. But a diseased woman is not fit for it; and actual marriage in diseased states of either party is--monstrous! The doctrine is nonsense, pure and simple. Magnetism may do, marriage no! But facts are facts, and the thing occurs. If love underlie it, well and good; if not, then not. It is disastrous. But if good results follow, it is Affection that works the miracle, nothing coarser! And more wives are injured in that manner than sextons can find spades to dig graves for!

That is a very poor sort of love which always exacts but never gives! "She prated of Love all day long, and neglected by one single act to prove her truth," is the story of many a man's life. "He says he loves me--but just look at me; does love waste one as I am wasted? My God! Let this bitter cup pass from me!" is the daily cry of millions of "Married" women!

-82-

I'm tired and sick of dead babies! They ought to fill out the term of three-score years and ten; but they don't; and those who escape the sewers, sinks, drains, and being carried out with the tides, or being snugly put away in a cigar-box and stuck in a hole in the garden, are mighty undertain of a safe deliverance from measles, scarlatina, croup, paregoric, or Mrs. Winslow's soothing syrup! Ah, but isn't it a soother?--soothing many a one to a sleep that knows no waking! But these dead ones are not all the offspring of the riff-raff, or hard-handed servitors at labor's shrine; but many a hundred of them might lay claim to aristocratic lineage; and I have quite enough experience to satisfy me that those who do, or who wink at, such deeds, are, many of them church-goers, full of deadly piety, who, behind the scenes, revel in debaucheries dreadful enough to shame a Satyr. Not a few of them are "Reformers," in public preaching perfect purity, but in private practising promiscuity, and the very ones--if male--with whom no decent, respectable woman could be alone with ten minutes, save at the absolute certainty of being insulted by the most villainous proposals.

In my Medical practice, and that of Teacher, three classes of persons mainly relief or counsel: 1st. Wives whose daily life was a living death; whose "homes" were tophets in petto; and whose "Husbands"--sic?--in one respect treated them worse than they did the dumb brutes in barn or stable--poor, waxen-faced martyrs, worse than sacrificed and slaughtered on the altars of a legalized sensualism, so low and mean, selfish, exacting, as to even shame the beasts of the field; and these wives human! 2d. Men and women whose hearts and souls yearned for affection which they found not; and which they were denied by those from whom they had the right to ex-pect it!--people who were either fretting to death under the awfully galling yoke of a bad marriage; or who wanted advice to guide them to the desired haven--and heaven, of Marriage, as God intended it should be. 3d. But by far the largest class of callers and correspondents must be reckoned that vast mass of people whose entire gender-nature had been broken up, or down, and demoralized until they had become mere phantom men and women, incapable of realizing the sublime meaning of the words Sex and Marriage; and so disordered and diseased that Hope itself, with folded wing and fouled anchor, perched upon a bleak cliff on some island far away. O my God! what utter horror and blank despair have I seen gleam from the eyes of thousands! --victims all, --to vampiral depletion; nervous and vital exhaustion; impotentia, barrenness; diseases of uterus, vulva, ovaries, kidneys, prostate, heart, lungs, brain--the terrible personal hades outgrown from society, society, society, with its falses and shams; its money-marriages; its deceit and hypocrisy, denouncing the Wrong with the breath, but with act encouraging concumbinage, cyprianism, libertinage; and by its repressions, fashion, style, display and airiness discouraging marriage, and fostering thereby the solitary vice now desolating millions, and decimating all the fair lands! I make the solemn statement and declaration that a very fair per-centage of that third class were from the dignified, wealthy, respectable, Christian, aristocratic, and even reverend stratas of society, not of this country alone, but of all divilized lands, including Cuba, Chili, Brazil, France, Spain, China, Australia Japan and England. In fact, the demand for sex tonics and invigorants is not only simply enormous but almost universal, and all springing from violation of the Love-laws of our common human nature. Of course, such a demand for such medicines speaks in thunder tones against the causes producing it, and equally loud against the private habits of us of the world. But the facts exist; and even the dreadful syphilis in modified form rages in the blood and bones of unnumbered thou sands-- not only of guilty debauchees,--who are scarce to be pitied!--but, alas, in those of innocent wives and prattling infants! What are these half murdered ones--of both the latter classes--to do? suffer and die like leprous dogs? or are they to reach forth and make desperate efforts for physical salvation? If the latter, then all legislators should at once look to the enactment of laws suppressing quackery; making syphilis a criminal offense; hanging abortionists; squelching "flash" papers,

and legalizing all unions based on blind trust on one side and villainous libertinage on the other; and punishing re-unions elsewhere as it now punishes polygamy
outside the favored Mormon and Perfectionist churches, institutions or bagnios,
"Religious" and "Theological." Shame on the Press--the First Estate of modern
nations, that it hesitates to launch its thunders at the class of wrongs just cited,
and hurl them forever into hades!

> "Firm in the right! the Public Press should be,
> The tyrant's foe, the champion of the free!
> Faithful and constant to its sacred trust,--
> Calm in its utterance, in its judgment just,
> Wise in its teaching; uncorrupt and strong,
> To spread the right and to denounce the wrong!
> Long may it be ere candor must confess
> On Freedom's hordes, a weak and venal Press!"

It is generally admitted that there's something wrong in society, but what the
cure is or shall be is not so apparent. One class of people advocate "Social Freedom" as the panacea, whatever that may mean. Before I went to, at, and until the
last day of, the Chicago Convention, elsewhere alluded to, I thought I knew the
correct meaning of the terms. I find I did not; and therefore look in other directions for the social cure. Spoiled cheese, and cheese spoiled, are the same to me;
nor for my life can I now see the difference in the moral grade and status of a
cyprian or libertine on the pay-rolls, and the same, impulse and passion being the
spur and motive. The cheese smells equally bad in both cases!

It wouldn't be a bad thing to make it a punishable offence for any M.D. to
call syphilis by the nicer name of scrofula, thus fooling honest wives, and screen-
ing recreant husbands--even if they are well paid for their white lies! For in
these days that scourge burns the bodies of unspotted virgins, in the shape of fluor
albus, womb complaint, etc., inherited from infected mothers. The evil is bad
enough if it stopped right there, but it don't; because, in the first place, it
brings on pruritis,--vaginal itching; creates morbid desire, and subjects girls as
pure as snow to the almost dead certainty of falling victims to the first graceful,
smart, and salacious scoundrel that comes along,--a scoundrel and victim too, it may
be of the same inherited-fluid ruin coursing like streams of fire through his
swollen veins! In the second place, these girls are to become wives and mothers;
these boys husbands and fathers; thus the curse is injected into the veins of
myriads of the yet unborn--children doomed before birth to endure a life of perpetual ill-health and morbid unrest; to know nothing of real happiness from the
breast to the tomb--to which latter they are likely to be rushed prematurely by
suicide, resultant from insanity begotten by the beings who parented them. Again I
repeat Syphilis is a crime, and should be held as such.

CXXVIII. Love is multiple in form and mode. Sometimes it will endure and
suffer long. At others it will die as if lightning-struck; but the "dying" sort of
affection is not worth tying to! Never!

Irish Love is gallant, but non-lasting, and is more affectional or amicive
than ardent and amative. Negro Love is diffusive, hilarious, sensual. Oriental
Love is sad-eyed, dreamy, vague, skyey, poetic, rapt, heavenly, divine, but not
keen, or passional. Spanish Love is fiery, ardent, impetuous, terrible, scorching,
consuming; tender, but not enduring. German Love is parental, maternal, filial,
domestic, dead-level, and mainly physical. It has no Italian heights; no sunbursts;
no mountains or valleys; no anguish; no great joys; no hill-tops crowned with glittering sheen. French Love is superficial, lascivious, and, when youth is gone, a

thing of memory, not of fact. English Love is domestic, but mealy. Northern Love is like that of the felidae—catty, scratchy, periodic, poisonish, often downright brutal, and never tender, delicate, or refined. Yankee Love is fitful, uncertain, changeful, passional, moody, seldom more than superficial, because the Yankee faculties are all engrossed in the one grand object of American life—dollars and dimes, dash and display. Western Love I know but little about, and, judging from what I saw in Ohio, is so-so-ish, not deep cool, calculating, and seldom drives its victims to suicide, because only the heartful sink to despair!

Lastly, Southern Love is volcanic, chivalrous, gallant, true, tender, jealous, safe when earnest, devotional and devoted, genuine and manly. The well-bred Southerners are the true ladies and gentlemen of America! I never met but one mean man among them in all my life (and he was descended from a French family, born in Limerick, or the Cove of Cork). They have less sharp intellect, perhaps, than the northern people, but more Soul; hence, while subject to fevers, amative weakness they are free from!

CXXIX. An old man should be very careful of the intimacies of wedded life; he should change his amative for AMICIVE ardor; because all old people are more or less troubled with Embolism—a clogging of the veins, nerves, arteries, muscles—all the viscera, with the limy, chalky, carbonaceous, calcareous refuse of the body —such as the organs cannot get rid of; and the accumulation means a cessation of physical joys and vigor, and ultimate death. When Embolism prevails to a considerable extent, the orgasm is a dangerous thing for that man, and death stands close by whenever he forgets that he is no longer a youth. But if such will insist on being foolish, they should first get rid of the Embolism, and cleanse the body of all superfluities in the shape of phosphates, alkaline or acid; dissolve the clayey refuse, and evacuate it at once, else some time he may, in repeating youth-like follies, so shock and shatter his nervous system as to rob him of what few years remain to him on earth. This cleansing process is quite easy of accomplishment, as I have elsewhere stated, and while alive, am ready to instruct about. And this point suggests another closely connected with it:--

CXXX. Self-venery is more often a disease than it is a vice or crime. In either case the fault or habit is easily corrected, cured, and broken. All that is necessary is to exhibit medicines that will repress the amative appetite, and for awhile seal up the ducts. The waste being stopped, of course strength accumulates, for the rich, vital life is retained, assimilated, and the diseases of nerves, brain, and pelvic viscera disappear before the returning march of vigorous and triumphant health.

CXXXI. I cannot resist the desire to repeat my warning against the ruinous and suicidal policy of "conjugal frauds," that is, carrying the marriage to a point short of completion; but I have additional reasons. They are these: The shock to the nervous system is at least ten times greater in such cases than in normal rite, or even its dreadful counterfeit; and I never saw a case where it had been a habit, that the man was not terribly injured, cerebrally as well as nervously. In all such cases Sanity was a diminishing ratio; and the brain injured almost beyond the power of reparation. The natural office must be naturally fulfilled, else the strain on the blood-vessels of the pelvis is so great, that premature impotence is sure; while that upon the cerebral arteries means insanity, paralysis, brain-softening, spinal disease, apoplexy, and death! Unless both realize what God intended, ruin, sooner or later, is the inevitable result. In cases where the senuous equations are not alike, the more rapid nervous action can be retarded by an effort of the will, and God's design be accomplished, not frustrated. One-half the sudden deaths of middle-aged men result from this cause!

CXXXII. Many husbands, by various means, have so impaired their personal vigor, as to be semi, if not wholly, impotent; but instead of imputing it to the right cause, they attribute it to some fault on the other side of the house, and poor she leads an unhappy life in consequence. Now this is all wrong; but the cure quite easy: 1st. He should occupy his own chamber _solus_. 2d. Breathe deeply. 3d. Be much in the sunshine. 4th. Drink no liquors. 5th. Bathe often. 6th. Eat solid beef, and unsifted flour--no potatoes at all; and in four weeks he will recuperate all his lost energies, and be a man again; for while he remains a weakling and a passional imbecile, he could not be happy with the best and fairest wife that ever was fashioned by the master hand of Omnipotence!

CXXXIII. It often happens that from some occult reason there is a great deficiency, even to the extent of horror and disgust on the part of some ladies; whose lords not realizing the enormity of such conduct, lead lives of _insistance_, and reap crops of passive, yet enforced compliance on the part of their--victims, shall I say? Such men should realize that it is in their own power, by delicacy and kindness, to change the morbid to a natural state; so that what was shrunk from with loathing, will, in six months, be accepted as natural and right, and be fully reciprocated--with a little noble and forbearing trial, and some patience; yet the reward is ample; and oh, how delightful! to feel that _she_ regards _you_ as a saviour from _yourself_! instead of as before,--a little domestic tyrant, bent on mischief, careless who suffers so long as you--_do not_!

CXXXIV. True Manhood, and all that it implies, proclaims itself in nothing so well and fairly as in the tones of our voices. When we are right in that respect, the sounds are clear, deep, round, full, sonorous, melodious, with an underlayer of music ringing out bell-like from our very souls. It then shows that we are right both at the emotive and brain centres of our duplicate being; but when they are cracked, shrill, sharp, acute, squeaky, false, coppery, gongy, it indicates little power and less Soul; for it is morbid, and its possessor is better fit for almost anything else than holy, honorable God-sanctioned marriage!

CXXXV. Soul-vigor, and what it implies, depends to a great extent on Lung capacity, and that generally indicates good digestion.

No great act or mighty though can originate in, or be accomplished by, one who is deficient in the foundational quality of absolute manhood. Just so long as we are morbid in that department, that long we are demoralized all over, inside, outside, head to heel, and soul and body.

Sexive health and purity is the price of power. We cannot have it on any other terms whatever; wherefore Truth to one love builds up the entire being; while any departure therefrom, any degree of promiscuity, beats the soul's wings to the ground, cripples its energies, lays it low, just as summer torrents lay low the ripening grain. As a thinker, I regard that as one of the most important of all truths. In nothing is this rule more imperative than in the cases of such persons as desire to cultivate the inner powers of the being; for any passional excess or "Variety" as certainly disarms the soul, seals up the spiritual eyes, blunts the inner power of perception, and ruins the capacity for psycho-vision, as that water and fire are antagonistic. It is said that one cannot serve God and Mommon at the same time; and it is equally certain that we cannot cultivate the better and loftier powers resident within us, and at the same time give a loose rein to the carnal passions of our nature.

CXXXVI. The force of Genius is the force of Gender, and both are the force of Destiny! No man or woman can be truly great unless their amatory natures are well developed!

In my medical practice I first cured people of innumerable diseases myself, and then taught my pupils how to do likewise, by, firstly, secondly, and lastly, getting them right sexively; after which dear old Nature carried them straight up the hills of death!

When a man is full of vigor he scorns to do a mean thing, because he feels himself so much a MAN. You pick out all the scoundrels and drivers of hard bargains, and that portion of their nature will be found missing; no color in their faces, no manhood in their being; too mean to live; too miserable to die!

On the other hand, when a lady's periods are sweet, pure, regular, she's mighty apt to be very pleasant company to whoever chances to pass by that way; and her very smile is a ray of sunlight straight out from heaven! But just as soon as the _fleurs blanches_ appear, she begins to sour right away; and a woman in either state should forever be held apart and sacred, for she is no more capable of _wifeliness_ at such times than is the weanling crawling on the floor. Why, every one can see at a glance.

CXXXVII. Death is but the beginning of some people's real trouble; and marriage is generally the commencement of everybody else's; for there's so much morbidity afloat that people are perverted before marriage, and remain so afterward. Such can never avoid slander, scandal, backbiting, but take thereto as ducks to water, because the foundations of nobility are sealed up; and neither man or woman thus characterized can live at peace with any other of God's creatures on the footstool.

Such wives either fool their lords, or make home too hot to hold them. Such men neglect their wives, and general chaos reigns supreme. Now if such would but take pains to revive and cultivate the true instinct, the road to happiness would open straight before them.

CXXXVIII. When the skin of the face, hands, arms, is loose and flabby, it is a sure sign of three things: kidney, bladder, vaginal, urethral, brain, or uterine trouble; originating in affectional disturbances; of chronic discontent; and of the need of cure by affection. Let this be done, and they who would love and be loved breathe deeply, and the physical ailments will disappear. Promiscuity can never do it. I have heard doctors recommend it; but I have no patience with them or with that other ilk who contend for "Variety in Love." To me they are but human toads bent on besliming the morals of mankind. I defy any sane man to love the wife whom he knows shares with another favors to which he alone by their mutual troth is entitled'. Public opinion sets in strong tides against such doctrine; and although it is sometimes pig-headed and wrong, yet in this it is unquestionably right; because no true, genuine man or woman is willing to, or capable of, sharing the love which ought to be exclusively their own. Lecherous human halflings advocate the doctrine; but it is always on _their_ side of the house, at the expense of some one _else's_ wife or daughter! It is simply monstrous and impossible for healthy people to be happy in "Variety."

CXXXIX. People who have no charity toward those who, by pressure of circumstances, place, opportunity, or magnetism, step aside and commit a social fault, will upon analysis be found not overly sound at heart, secretly unprincipled, and wofully lacking in the basic elements of genuine man or womanhood.

Prudes are not perfectly clean in all corners of their souls.

Those who demolish bagnios are usually bagnio-patrons! Rakes and libertines have less mercy than their opposites; while those who say a good word for the fallen are the ones who know how it is themselves to be spat upon, maligned, lashed, scorned, neglected; and that too by those unworthy to latch their shoestrings! while they who hate the opposite sex give proof positive of foul personal habits within the secrecy of their own rooms!

CXL. Men often *like* their wives, as household conveniences, yet never really *husband* them; and that's exactly what every woman wants but don't get--as a general rule! Now if there is one fool greater than another, it is either the wife who submits to such treatment, when she has her remedy in the exercise of the three principles named elsewhere in this book; or the husband who expects that a neglected wife can really love him, and honestly be sorry when he dies!

CXLI. Virtue, not its opposite, is the normal state of man! Affection, not passion, is what we crave and yearn for; and finding are blest. When we go astray it is more from the pressure of circumstances than the natural inclination of our souls. Most of us were born wrong, and inherit tendencies not good for us; still in the cultured will we have a never-failing remedy.

The heart's allegiance must first be turned aside before the body yields to passional breezes blowing from off the home-shore; wherefore I hold it better to not try to break the bad connection by force, but by the applied will rewin the straying one to love's arms again.

CXLII. The essence of Marriage is consent. Ceremonials merely publish the fact; wherefore it should be the law of every land that he who finds a woman worth seducing, and does it, should, by that act alone, be compelled to maintain and acknowledge her as a lawful wife, unless she sees fit to waive her undoubted right to claim and hold him as a husband. The fact that a man has done such an act should in law bar him from marriage with any other woman. Such is the way in which I look at it; and if society would but adopt the idea there would be fewer libertines, and some millions less of ruined girls and forlorn prostitutes.

She who robs a woman of her husband; or he who ruins a confiding girl merits a season in Tophet, and if I were Brahm would get it--sure!

CXLIII. The more familiarities a single woman permits a man to take, the more he is sure to undervalue her, and the less she respects and honors him. It is natural for him to despise one who allows too great freedoms. So also within the sacred pale of wedlock: the very first immodesty on either side blunts the edge, takes the bloom from the peach, lessens them in their own and each other's eyes, and is the beginning of folly which often ends in the divorce courts, the brothel, bagnio, or the grave! Modesty and circumspection build up tottering loves. Their opposites bring disrespect and finally dissolution. I say these things here, because I have long known them to be true.

What a pleasant thing it must be to a sensible and senitive woman to have, whenever her heart prompts her to express affection--her better half meet her with a storm of coarse and disgusting passion,--the base idea of which must be perfectly withering to her soul. Poor She!--one of thousands!--how ardently must she long for death, and dread even heaven itself, if there is marrying and giving in marriage away over in the upper Land! And how such a woman must try to be a Budhist and long for nihility rather than continued life. But then such states are begotten of her-- their, deep unrest, causing them to long--as have I ere now--for whole eternities of sweet and restful sleep. But then women capable of such yearnings are immortal;

will survive death, and, let us believe--their longings will be appeased, their pangs assuaged over there where it is certain they, like myself, will at last be understood; for such seldom are on this earth, and at thirty odd, it is too late to hope to be while in the flesh.

Helen, a loose one, caused the wars of Troy, and from her down the lane of ages, men, and women too, have practically adored body, and worshipped Lust and Fashion, openly or sub-rosa; and until some decimating scourge, originating in Lust, shall sweep the earth--as it will within a century!--of six-tenths of its human denizens, the same wild worship will continue as before.

CXLIV. How very seldom married people praise each other! yet nothing on earth goes so far toward rejuvenating a waning regard, as the expression of gladness at each other's points, acts, trials, victories, industry, perseverance; yet all this power for good is practically ignored; and while others are praised and cheered to the echo, we never get the slightest token of appreciation, even though we toil like abject slaves to deserve it. If love exists between couples, it ought to show itself in something better than mere empty words. If it does not, whole troops of discontentments come crowding at our fireside; for neglected duties, broken promises, lip affection, magnetic, or passional attraction, will not fill the bill of an anxious heart! They paralyze us, render us cross, selfish, non-ambitious, careless, hopeless, solitary, and despondent. That affection which words itself by daylight, and snores when Night veils the world, is not worth an hour's purchase. Palsied affection seldom gets entirely well again! and non-reciprocal marriage infuriates all males; and too many wives make not the slightest effort toward mutuality; and by so neglecting one of the first of wifely duties, clap the lid on the coffin of their happiness, and hurry their joys to an untimely grave; and after thus committing marital suicide, they weep and wonder that their lords do not fall down at their feet to worship and idolize them as of yore, in the halycon days of courtship and the honeymonth; not realizing that he, poor fellow, has found the lace all paper, the diamonds all paste;--and no man likes either of these! She is not wise, who expects to hold a man securely unless one of her strongest cords is reciprocation, which every husband has a right to expect and realize; and every wife, by ner vow, is bound to culture and accord. Otherwise their union is but a mockery and a sham.

She who habitually fails in that wifely duty helps to support the females who occupy the palaces of sin--and gin, to whose society her husband is, as "they say," driven by her coldness. The strange woman at least simulates accord; while the honorable wife expresses frigidity, horror, indifference, or disgust; neither of which are well calculated to keep a man in good training for his constant combat with the world!

I hold him not a good man who ever seeks what can never be sanctioned except by mutual love; for it is a profanation of the divinest sanctities of the human soul; and he is a poor specimen of a man who can seek solace in a cyprian's arms, or revel in passional debauch bought with current coin either in or out of wedlock; for nothing but Love can ever justify an act which may launch an immortal soul into being. Under these holy conditions marriage generates glorious thoughts, noble resolve, courage to endure; gives a better zest of, and hold on, life, fortune, goodness, God!

Under the false condition every participant rests on the edge of Hades, ready to roll off into it at any moment; and if there is an especial curse, they deserve it who, with their eyes open, as mine now are, and for some time have been,--violate that sacred law. That and "Variety" are death to true affection, and also destructive of the power and ability to experience any but coarse and gross emotion; besides brutalizing human nature, destroying nobleness of character, they totally unfit us to become parents of pure children and good ones; but only of such as, born of passion, shall rush on passion-tides adown the stream of life, cursing their progenitors at every inch of the dreadful way! But true love, thank Heaven! antagonizes, and finally destroys, lurid, baneful lust. The twain are incompatible; but the angel slays the fiend whenever they meet in combat on anything like even terms. Thank God for that again! So be it forever !

CXLV. There are too many million outrages inside, as well as without, the pale of matrimony; but these won't be, when both sides understand and obey the law which underlies human nature everywhere. Men are chronically inflamed by reason of wrong life; are too excitable, hence unreasonable; and are apt to obtrude offensively, and far too frequently, for the best interests of all concerned. Wives yield when it is clear that from ill-health they ought not, and cannot without injury. No human season occurs oftener than thrice a month at most;--before, after, and midway, of her lunar period. The first two being ovarian seasons, maternity may result. The latter is her periodic soul-season, when motherhood is impossible, but soul-blending the divine resultant. Here is another new revelation of Sex, and the statement of a law discovered by carefully noting hundreds of cases in a medical practice of nearly thirty years; and it is one that ought to be conformed to, because it will yet prevent innumerable child-murders that else would result from ignorance of it. In announcing this law I do mankind a service, and save many a woman from risks that they may not wish to encounter.

It is held by some modern physiologists to be a law, that if the wife reaches the natural demise of marriage before the husband, and conception occurs, the resultant will be a Boy, whose nature will resemble her own far more than it will her husband's; but if the father anticipates, the product will be feminine; but she will be more like him than its mother. Thus the gender of an inchoate human being can be predetermined by the Omnipotence of Will; all that is essential is the agreement as to what it shall be.

Before ending this section, I desire to re-impress the great truth and vital law. It is this: Where husband or wife is ill, mentally, morally, emotionally, or in any other way, that illness can be assuredly remedied by them, if when lying by each other they will but place their hands on each other's breasts, and will an interchange of vital life. It will instantly pass and repass, affording an exhibition of soul-power that shall astonish most people; and this mutual impartation becomes not merely a physical-nervous joy, but a most powerful magneto-vital, health-engendering force; an invigorant of the most wondrous potency; a direct and holy prayer, certain to be honored and answered by the everlasting and very loving God!

CXLVI. Couples fail in being happy or rendering each other so, from muscular flabbiness, and consequent pulpiness of brain. Now if they will but lift all they can, gradually increasing the weight of the bags of sand, or whatever else it may be, five minutes before retiring, and two on arising, while in night-dress, ovarian, uterine, vaginal, kidney, bladder, testicular, and prostatic weaknesses will vanish like mists before the morning sun; and with the increase of muscular strength will come an accrement of Love and its cognates, thus dispensing with the aphrodisiacs now so largely used. In three months this course will revolutionize a household. Because it will give the soul a better vehicle to operate through; clear the channels of the body; remedy constitutional weakness; prevent and cure Embolism--the great impotence-creator, and will give a prolonged lease of life and all its nobler pleasures.

CXLVII. Love-starvation is a terrible thing to endure, but one which is not at

all necessary; for by _posing_ the soul for a mate or a love;--by _willing_ and decreeing it _as a system_, the love-power will go out from you and centre on your _adapta-_
tion, just as surely as that you make and persevere in the effort. The same principle
applied to amative disorders will repair the impairment.

CXLVIII. Accursed forever must he, she, or they be, who counsel either conjugal
frauds, condanuism, or any other destructive social abomination. They are seldom
anything else than murderous. They lead to abortion, _that_ is MURDER; and its per-
petrators, non-professional, should be paraded through the streets on a mule's back,
placarded "ABORTIONISTS!" while the professional baby-killers should swing by the
neck to the nearest tree or lamp-post !

Another class of wretches need legal attending to. I refer to the makers and
advertisers of peculiar stimulants, because they are compounded of villainous drugs,
which agitate for a while, but are dead-sure to land the takers upon the bleak shores
of sterility and hopeless impotence. There are cases wherein sex-tonics, invigorants, and direct aphrodisiac agents are absolutely essential to the restoration of
amative and general health, but such are incapable of harming even a child, because
their action is tonic and constitutional, and not sudden, fiery, lust-begetting,
and destructive.

There are plants, essences, tinctures, and extracts, which, in the hands of
good physicians, are effective for the purposes sought, while utterly non-dangerous,
and free from harm. Let such be used, or none at all.

Elsewhere, herein, I have alluded to a paper upon the esoteric part of the
grand topic of this volume--called the _Ansairetic Mystery_, in which form I have opened up certain knowledges which I deem quite essential to the complete education of
every true adult person. Concerning it, while I live, letters can be addressed
to me; when dead, to my heirs, and those who will then become sole publishers of
all my works.

THE END OF THE VISION.--I promised to give the sequel to the curious Vision,
related in the forepart of this book, concerning The Woman and the Man.

1st. It will be remembered that I sincerely loved and sympathized with my
friend, to such an amazing magnetic extent that at times I was in absolute _rapport_
with his entire soul; and at one time, believing the vision to have been true, I
pitied him, and the millions who have sailed in the same boat, and been wrecked upon the rocks of treachery, adultery, and deceit. But in this case the vision was
not true, for the lady was then, and ever after, as pure as snow-flakes winging their
way from space to earth, while still floating in mid-air. But she had, prior to
leaving, associated a day or two with a woman of the world, who had suggested the
strange question upon which the man had long pondered and morbidly brooded; and his
loneliness, and her long silence, had strengthened his evil suspicions, which
suspicions he had imparted to me, and I had entered into full sympathy with him,
believing just as he did.

2d. My friend was an artist of wide celebrity; very magnetic, and ties of that
character were easily formed by him; and to sever them was often as fraught with
agony as would be pulling teeth from a sensitive soul, were that possible; hence he
was quite easily vampirized by unprincipled women, just as I have been a score of
times, in as many lands, in my own strange life, by female leeches, who attracted by
the magnetic fulness of the nature inherited from the dear mother who bore me, came
to feed upon it, and deplete my very soul; this, be it known, being possible without
the slightest guilt of a sensual character, for such is not always essential to the

attraction of the vital life of a full soul by an empty cormorantic one. It was from the abundance of these she-fiends who clustered round me, that for a time a semi-libertinish odor attached itself to my name; because, being foiled in their desperate game and diabolic intent, they generally went off and took sweet revenge, a la Mrs. Potiphar, and scandalized me far and near, right and left; cyprians, vampires, ghouls, all!--without a single exception!--penniless adventuresses, who came to learn of me how to victimize mankind, because I knew all the higher, white, as well as the lower, and black, magic, and they panted like the hart after the brooklets for the information they knew I alone, if I chose, which I did not, impart, but dismissed them empty as they came. It is a curious circumstance of my life that the worst foes I ever made were, 1st. The people to whom I lent money; and, 2d. Those whom I refused to initiate into the mystical secrets adverted to above; for the fellow who invited me to Massillon, after the Boston fire, finding I would not instruct him how to be a greater scoundrel than Nature made him, or God intended, perjured what soul he had, and thereby extorted nearly all I had saved from the fiery wreck two months before. The old "Man" of the Letter and young girl notoriety, also turned upon me for identical reasons. The Ranks of "Reformers" are thickly strewn with unprincipled males, and females, too, and I have been "done" to the tune of thousands by adventuresses of that peculiar ilk, as in the La Hue case detailed in the book called "My Curious Life;" and in the case of "La Blondette," of the "Woman's Book."

So much for victimization through magnetisme mauvaise, to say nothing of another instance where, through a cleverly morphined pint of ale--"Bitter beer" it proved-- my mother's only son was relieved of some hundreds of dollars; compelled to execute a will, and acknowledge a fact which never existed, by the persuasive eloquence of a six-barrelled revolver in the hands of a male, and a four-barrelled one in the pocket of a thieving she-zingara. I therefore could pity the Man. 3d. If you turn to the section of the Mirror Vision, you will see that it had prophesied coming trouble, to be followed by a calm; and also that I had utterly forgotten the fact for the time. About the same period in which my friend was in the trouble about the woman, that trouble was enhanced and exacerbated by the arrival of a female from California, who had crossed the continent expressly to lay seize to his heart and-- passions. She was strongly sensuous; of fine presence; voluptuous, sharp, keen, practical, and totally devoid of honor and principle; yet fearfully, desperately in love with him; so that, between all the powers bearing on him the man was entirely distraught ; and that, too, at a time when from other causes he was ill, morbid, downcast, and very negative; he, therefore, had brooded on his wretched fancies till himself was half daft, and I, his friend, through sympathy, was in full rapport with him. 4th. He had entrusted the absent one with certain very important financial business, which she, in thoughtless mood, had utterly ignored and totally neglected; consequently he was angry. 5th. He wearied me with the constant recital of his troubles, while I myself was ill, tired, worn out with excessive loneliness, mental toil, and financial embarrassments, all of which combined, threw me into a very morbid physical state; and his injuries and my absurd fancies took the dreadful form they did, which state of soul was taken advantage of by the teaching dead!-- the viewless powers of the empyrean, to inculcate the most solemn, if most painful lesson he or I had ever learned; for there was not, and never had been, the slightest ground for either jealousy or suspicion; for their object was as pure as the sweetest angel who flits in glory about God's eternal throne!

The lesson cured two of us of jealousy in the first place. 2d. Rid him then, and me, shortly afterward, of all vampiral influences, whether from California or elsewhere. 3d. It brought us both nearer to those to whom our hearts went out in craving, longing, yearning, for the bread of life--Womanly affection. 4th. It led us to bend our stubborn souls at the shrine of the forgiving God! 5th. It taught us the mighty lesson of God-reliance and self-control. 6th. Taught us the folly of indulging even in occasional bibulant habits. 7th. It opened the road-way to a higher possible life, though the lesson was a terrible one; taught us the folly of unjust suspicion, and to ask pardon, while extending charity--of all, to all, and to ask it, too, of that good and compassionate Lord whose chastening hand had brought us face to face with truth and human duty, until at last the glorified beings flitting by that way peered into our humble rooms, beheld us there on bended knee, --contrite souls pleading for full redemption, and, turning their holy gaze heaven-ward again, they sent a message home to God:--"Behold! They Reason _justly_!" Reader, go thou and do likewise!

MORAL!--1st. Never let your love be drawn out till you are _sure_ it is right that it should be. 2d. If you are magnetic, take care to restrain its flow, and do not allow yourself to permit it to saturate a vampire, and then fall in "Love" with your own spheral emanation. 3d. Pray for deliverance _all_ the time, else embodied and viewless leeches will sap your body and soul to the very lees, and then laugh at you when the certain Horror comes! 4th. Trust no one who seeks to separate you from your mate. 5th. Bear and forbear, give and forgive, and trust ye each other. 6th. Never be jealous, no matter what the proofs be, so long as your two bodily eyes do not sanction it. Remember my LESSON! 7th. Fulfil the part of husband and wife as if both stood on the verge of death; so shall ye be holy, pure, and fully, truly Human!

Upon good physical conditions, soundless, health, normal play of electric, nervous, magnetic, and passional forces, depends, unquestionably, much of the weal or woe, happiness or misery, sanity or insanity, attendant upon us in our journey through life. An experience of many years, in many lands, has familiarized me with all methods extant for creating the best conditions of vital health; combating obscure diseases of the nervo-vital organization, and for overcoming the effects of both excess and violated natural law. That experience, travel, experiment, and observation enabled me to not only found, but firmly establish a NEW SYSTEM of Medicine, embracing all that is good of Homoeopathy, Water Cure, Magnetics, and a dozen other methods. I am nearly at the end of my career as a practical Physician, but desire that my methods and systems may survive to bless and relieve mankind, when my body shall rest beneath the hillside, and my weary soul shall sweetly sleep near the Throne of my Redeeming God,--the Ineffable One, whose hand has brought me out of the deeps, and given me a crown of victory at this end of my half-century of life; wherefore I propose to teach others a part, or the whole, of the magnificent System evolved during all these years of toil and struggle; and these are my reasons for desiring to do so:--

Very many of the large-brained, active-minded People of this Country, as is the case with the same class in Paris, London, Berlin, Vienna, Constantinople, and other large centres of population, labor under some form of Nervous disease, caused mainly by cerebral exhaustion from mental overwork. Another large class, including both sexes, suffer the same troubles, but from different causes,--the distressing symptoms being difficult to alleviate, much less to cure, with the means at hand, for the reason that until my discoveries and improvements there was no absolute medical agent, or Pharmaceutical preparation in existence, capable of meeting such cases successfully; and since my preparations--during 25 years of trial--have proved their unexampled power over all diseases involving nerves, brain, lungs, kidneys, and sexual organization, their popularity, without the adventitious aid of advertising, paid-for certificates, and other modes of puffery, demonstrating this fact,--I am proud to say, the field of their usefulness is wholly unchallenged by the products of the Pharmacopoeia of the civilized world.

In the experience of every Physician worthy the name, numerous cases present themselves, which may be generally defined as _loss of magnetism_, depletion of magnetic force; in other words, Vital Exhaustion; to cure which, thousands have resorted to the various hypophosphites, preparations of Lyttae, Valerian, etc.; some of which undoubtedly afforded temporary relief; but all of which are impermanent, and, as Dynamic remedies, and no other, are adapted to that class of troubles, wholly and utterly unreliable. Patients who need and resort to such remedies--and in vain, for reasons self-apparent--may be classified,as, First, those who, forgetful that Vigor is the gift of God, have exhausted the brain and nervous system by indoor life, too constant mental applications,--of course involving loss of lungpower,- and hence, like plants in a cellar are bleached out. The Second class have lived too fast; and late hours, wine, and personal excess have stranded them midway of life's sea; the Nerve fountains are run dry; vital energy is sapped and gone; and existence is dull, feverish, wholly spiceless, and insipid. A Third class have led such fretful, vexed, and troubled lives that, without intentional error, they have nearly extinguished the fire of life. A Fourth class, embracing both sexes and all ages, from ten years to threescore, consists of those unfortunates who, by neglect or other causes, have become inverted, and by solitary habits (not to be mentioned, but whose terrific consequences must be met and conquered), have sapped and drained their vitality, till their flesh is waxy, nerves unstrung, brain softened: they have become unreliable, changeful, angular, crooked, wild, shiftless, aimless, suspicious, lonely, nervous; easily affected by the weather, bad news; are gloomy, morose, scary, discontented, dreamy, fidgety, suicidal, secretive; now tender, then coarse and callous; now gentle, then the opposite; vapory, fretful, easily worried; wholly unfitted for life's most solemn duties; disquieted themselves, and estranging their best friends; they have become worn out, exhausted, and, in the case of females, loaded down with troubles that would kill half the men living; often, in their cases, resulting in morbid state of mind and body; and in men resulting in Impotence, and worse trouble. There is a Fifth class, whom Disease has wasted and reduced so that there is scarcely life enough to make it at all desirable; and a morbid melancholy, almost utter despair, follows. They have frightful dreams, flashes, headaches, palpitations, anger fits, hysteria, and angularities without number. A Sixth class have gone to waste, impotence, and senility, at 30, 35, and 40 years of age,who with a little care could retain full vigor till threescore years and ten!

The above list embraces, 1st. All that vast mass of people who are exhausted by mental labor and sedentary occupations; who from various causes are angular, excitable, nervous, and, at times, unaccountably morbid; 3d. All who are passionless, cold, non-attractive, non-attracted, or, if attracted, hopelessly so, from lack of responsive ability; who are unsettled, uneasy, subject to mental, temperamental, gloomy, longly, and passional storms; 3d. All who have half-ruined their minds and bodies, sapped their health and vigor, and are now crooked and fretful, despondent by passional excess, normal or otherwise, or from any cause whatever.

Who can doubt that, in reference to very many of these troubles, perverted, excessive, or abused Physical Love lieth at the foundation? No woman is ill whose Nervous apparatus is sound; no man is so whose natural appetites and brain are strong and vigorous. Life and power, strength and force, beauty and love, talent, genius, endurance and longevity, all depend upon the normal health of the vital-nervous organs, for when these are disordered the whole being must and does suffer, and ninetenths of all the diseases of "Civilization" originate in the disturbances of that portion of the human economy.

The remedials I propose to teach how to manufacture, will revive energy lost from whatever cause, for they are nervous force and vital power in tangible form, and act, not by stimulation, but by INVIGORATION, restoring magnetic and dynamic power, when nothing else on earth can do it.

Physicians and others are hereby given to clearly and distinctly understand, that in no sense whatever are either of these preparations empirical productions, or "Patent Medicines." Their discovery opens a new era in the curative art. They are not Medicines, but DYNAMIC AGENTS; have been thoroughly tested in France, England, and 35 States of this Union; and, where properly administered or taken, it is doubtful if a case exists of Incipient Consumption, Wasting, Nervousness, Hypochondria, Hysteria, Nervous or Vital Prostration, Leucorrhoea, Sterily, Brain Softening, Dyspepsia, Mental Wandering, General Debility, Whole or Partial Weakness from Nerval Exhaustion, that they will not speedily and radically cure, because of their extraordinary dynamic power.

IN THE MEDICAL PROFESSION, the great want has long been that of a powerful, positive, certain, yet harmless Nervine-Invigorant, capable of direct action upon the brain, nervous centres, and pelvic apparatus; an agent that will allay morbid inflammation, yet stimulate, exhilarate, tone up, and permanently strengthen; that will supply nervous energy, correct all morbid action, and furnish the material lost or wasted by excessive mental toil, venery, masturbation, onanism, and other forms of vital prostation. Every Physician of any reasonable amount of practice frequently has cases of weakness, mental and physical, demanding the exhibition of peculiar tonic stimulants and aphrodisiacs, that shall be certain in effect, yet non-irritant or reactionary. This want is generally met in my remedials, beyond all question the most perfect vitalizing agents known, and hence peculiarly adapted to all cases of Female disease, Marasmus, or Wasting, all anaemic cases, and those morbid states resulting in Hysteria, Despondency, Melancholia, Insanity, and Suicidal Depression, all of which result from Uterine, Ovarian, Cerebral, Nervous, Prostatic and Seminal Exhaustion in either sex respectively. To meet and conquer, especially, severe and stubborn cases of all such, I propose to instruct suitable persons how to prepare and use the following list of remedial agents, hitherto prepared by no one but myself; viz., 14 Formulas, embracing 1 Barosmyn, 1 Lucina Cordial, 1 Protogene, 3 for Eye diseases, with instruments, 2 for "accidental" complaints, but whose effects are supremely terrible--(these formulas are the ONLY perfect cure on earth,--Hope for poisoned wives). In short, I purpose to teach the best of my discoveries, and to give Parchment certificates to Prove the purchaser has actually been instructed in my system and my formulas.

Through these remedials many have regained health; old men and barren women have become happy parents, and patients standing on the verge of death have been rendered strong and vigorous,--of course not alone by medicines, but by the course laid down for their guidance, especially those set forth in my Pamphlet on the Prolongation of Human Life and Power, called "THE GOLDEN SECRET."

Where Parties expressly desire it, the above system will be supplemented by a Series of Esoteric instructions, involved mainly in the Ansairetic Mystery.

Those who have read my Works, need not now, at the end of 30 years, be told that, as an expert, in diseases of the nervous and genital systems, my fame if too well established to be successfully contested by any man, men, or party, nor that the ablest Physicians in the land are glad to accept my teachings and improvements upon original discoveries. During the past year I have by a new discovery revolutionized the entire treatment of such diseases. By it the physician and patient need no longer "guess," but go at once to the cure of the case. The discovery is entirely original, and will be imparted to practioners,--those who wish to make a specialty of treating that class of human ailments. Terms by mail. The cardinal principle of both the treatment and remedials, is that, contrary to all the "schools," I hold that LIFE itself is a principle; that we are not born with a given amount of it, which, when exhausted, gives us up to death; but that we can not only accrete and gather in NEW LIFE, and thus add long years to the sun total of its duration, but also that we can intensify, deepen, broaden, and expand it in _every_ _direction_, thus preserving our fire, beauty, vigor, energy, magnetic and personal force, to an un-limited degree. And not only that, but--and here is indeed a mighty discovery--that the very source of exhaustion, is, properly understood, the _actual_ _fountain_ _of_ _perpetuity_, _endurance_, _long_ _life_, and power, mental, physical, moral, emotional, and magnetic. In a word, I hold it possible to almost wholly rejuvenate ourselves and become young again in spirits, vigor, mental power, and endurance,--that loss of love is loss of life, and that both can be restored. These things I teach, and among others give much practical knowledge of inestimable value, on the observance of which fills the land with vice, murder, suicide, divorce, and wretchedness in-calculable. (This knowledge is broadly laid down in the large work, "The Master Passion," and the greater one "Good News," Tables of Contents of which will be sent to any address on receipt of postage thereon.)

My instructions will prove of inestimable value and importance not only to Physicians, but to other men, and especially to women, for a _great_ _many_ reasons which I do not choose to set forth herein.

Lastly: this book will inevitably call attention to the B. O. E. (Brotherhood of Eulis), the Hope of the world and Sheet anchor of Mankind. All such are informed that a handbook of the Order will be issued from this Grand Lodge; to the officers of which application for information should be made; and to no other authority, save myself, until death.*

My address at present is Toledo, Ohio; when it is changed, due notice will be given.   P.B. RANDOLPH
See second not below.

There are quite a number of exceedingly important and inexpressibly holy and delicate questions connected with the subject-matter of this work, which, although alluded to, have not been openly and freely discussed herein, for self-apparent reasons. These things relate to the inner mysteries of the human being and of Eulis, (or the Philosophy of Love, AGAPE, not _stogu_,) and are only to be given under the sacred conditions of Patient and Physician or Teacher and Pupil. How long I may remain to teach of course I do not know,--only this I do know--that I have suffered much and am weary; but while able I shall take great delight in clearing up the doubts and mysteries besetting those about me; and all who need such counsel as I am capacitated to impart, are hereby freely warranted in asking or writing for it, --assured that I will do my best toward alleviating the distresses of body and heart, Soul and Spirit; and although I cannot bear the burdens of all, still I have done somewhat of good in that line, and am ready to continue so doing while life lasts.

*In March, 1874, I organized a society, _provisionally_, down in Tennessee--"The B. O. E." to which it was my intention to teach all the occult branches of esoteric knowledge, constitute it my literary heir, and through it spring many lofty truths upon the world; but

"The best laid of mice or men
Aft gang aglee!"

And so did mine with reference to that society; for owing to irreconcilable misunderstandings it became absolutely necessary to dissolve the provisional society <u>as</u> the B. O. E., and to utterly decline to permanently organize it, owing to the presence in it of a person with whom it became impossible for me to break bread and taste salt--things which no man of Eulis or Rosicrucia will ever do under unpleasant conditions. Consequently, hereafter as heretofore, I shall do what good I can, single-handed and alone--yet not alone, for God and I are a clear majority. I'll help myself and others, and He will help me.

JUNE 30, 1874.

PART II.

IMMORTALIZATION.

————

"PHILADELPHIA, Sept. 30, 1873.

"DEAR SIR,--I am deeply interested. I have never read anything of your Publications except the NEW MOLA.* On the 61st page of that work, under Section XIX, I
find a single sentence in <u>capitals</u>: the same thought I have been inclined to believe
for more than thirty years:--'ALL PEOPLE DO NOT HAVE SOULS!' My dear sir, do you
mean it? Have you said something more about this somewhere else in your publications?
. . . Oh, do you guess how my soul hungers in viewing the table of contents of the
extraordinary Works published by your House:--and you will guess I HAVE A SOUL?

"Praying that your valuable life may be long preserved, and that you may continue
to enlighten the millions as <u>only</u> <u>you</u> can,

"I am, your true friend,

E. B. MERRILL,

308 WALNUT STREET."

E. B. MERRILL, Esq.--Sir: The following Paper, in substance, is the reply to
the questions involved in the "Mola" and your letter. In response to your inter-
rogatories, allow me to say that:--All things are generally reputed and believed to
reproduce their kinds. That is regarded as a determinate rule, and strict, unswerv-
ing law of nature. But it is not wholly true, nor an unchangeable law, because there
is a law of spontaneous generation both in the faunal and floral departments of
nature,--both vegetable and animal life produced by other than seen germination,
some of which have, and others have not, the power of reproducing their kind; instances of which are altogether too numerous to need special mention--as, for instance, the various <u>acarii</u>, produced from powdered flint which had first been
calcined to white heat; and the familiar phenomenon of lizardesque beings originating from salted cabbage in dark, moist cellars; and still further, the occasional
production of the low-type baboon, by the arrestation of gestation in pregnant
negresses,--an instance of which occurred in Charleston, South Carolina, but a few
years ago. So it is not always <u>strictly</u> albeit <u>generally</u> true, that things reproduce
their types and species.

In the case of man, his origin by the methods and processes universally believed,
in a few years ago, is not almost as universally discredited, for the Science of
To-day rejects all that cannot be demonstrated accordant with Law; and the human
being is proved to have been a gradual, and by no means a sudden or miraculous
creation. (See the Volume "Pre-Adamite MAN," Published by this House.)

It is difficult to determine the precise point at which the purely animal left
off, and the purely human began. Every recession from the highly human type is an
approach toward the Simian, or ape-type, and ape-like forms, shapes, hands, facial
angles, faces, noses, mouths, and features meet us among all races, colors,,and

----

* See notice at end of Vol.

classes of mankind at every turn; while embryology clearly demonstrates that the human being in utero passes through every stage of the world's animal growth and products, from the jelly-point to tadpole, fish, monkey, up to man; and the farther each gestative stage is pushed, the more perfect the resultant child. The lower types and forms of the Simiana are not, cannot be, immortal, by reason of paucity of cerebrum, or fore, top, brain, and redundance of back, low, brain, or cerebellum.

If a man is, as science proves he is, a growth, then his immortality is a growth also, and not a miracle or gift, or the result of any sudden force applied from a non-immortal ancestry. We need a new exegesis of early scripture, for in the light of the daily resurrections of the remains of dead nations and absolete civilizations; of the constant exhumations of the remains of Prehistoric races, some of which, reckoning from geologic data, date back not less than from three-quarters of a million to two whole millions of years ago, it is impossible to accept the literal account as we find it. People used to hold and believe that all mankind were the progeny of an original pair of Protoplasts, the autochthonas or primal couple--Adam (Kadmon) and the fair Eve, his rib-originated compagnon du vie, or wife. But that dogma is a dogma no longer. Black, brown, white, yellow races, are all as clear cut and distinct from each other as are grayhounds from poodle dogs, or bantam fowls from headstrong, long-spurred, do-or-die game; nor will one race, even by admixture, produce a perfect speciment of either of the others.

In these days science explodes the fables of antiquity, and has already gone far toward dispensing altogether with the Edenic couple,--insisting that Tartar, Caucasian, Indian, and the Nigritian race came from diverse centres and sources, and Darwinian theorists hold the reins and drive straight from Palace to cavern; from man in pride and pomp, to man the cousin of hairy chimpanzee and red-rear baboon; and she demonstrates him to be a natural outgrowth of nature; and that his ancestors were some sort of superior ape-monkey or baboon, gorilla, nschiego or chimpanzee; and that he is himself a grand improvement, by natural and sexual selection, upon his progenitors, who slowly advanced from monkey-hood to be cave-dwellers and weapon-users; who gradually learned the use of fire and fighting, monogamy and mating, but-building and clothes-wearing, and who, developing still, finally, through the lapse of thousands of--centuries, grew to be what he is now--generally, half-civilized; for he yet hangs, beheads, cruelizes his kind, and at best delights in carnage, drums, war, glory, gibbets, jails, Alcohol, Tobacco, Robbery, and Force, meat food, and fiery drink, still laying claim to survive the ordeal of death, in an etherealized form, but without knowing really how or why; Holding firmly to the belief that his life on earth is but the prelude to his music of perpetual being beyond the grave, while all nature chants the low, sad requiem of all other sentient forms, the totality of which topple over into their original dust, and are no more as Individuals, but only survive in their respective species. This belief gladdens him, yet it is a sad thought--Nothing sentient beyond the grave but man alone;-- while all other forms of life and beauty go out forever?

Doubtless this development theory--of Darwin and others, is mainly true--so far as it goes,--but it fails to go far enough. It is eminently unsatisfactory to every true thinker and hoper for life beyond death; and the same class of persons find it utterly impossible to predicate immorality upon the materials furnished for that purpose by those who are mainly interested in the firm establishment of the grand idea. They ask WHY? but no logical reply is given. I shall present it here and now.

No one, that I am aware of, contends that monkeys, either large or small, are capable of overriding the billows of Death, and swimming safely to the etheral shores beyond, (they probably deserve that power quite as much as some men do), yet man is, physically, but an improved ape, which fact has a singular proof in this: viz., the higher simia will, and do, inter-breed with the lower human. Proof--the tailed "Men" of Namaqua Land: the dwarf peoples of gorilla-land, and the offspring of Hottentot women captured and impregned by the giant apes of Nigritia. But it does not follow that the monstrous progeny thus generated are immortal, even if, as is doubtful--the human esque parent may chance to be so; nor does it follow that all who are undoubtedly human, are also possessed of power to exist consciously subsequent to actual death; for unquestionably all are not thus endowed who possess the external and ordinary characteristics of humanity; and there are thousands who pass and re-pass us in the streets every day of our lives who are no more immortal than the fish they ate for dinner; for that power, fact, quality, call it what you will, is a development, an outgrowth, a result, the principia of which I herein purpose to briefly set forth an, so far as my limits permit, explain. And first let me define what the world and myself understand as the true definition of the term I Immortality: --

The body is supposed to contain within itself an electrical form just like it-self--head eyes, brain, tongue, arms, legs, sex-organs; that at death that AEreal form escapes the body, and goes to spend its eternal years in heaven or in hell; that it can die no more, but lives, loves, suffers, thinks, enjoys, in that other life; and that it is in all respects a human being still. This brief definition is as good as one occupying a hundred pages.

Now if man is--and the affirmative proofs are strong--the descendant of any sort of ape, existent now or extinct for a hundred millenia; if he is immortal and the ape-parents not so, it is clear that those immortal human beings must have con-ferred on their off-spring a power and quality themselves had not; so that at death the progenitors returned to dust, while the progeny exulted in perpetual life, and renewed existence; immigrated to other worlds in the Vault, immortalized beings, but with no parents to meet and greet them on the farther shore--the lands beyond the swelling flood, the kingdoms o'er the Sea!--and, undoubtedly, such was actually the case. Of course these first fruits were not of the high and fine grades sub-sequently developed on the earth by dint of time and better physical conditions. Logic is a good sieve, even if a grain or two or error does occasionally fall through the meshes among the finer truths. Now either the parent-apes were capable of conferring what they had not themselves--which is equivalent to extracting the greater from the less--an absurdity on its very face,--or man is not immortal by right or dint or reason of birth, and must, therefore, reach that condition, or attain that quality in some other way, by some other method, through some other rule or Law; that is, children must have the quality conferred upon them at the very instant of generation; must acquire it during the gestative period; at some other point or moment of their career, or, finally, gain it in some mysterious or miraculous manner not generally known or fairly understood. But it is sheerly preposterous to believe, and impossible in every way, that an immortal thing could, or can, derive its death-defying nature from that which is itself death's common prey and victim. To take a gallon from a river is easy; but a river from a gallon is impossible, yet not more so than to predicate the immortality of the offspring of apes as a derivative quality. Yet I hold that a non-immortal human couple may generate immortal offspring; but then that comes of the magnetic unction and appul-sion of the parents, who thereby impart the immortalizing bias, which bias or tendency the subjects may either increase or destroy, by methods hereinafter explained and set forth.

Now let it be distinctly understood that we of EULIS hold that the general pur-pose of the material universe, the end for which it exists, is the crystallization of mind,--the immortalization of Soul; but it does not follow that all human beings are death-proof, any more than that all the countless myriads of seeds produced every year in the floral departments of nature are endowed with reproductive vitality; for by far the greater number is wholly inert, while others possess but weakling life, and even if they do germinate soon perish and decay. Transfer the view ot the animated world and it will be seen that the union of the genders fails of one of its purposes--reproduction five thousand times for every single success, taking the lower planes of life only; while in the case of man, the union, so far as offspring is concerned, fails nine hundred and ninety-nine times for every single successfully implanted germ.

Again: Every healthy man--of course excluding libertines, debauchees, habitual passional transgressors, and all injured persons--in fair spirits generates from one-quarter of an ounce ot an ounce and a half daily of the three forms of fluid life--semen, prostatic lymph, and the exudation of Cowper's Gland; and every normal evacuation thereof will average half an ounce, containing, as I have repeatedly demonstrated under a powerful microscope (one magnifying 35,000 times) from nineteen, the lowest number, to seven hundred and eighty-three, zoospermes, every one of which was capable of being developed in utero to perfect human proportions. Take the first case, and it is clear that eighteen must fail if one succeeds; and seven hundred and eighty-two lose their chances if one is fortunate enough to reach the ovum, and become incarnate in the mother's bosom. But, the chances are billions to one against even one of them effecting a safe lodgement; and we conclude that for every successful human union there are not less than nineteen hundred and fifty-seven billions of human germs doomed to quiesence, if not to perpetual death, taking the adult population of the globe to be about thirteen hundred millions. Another thought right here: Nature selects the fittest to perpetuate species; and the strongest and most active zoosperms always override the weaker, and reach the ovum, dooming, thereby, all the rest; but it is clear that they too must perish if there be no ovum to invite them. Precious few ripe zoospermes reach the ripened ova, because deprived of the element time, essential to their perfection, the consequence of which is, that the great majority of people spring from unripe conditions, and remain unripe from the cradle to the grave. I will tell you a profound secret of generation, whereby the most magnificent results in that line are producible at will. It is this: (Here follow the glorious truths hinted at, but of such a holy, delicate, and private nature as to be only impartable by words or ink. The publisher hereof has no desire to exclusively retain it, and will, therefore, impart it to such noble souls as can appreciate it.*) These principles alone can redeem the world, and clinch the rivets of Immortality. Nature makes many attempts, but only few successes, and as it is with trees and grasses, shrubs and flowers, so also is it with mankind. She tries, and tries hard, to immortalize a species, but only succeeds in doing it for individuals; and it is as easy to pass along the streets and pick out those of Perduring souls from those whose future is nihility, as it is to select a negro, Indian, Hottentot, or John Chinaman from a crowd of Digger Indians. The truth is, that while man, generally, is immortal, he is not universally so. The development theory is good and true to a certain limit, but it at any stage or rate is wholly incompetent to the tremendous achievement of accounting for the existence of Soul. It needs improving; and it is astonishing that its chief priests have never even attempted to demonstrate man's immortality, but rather have studiously evaded contact with the troublesome question. Their theory fails them from the moment they reach the psychical and metaphysical phases of the grand subject. They take no cognizance of soul per se whatever, because fully aware that they cannot give a reason why Souls should be at all. The fact is, that immortalization could not, cannot, be at all on their hypotheses. It is not inherited (of necessity); it is not a gift, nor the result of fiat or miracle, but is a process, an evolution, the principia of which are as clear and plain as one, two, three, or a, b, c.

---

* See the Asian and Ansairetic Mysteries--Passim.

Three brothers may live: one of them shall survive the process of Death; the second shall die forever, as that specific Person or Individulaity; and the third one having once been possessed of the elements and conditions of immortality may <u>lose</u> them and <u>go</u> <u>out</u> like an extinguished taper or snuffed candle, by reason of his repeated violation of either one of the fundamental or organic laws of his nature; while a fourth brother may nearly lose the great boon,--if boon it be,--as some believe it, and millions of others do not; but this fourth brother, by prompt action, the instant abandonment of all his pernicious, soul-wasting, mind-dwarfing practices and habits; the total and persistent avoidance of all infractions of the fundamental love-laws of his being, and a steady, manly course and demeanor, may regain what he has so rashly jeopardized and imperilled.

Some human infants are born immortalized, death-proof, and indestructible from the moment they were conceived; while others require long years and terrible disciplines and experiences ere they reach the coveted goal. For thousands of years the followers of Gantama, the Budha, have considered what we call immortality as an unmitigated curse, and continued existence as the most terrible and tremendous evil that can possible befall a human being. They regarded Narwana, or the final cessation of existence, as the grand desideratum,--the Ultima Thule of all possible human hope, aspiration, and endeavor.

Dissatisfied with life, its pains and penalties, there are millions of us who would gladly cease to be. (Time was when the penman of these lines, disgusted with the sham Philosophies and Philosophers of the age, actually tried to accept the doctrine of Budha; but, having reached the power--through the extraordinary means recounted in Part III.--of glimpsing the mystical states beyond, he changed his faith, and raised his hopes, and all the more so by reason of his discovery that Nihilism and immortality alike are reachable through the continued exercise of the human will.)

The discovery alluded to in the bracketed sentence is this: There are <u>two</u> kinds of immortality: 1st. A man may survive death, and escape the thrall of his physical form, and maintain his ethereal state for a while; yet if he shall not have received the proper and essential love-impulsion before birth, or else have subsequently developed love, he is as certainly doomed to GO OUT, fade, dwindle, go back to the monadal state, as that gravitation in a law. He will be like the huge soap-bubble at the end of a pipe-bowl, which only requires to be let alone in order to grow smaller by degrees until it is again all within the rim of the bowl, and then bursts forever beyond the possibility of reparation.

Since the advent of the modern phase of Spiritualism, there have been thousands of people who have sought to commune with their deceased acquaintances, but wholly unavailingly. Why? Simply because their friends thus sought have ceased to exist. 2d. A man may have received the proper impulsion before birth, or have gained it afterwards, and he may enter the ethereal lands with, to use a common but very expressive phase--such a good send-off as to be able to continue on forever. The two kinds of immortality may be likened unto this: one is as a seed planted in good rich soil, but only an inch or two deep, with a hard pan of solid, arid rock beneath it, which defies the roots to spread; wherefore, that plant looks well and promises much for a while, but it soon withers and is seen no more forever. The other seed, planted in the same soil with plenty of water and root-room, grows gayly, waxes strong, spreads, blooms, flourishes, triumphs, and perpetuates itself; yet the seeds were alike, and so was the soil.

There are, also, two kinds of Nihilism: 1st. That of the brute and the brute homos, or brutal-man,--both of whom are doomed to sudden and total extinction--a extinction--a cessation of being as complete as that of exploded powder, or extinguished light, which, <u>as</u> powder or light, can exist no more forever; and, 2d.

A truly human nihility, rest, divine Narwana,--a state infinitely harder to reach than any phase of active immortality, whether transient or permanent!--the man dies with a celestial strain or note of divinest harmony and seraphic melody ringing sweetest music through every avenue, vault, and chamber of his being. Now observe, and mark well this definition of Narwana; On earth the longest duration of any single musical note never exceeds a few moments; but this Note of which I speak, this Sunburst of celestial music, this instantaneous rapture lasts unchangingly FOREVER, and FOREVER! It is unaltered, the sound, the music, the man, eternally the same, without an interval to suggest even the idea of monotone! It is an infinite melody, struck on an Eternal harp, enduring forever and aye!

Such is the Narwana of the good! The other, the Nihility of the evil and imperfect. Thus death has three Gates: the Iron one opens on Night--total extinction; the Silver one, on Immortal fields; the golden one on--What Gods may well aspire to!--if we are to believe what lordly and loftiest Seership tells us--and I am one who thus believes.

I, within the year 1873, met people whom I knew were under the ban of the bad Nihility. Elsewhere, in the volume of which this is a chapter, an account is given of a hoary-headed "man," of nearly seventy years, who sought, and expected, to prolong his own miserable and wretched life by absorbing that of a third young girl, --one of sixteen years,--he having already performed the burial-service over two prior victims; that old man is doomed to absolute extinction, unless saved by repentance, physical regeneration, and the growth of affection within him. It was not passion of lust only that urged him to prolong his own existence at the cost of others; to stretch out his wasted years by the awful crime of drinking the young life, and wrecking a child of so few summers; but the conscious and unconscious want of love was what urged him onto the deadly, selfish deed; he felt the need of the great base upon which immortality must be builded, or not at all. Many such as he there are.

But it does not follow that the monadal point, spark, or germ, constituting, underlying, and animating the old lecher, and others of his ilk; the detestable crew in whom lust reigns supreme; the infamous "Hullites" of the year 1873; and the still more infamous followers of the example of the thrice-dyed scoundrels who ravished young children, and were burnt for it,--it does not follow, I repeat, that the germs, or monadal points, basing their existence, will, at their demise, cease to be forever; but they will only cease to be those particularly villainous and vicious personalities; while the germs basing their being may appear and reappear here again and again, clothing themselves with new elements, and, of course, for that reason, running new careers. No one can go to the heavens until he shall have gotten all of good the earth or earths can give him; and not till he has undergone the full ordeal and disciplines incident to material life can he reach that golden supra-immortality whereof modern thinkers, outside the pale of us few, have never even yet dreamed, imagined, or surmised.

Nothing organically imperfect can ever enter and remain in the superlative and ineffable land of pure Souls. The imperfect must go back to the domain of chemics and matter; nor can they, with hope, knock at the doors of the golden temples of Eternity, except they be full, fair, pure, free, and good, even though their discipline extends through a billion of ages; and the greater the gifts or talent, genius or innate power one has, the heavier shall be the price paid for all accorded unto him. It may be well and truly said that there can be no peace in high places,--for storms, hail, and tempests, hurricanes, fierce lightnings and crashing thunders play and break around the mountain's brow; and he who would win the game of triumphant immortality must do so by loving well and much.

-103-

But to return to the subject: Darwin and his co-thinkers saw clearly that a different genesis of man than the usually assigned one was imperatively demanded in presence of the startling discoveries constantly being made, and they adopted the theory of selection, and, so far as externals went, were right; but instead of immortal souls, originating in, among, from, or by, the Simiadae, it was only the soul-case, the mere physical body, the outer form that was thus developed, thus grew up through the slowing ages, while the inside, the works of the grand watch, the imperial soul itself, originated otherwise and elsewhere.

Now by soul is here meant the thinking, conscious, knowing, hating, loving, aspiring principle--that mysterious something about whose origin, nature, perdur-ability or co-perishability with the body, so much has been said, sung, and written, until philosophers generally have got by the ears, while waging the fiercest of all intelectual battles. I propose herein to settle the controversy, or at least to indicate the clear road to such settlement, being perfectly confident and conscious that herein will be found the only possible method and route to the final adjudica-tion. It is hard for a true thinker to have much patience with those whose highest conception of Soul and Spirit is that of a rarefied gaseous ether evolved from gross substance as light and heat radiate from flowing coals of fire in a wintry grate; be-cause such a conception is wholly untrue, seeing that no possible refinement of solid substance or matter can ever approach the state of even the magnetic AEth of Space, much less that diviner thing of which we are treating. It is clear that matter does not think; Soul does, therefore Soul is one thing, matter quite another, requiring a bridge to span the gulf between them, and that bridge is some subtle form of magnetism; nor can Soul be evolved from it by any process of rarefaction or refine-ment; for Soul it was from all past Eternity; soul it is, and such it will remain to all possible eternities to come; while matter, either in its solidified or con-densed, or in its far-particled or fluid states, will remain matter until all its life is exhausted, and Deity shall have become senile and decrepit from the weight of Time and lapse of hoary centuries!

We know, can know, but little concerning God, notwithstanding so many people claim to be quite intimate acquaintances, and on familiar terms with Him! yet we have every reason to believe the Ineffable One to be pure SOUL; and I, the writer hereof, so believe; and furthermore, that he is A Sun, emitting countless billions of beams and rays every instant--and that each contains myriads of scintillas, every one of which is an embryon, or soul-germ, capable of development into perfect man or womanhood!

While God is clear Soul, matter is pure body; one is a unit, unparticled it-self, yet emitting and irradicating, besides the countless scintillant sparks or monads just alluded to--a glory-sphere, aroma, aura, a portion of his divine Life, which is the breath of life to all these monads, and all else that exists within the radius of the universe. Soul, like God, is homogeneous, unparticled, indivisible, necessarily death-proof, in itself considered, and we conclude therefore Eternal, albeit no one can tell what "eternal" means, for we cannot clearly grasp a thousand years, much less millions of --ages! Matter, on the contrary, is heterogeneous, divisible; its Spirit is CHANGE, and that is the quintessence of Death itself.

Erewhile I spoke of the menstruum wherein floated the rain of soul-germs, and I gave it a name. I now give it another, LOVE!--which is the life of All,--the celestial influence of the Eternal One. In beasts, apes, et caetera, this vivific force is diffused. In some human beings it is condensed and crystallized. In some it is not. The first is immortal. That latter not so. Beasts, apes, Low-grade people, have instincts, attachments, magnetic attractions, and affection:--Man,--true men--alone have love! Beasts die. Immortal man lives on; but if man be more

-104-

beast than human he must share their fate and lot, and as that specific individual dies out, and the divine spark, losing its consciousness, escapes, and once more floats freely i' th' air, until God once more breathes into some man's nostrils, and it again becomes not a quiescent, but a living, active human soul! If he be more than animal he may challenge Death, defy ruin, laugh at destruction, snap his fingers in the face of the grave, and ride triumphant and victorious o'er the mazy wreck of worlds and countless starry universes!

But, as I have hinted, there is such a thing as being ultra-human, not only in the line of Narwana, but in quite another direction. If a man reaches that mystic plane, then he comes beneath the sway and rule of supre-human, and ultra Law, and attains a destiny better, greater, higher than is afforded by the ordinary immortality which gives him so much care and trouble, and for which he so painfully years and sighs!

What the destiny, state, condition, better something is, I am not yet ready to inform the world--but may leave it for the Brotherhood of Eulis to impart.

There are limitless regions of unexplored thought toward which that fast-increasing multitude, who think as I do, push; nor do we, as do many of the supernalists,--though not all,--confine ourselves to the mere outside, i.e. soul-facts of the universe. We believe a few things as do they, but not all that they do, for which they rate us soundly. They rejoice in the physical demonstration of the reappearing dead, but are not quite sure always that the manifesting powers are really their departed ones, for they have not, as have we, the means of establishing identities through an unmistakable agency alluded to elsewhere. Vast numbers of, but not all, the Spiritualists concern themselves mainly about raps, tips, quarreling, scandal, mutual vituperation, backbiting, libel, misrepresentation, "Social Freedom"--things of earth; while we occupy ourselves in actual research and inquiry into what happens to man after his flight over the river of death to that mystic state alluded to; to Narwana and Nihility; or to the upper spaces of the blue Empyrean. At and across the borders of death-land, we strike hands with all the Spiritualists, and there part company with some of them, because we seek to know more; they are content to drink fourth-class mental vinegar, acrid as gall, flavored hellaciduously, and call it wine; while we quaff the waters of life on the very brink of the mighty River.

Just so far do we go with the cold, hard, dry, materialistic, uncheering Darwinism--a system which lands us in the grave, there to stay until we turn to grass, trees, beans, pineapples, or bananas--according to the locality where death overtakes and trips us up; but at that point we separate from Darwin completely,--because the system ignores Soul altogether. We are not wholly content with the modern spiritual doctrines, seeing that they fail to fill the great bill--of human want; and because it is all head and no heart; has no warmth, fervor, ardor, religion, about it; not because it fails to make men better, but solely because it affirms and accepts the development theory as opposed to the genesic account of man's origin, yet fails to tell us how, when, where, or by what agencies immortality became a fixed fact. It accepts the dogma, but gives no valid adequate reason why. It originates no thought, but boldly borrows and appropriates the mental stock of others. In all lands it depends upon, and bases its faith on media, whom it teaches man to accept as oracles, yet no two of whom tell the same story, or see facts alike. George, Peter, and Thomas, communicating through Medium A, in latitude 16, have no recollection of communicating yesterday with the same party through medium B, in latitude 17-30. We, in our investigations of the recondite, occult and mystical;-- ay, even in matters of mere finance, such as specution buying, selling, contracting, or even in purchasing tickets in a lottery, prefer the better agency of a surer power--because it never lies, falters, prevaricates, and it ever tells the same story of the same _thing_, to all alike, no matter what the latitude or longitude may be!

But stop we here? Oh no! for by the same instrumentality we enter the Slumber of SIALAM, and with keen glance and quickened consciousness, scan, and leisurely survey realties denied to "Media," and with sure and rapid gaze trace the awful and majestic rush of hurricanes of glowing galaxies,--the wintry storm of falling worlds!--lamps of God flickering in the Vault! starry eyes glimpsing down into the Deeps!--pregnant earths waiting patiently to be delivered of the Humanity gestating in their bosoms.

Seers, ancient, mediaeval, and modern, alike, inform the world that the supernal country is peopled by all grades of persons from the low and brutal barbarian to the high and polished civilizee; which, if true, proves that intellectual power and capacity is not a passport thither, nor a perquisite of immortality; for there are myriads--not merely of people--but of armies of savage races, tribes, and nations dwelling in that starry land.

Moral goodness is not the touchstone or key either; for no amount of that alone will warrant success, or prove the "Open Sesame" to the farther gate of the grave, nor be potent enough to ensure a man's safe arrival at the golden portals of dis-bodied glory; for ef all mendacious people; of all pullers of the longbow; all perfected liars--on the authority of those who claim to know about it--the disem-bodied ones are champions, able to give long odds, and then heavily denied his Lord, down to the level of--who you like. It is not race, nation, or complexion, that determines a title to supre-mortal existence; for there are people of all kinds there, even "Niggers" and _Sangs Melees_,--lots of them too, _vivat_!--and the dark-hued Southern and Oriental races and peoples outnumber the Northern and fair ones in the ratio of about twelve thousand to one hundred; besides excelling them in the same degree in mind, love, knowledge, force of character, and power of soul. The white Yankees, as a general rule, occupy, according to one A. J. Davis, a large tract known as "Diakka-land;" while but few dark-hued beings can be found there, because _they_ constitute the population of the heavens proper,--along remove from the stormy realm and imperfect people alluded to and named above, albeit myriads of the Light-hued races help to people these choice abodes of spirit-land.

It is not age or sex either; because, if reliance can be placed upon the state-ments of investigators--thousands of infants and people of both genders are continu-ally demonstrating that they still live--and lie! Nor is it talent, genius, or social status. What, then, really constitutes the passport to the ethereal worlds beyond and above the earth we live on? Reply: All who return evince, express, and counsel LOVE! and so confirm the faith of us, who hold _that_, and that alone, to be the great _sine qua non_, the grand desideratum, without which it were as impossible to survive death as it would be to shoot out the centre of Donati's comet with a pocket-pistol! This establishes one pregnant fact, vix., All who are deathless have love at the core! It, alone, is the life-boat in which man sails o'er sounding seas to triumphant existence beyond the grave! Whence it assuredly, ay! and remorse-fully follows that they who waste love, waste soul (see further on), and will assuredly dwindle back to his or her pre-existent monad life or state, there and thus to abide the chances; patiently waiting for an opportunity to begin a better and a fairer race on earth toward the glittering, golden, sunny, shining shores be-yond!

How large the number of those who have written and preached about the immortali-ty of the Soul; and yet not one of the whole vast host, with a single exception, has ever attempted to give a scientific reason why man is endowed with the power of death-survival, for which reason I attack the problem here, and for the first time in the world's literary history give the reasons why, enlarging somewhat upon the theory advanced years since, from the same source, in the book now called "Soul: The Soul World, and Homes of the Departed," then known as "Dealings with the Dead;" and I now proceed to state the argument; and start with the propositions, that:-- No Apes are Immortal: Man is an improved Ape; therefore man is not immortal--by reason of descent. But some men are immortal; they ascended from Ape-ancestors; therefore apes possessed the elements which, in man, conspired to produce immortality. No apes being immortal, or endowed with death-proofness, it follows that his Simian ancestry could not have endowed him with such qualities. Then where did he get them, or it? and How? If he obtained it subsequent to birth, may he not lose it? If his origin is purely mortal, whence his immortality? A stick must have two ends. If man begins as a soul, what hinders him from coming to a full stop; a final cessation; for commencement not only implies, but inexorably means, END also? If he is death-proof in part, or totally, what is the rule and law underlying the tremendous fact? Is it gainable? losable? If either, why?

Now all of these are fair questions, worthy of fair reply. In the first place, there are what, in one sense, I may call apparitional or phantom men; individuals who are only so in seeming; who have little mind, less "Soul," and none of the higher, nobler traits, which we associate with the terms MAN and Manhood. Such may have been born so; or, as in civilized life, may have worn away the jewel, and deprived themselves of the very first essential to the attainment of supra-mundane existence; people who talk about, but will never even glimpse the "Summer Lands," of scent their blossoms afar off, because they have wasted their substance, and steadily declined from the first, exhausted soul, spirit, body, therefore Love, consequently are not true Men, but mere phantoms, who at best become but the sentient vehicles for the exploitations of disembodied wags.

Some, so far as immortality is concerned, die in bringing forth some work, or mechanism;--laboring without recuperation, until the ability to build up soul is forever and forever lost; they having injured the heart-valves, kidneys, supra-renal capsules, prostate gland, and seminal vessels, rendering it wholly impossible for them either to propagate their kind, equal their former mental efforts, or elaborate the electro-ethereal body without which immortality can not be. There are very many in our midst who never received the proper congenital impulsion; and acquired it since birth; or who have lost or wasted the power by too faithful worship at the altars of Mammon, Venus, or Onan. But it is gratifying to know that such even may escape nihility, and gain enduring life beyond the grave; aye, and by stern resolve and persistent endeavor, aspire to the sublime destiny reserved for noble souls,-- that magnificent future awaiting the choice spirits of mankind--the Peers, princes, and Powers of the starry skies!

Soul, per se, I hold to be Eviternal, Sempiternal, and Eternal, just as is that Supreme Deity whom we believe to be, not because His existence is demonstrable, but because we cannot help it, for God is Soul, so is man--existence ergo sum! It has been from Now to all past Eternity; is, and probably will be, from Now to all Eternities to come, and its one orbit is the grand Eternal year. Of course there will come a moment in the far-off aeons when matter will have yielded up all its electric, magnetic, and ethereal life and essences, which it will have contributed to form the electric bodies of the Imperial hosts of the dead; when the last monad will have been incarnated, and no more new souls will be launched into being, and the mighty armies will migrate into space; the refuse of Matter prepare to again renew its forms in loftier moulds; the second act of the transcendent drama be ended, the third begun, and the true and real purpose and meaning of the vast universe begin to be realized and understood--as not Now!

Soul is an Empire, or rather a Republic of States with a central, controlling, governing power. So is Deity--a sun radiant through all space, yet central at Home, just as man lives all over his body, but mostly in a tiny point at the centre of his brain. Deity is conscious at all points; but supremely and infinitely so at the centre of that vast Brain whereof stellar galaxies are but tiny convolutions. and astral nebulae mere nervous fibrillia! Soul is a radiant, invisible, crystallized globe of white Fire and Light located topographically, so to speak, in the middle of the head; and metaphysically, at the centre both of the conscious being, and that other existence of which we see the effects, but are not, and never will be, conscious.

All things whatever emit a sphere, aura, air, aroma, or atmosphere peculiar to themselves. So does man; so does Deity, and, as said before, His nervous fluid, or sphere, is Love, which, like all other fluids, is governed by Wave-motion, not linear Proof: We are suffused with love, not merely penetrated by it. When a love is sharp and cutting, beware of it, for it is electrical passion, not magnetic affection. Love is the effluence of God's body; upon it souls feed, for Love is their life, and they derive sustenance from it in two ways: First, from the AEth-Love pervading the Empyreal Vault; that universe-life which flows out from God. Second, upon that fabricated by, and supplied it through, the nervous and pelvic or genital apparatus of the human frame; for that entire organic system of each gender is but a mighty, powerful, intricate, yet wonderful chemical laboratory and electro-magnetic battery, whose function and office it is--giving us pleasure, comfort, peace, and joy, while performing the strangely esoteric task--to elaborate matter's highest, purest, subtlest essences from food and drink, and absorbed imponderables, and send it to the central brain,--Material whereof Soul fashions the deathless lining of the fleshly frame, the electric body within and beneath that of clay, and which it will wear in the spaces where gross substances are unknown. Now it is easy to see that this great end and aim of Nature may be, and is, defeated in a variety of ways, some of which I will point out,and thus this monograph may be the means of saving many a being from ruin, utter, total, eternal, and complete. And first: It is clear that all diseases, injuries, disorders, or misuse of the sexual apparatus have a direct injurious effect upon the soul, and may, and do, often bar it from building the silver-hued body intended for eternity, and may thus doom one to Nonenity--the equivalent of complete Annihilation! Why? Because no mechanic, not even Nature, can perform perfect work without good materials and tools; and if the Prostate Cowper's glands; the uterus, ovaria, and supra-renal capsules; the testes and vaginal fibrilia --which are the implements with which the spirit-building is accomplished--are not sound, active, healthful, normal, non-inflamed, the soul can no more erect its desired electrical body than a good brick-house can be built without mortar; for such a house would tumble in the first gale, while the touch of death would crumble the half-formed spirit into atoms finer than sparks of Light! Thus it is literally true that every excess and bebauch adds a nail to a man's coffin; but, alas! in more senses than one! It is from the source named, alone, that the soul obtains the materials and elements whereof to construct an ethereal body--from the finest essences of matter held in absolute coalescence by the highest law, and, therefore, proof against death, division, decay, or dissolution--within its fleshly one, by processes analagous to that of gestation--and completes it as the vehicle whose true use only begins subsequent to the fact of physical death! The problem is Solved!

In my day I have encountered thousands of Lust-fired, passion-driven human beings of both sexes who I am sure were quite as pitiable as blamable; and I made such cases an especial study for many long years, in very many lands, the result of which is that I know, with more than mathematical certainty, that it is utterly impossible that such beings, as those described a few lines above, or the old man whose criminal longing for the lives and vitality of young girls I have elsewhere alluded to, can by any possibility have been rightly formed en utero. There was something lacking: too much mortar; too few bricks; nor did they receive the proper immortalizing impulse before birth, or have acquired it since. Such beings are semi-conscious of their lack of elemental soul; that it was and is attainable; that Love was a grand Fact, but not theirs; that it alone could satisfy their longings, and confer the boon they craved; that young girls were generally over-full of soul, life, animation, vivacity, and were easily drainable; that magnetism is a soul-conveying vehicle or fluid; and they rushed headlong to the conclusion that possession of such would, in some mysterious way, cause the young life to pass to the old frame, renew it, and confer upon them what themselves had not--the power of death-survival. Such beings--for Men they are not--have a secret craving for, and sense of lacking of, the magnetic unction and inner power which alone is the assurance of ethereal life beyond the grave; and this half-conscious sense constitutes the impelling spur and motive to the unhallowed wish, and the diabolic and detestable crimes it leads to.

Furthermore: My investigations with all the powers at my command, and facilities accordant, let me to the irresistible conclusion, and deeply solemn religious belief, nay, absolute knowledge, that no confirmed Onanist, or correspondent transgressor of the other gender, is immortal, for reasons set forth elsewhere herein, and which cannot be repeated in this chapter, except to observe that the mechanical, vegetable, tree-like life of the insane from that abominable and most accursed cause, absolutely demonstrates the lapse and loss of Soul itself, leaving nothing but a mere human-esque automatón behind to show the world what once was, but is no longer, an immortal human being! Familiarity with, and investigation of Spiritualism, proves beyond all cavil, that while thousands of all other sorts of debauchees claim to reappear and manifest, yet that not one single Onanist has ever been known to demonstrate. THEY ARE DEAD!--just as all such transgressors must and will inevitably die--soul and body, unless they turn right about and begin the salvatory life as recommended in this and other works by the same author.

Attraction, gravitation, selection, are regnant and unbending laws alike of Soul, Spirit, Mind, and Matter. Oil and water wont mix, neither can the floating germs or monads be attracted to, or be inhaled by, any non-human being now, because that possibility exists no more. Apply the law just stated, and you will see the reason why; for they can only be breathed in by, and come to active, conscious life within , brains of the very highest bimana.

The Simian progenitors of man did not endow him with immortality; but, by natural, which is sexual, selection (of the finest and fairest by the strongest, bravest, and most intelligent), at length produced beings a great deal finer, superior, higher, better, than themselves. Their parental affection enabled gestation to advance a step toward perfectness, and the consequence was superior bodies, and affections, in their young. "Cowper's" and the prostate glands were developed, enlarged, perfected; as were the testes, ovaria, uterus, and nervous systems of the females; and, for the first time, an organization existed of such potent, magnetic, and chemical power, that these organs in the course of generations--still by selection--were enabled to evolve and elaborate that which coalesced with the animal life-principle, elevating that specimen of the pre-human, until it was enabled to inhale monads of the strictly human type. Thus it is true that God breathed into his--her, its, their, nostrils the breath of life, and man became a living, conscious soul, which, being competent to evolve the finer essences, at once immortalized the being!

Now take notice. Magnetism is the power of man. It is of two kinds, physical and mental, or of the body and the soul. One may abound in the first, and have

-109-

nothing whatever of the other, else would we expect to see men of strong build, firm health, any amount of physical, magnetic plethora, capable of being fathers to the very finest specimens of the human race; but such is notoriously not the fact, but quite contrary; for they only who abound in mental, emotional, soul-magnetism, are capable of generating a superior breed of human beings. Again, Magnetic strength is one thing, magnetic unction quite another. The first is material; the second psychal; the results of one are superior physical specimens of the species; those of the second, mental and moral giants; and in the scale of soul-weight puny people, with large spiritual souls and magnetic unction, will produce children a myriad times superior to the other. Bear this in mind, for on it hangs the solution of the problem before me; for if the breather have not love-unction sufficient to plant the germ of immortality, by bequeathing strong love-power to his offspring, how can that child have a starting-point wherefrom to go toward the land of spirits? or force to elaborate the electrical body essential thereto? And if he does not then endow his babe, at death its soul will dwindle back to the monadal state; its present identity and individuality be lost, and the monad will escape into the spacial AEth, to be again breathed in under more favorable auspices, until at last success crowns its efforts in the process of immortalization. This often, very often, occurs; and these reincarnate souls frequently partially awaken to a vague, dim sense of their then pre-existent states; and this explains in a few lines what has been an insoluble problem all along the ages, from Budha to our own day; and it is the only satisfactory solution ever given to the world.

Were Darwinism all true, and man merely a developed Simian, there could be no such thing as destiny or Fate. But there is, and men are cast to a certain lot and career as positively as that they are born, and are compelled by a resistless power to move in given lines and grooves, hopelessly, and are as certainly and solidly bound to the wheel of a peculiar fortune, for good or ill, as was the fabled Ixion. Some are doomed to perpetual strife, struggle, poverty, hopeless effort, from the nipple to the grave; they fail in all things, and disappointment, disaster, ruin, and defeat stalk by their sides, turn whithersoever they will or may. Love, wealth, fame, comfort, rest, joy, happiness, success, all elude them, and if apparent triumphs come, defeat invariably ends the game. Other people do or say with impunity things that are sure to bring down storms of obloquy and pain upon their devoted heads, and sorrow and agony is their lot forever on the earth. On the other hand there are those exactly opposite; whose every step is a triumph, and whose touch transforms everything to gold, money, fame; success flows in upon them like a rolling tide, and they revel in delight without a shadow, till life on earth closes on them in a blaze of wealth and glory; yet these people are not half as able, good, noble, true, as the other class. Now all the Darwinism on earth cannot account for this, yet the solution is easy. The successful class are those who are embodied for the first time, and all their ranks can not furnish a first-class man. The others, the failers, have undergone prior existences on earth, and are either paying penalties for former transgressions, or are undergoing ripening disciplines preparatory to special sunbursts of usefulness, joy, and glory on the further shores of time. Weigh a soul of each class in the scale of actual worth; and the Failers touch ground while the victors on earth kick the beam; and one of the former is of more real value to earth, life, God, and the universe, than scores of the others. It is as the Atlantic to a brooklet.

Children begotten without love are not necessarily immortal; but a proper culture of their better parts may easily make them so. They who do generate offspring by loveless marriage commit a crime against nature and the Deity; for all human beings have a right to receive the immortalizing impulse at the moment of their generation; and also to that culture and training thereafter which alone can make assurance doubly sure in respect to this, the most important of all human matters.

They who become parents under Love's sweet influence at once give the required impulsion to the new being; enable it to survive death's ordeal, and help God Himself to empeople the starry homes of the dead!

It follows that the low, harsh, crash, selfish, hard, crusty, dry, ungenerous people are not entitled to, nor without Very strenuous effort at self-redemption from the lot of beasts, can attain, immortality, much less the other and vaster glory reserved for greater souls, mainly those who, themselves abounding in love, yet languish unto death without return.

Of course a child receiving Love's impulsion will ride triumphant over death's dark tides, even though its bodily eyes never open upon or glimpse this world of ours!

Many and many a full-grown man or woman, stepping into the grave at ripeness of years, only step out of it again as dwindled monads; and when reborn they too have vague, shadowy reminiscences of the, to them, foretime. They who are loveless are no more immortal than the ox which falls beneath the butcher's axe; while, per contra, myriads of savages, Indians, blacks, and the uncouth of all races, ages, and climes, attain to immortality, because of the love and love-generating power within them; for that alone lies at the foundation, and is the sole process of its attainment--or Immortalization.

In conclusion: Let all who wish for immortality learn to Love, and cherish the better feelings of the human heart; take good care to preserve, regain, and cultivate affectional, amative, and psychical Health! Where the nature is injured take immediate means to restore it; thus the point will be gained, and goodness reign. Let no one despair; for while there's life there's hope; and, however dark the outlook, don't for a moment forget that God still lives! that the darkest hour is just before day; that the densest clouds have silvery linings, and that, though love-lorn and wretched, friendless, isolate, and alone, still

WE MAY BE HAPPY YET!

PART III.

CONCERNING SOUL-SIGHT AND MAGIC MIRRORS.

_____

I ADD this chapter to the present work for two reasons: 1st. To gratify the
hundreds of correspondents who, for five years past, have pressed me for something
on the points involved; and, 2d. To give, in a concise and condensed printed form,
information which it would be wholly impossible for me to write out for even one-
fifieth of those who ask it of me. This and "Seership" contain all that is necessary
to be known upon that occult subject. But first I quote the subjoined article:--

The far east must ever lead the world in the practice of necromancy. All the
skill and mechanical ingenuity of the most expert prestidigitateurs of Europe or
America cannot produce a single exhibition which will compare with the feats of the
commonest Indian juggler. The Japanese have taught us the greater part of the
slight-of-hand illusion which is now paraded before staring audiences in this
country and in Europe; but the necromancy of Japan is as boys' play compared with
the mysterious jugglery of the nether and farther Indies, and especially of Siam.
In the latter country there is a royal troupe of jugglers, who perform only at the
funerals and coronations of the kings, and then only in the presence of the nobles
of Siam, or those initiated into the mysteries of the religion of the country.
These necromancers do not perform for money, are of noble blood, and it is seldom
that a European sees even their faces. Last year, however, an English surgeon, who
was in the country, performed a somewhat remarkable cure upon a princess, who had
been treated in vain by all the physicians of the country. Great was the gratitude
of the Siamese court at the doctor's performance; and, as a reward commensurate with
his great service, he was permitted to witness the performance of Tepada's royal
troupe of jugglers. This exhibition was given in the sacred temple of Juthia, on the
16th of November, the occasion being the coronation of the young king. The surgeon's narrative, stripped of a large amount of description, and materially condensed, is given below:--

" IN THE TEMPLE OF JUTHIA.

"Woun-Tajac called me very early, and he and his father's cousin, a jolly, fat
old gentleman, called Soondatch-Tam-Bondar, set to work to prepare me for witnessing the performances in the great pagoda. A white turban was wound around my head;
my skin was stained the color of new bronze; my mustache ruthlessly trimmed down,
blacked, and waxed till it had the proper Malayan dejected droop and tenuity; my
eyebrows blacked; and native garments furnished me, over which I wore the long white
robes which, I was told, were peculiar to the 'initiated.' The pagoda of Juthia is
more celebrated for its sacredness than its size, or the splendor of its architecture. It is, nevertheless, a building of some very striking features. It is
situated without the city, upon a broad and commanding terrace, elevated consider-
ably above the level of the river-plans. It is approached from the city by a long,
brick-paved avenue, wide, straight, and imposing.

"ADMIT ONE.

"Soondatch and Woun-Tajac, each holding me by an arm, now directed me toward one
of the doorways of the temple. It was guarded by two men, with drawn swords, and

very fierce aspect, who stood in front of a heavy drapery of red cloth that concealed
the interior of the temple from outside eyes. At a triple password these men admitted my companions, but crossed their swords before my breast. Soondatch whispered
in the ear of the elder of the two; he started, gazed at me intently, but did not
withdraw his barrier. Woun showed him a signet. He took it, and reverently placed
it upon his forehead; yet still he refused to admit me. There was a controversy
between the doorkeeper and my companions; and, at last, the elder guardian whistled
shrilly upon a bone-pipe tied about his neck with a strand of silk. A tall man
suddenly appeared, I could not see from whence. He was middle-aged, athletic, and
had a most peculiar, cunning, self-possessed look of person and intelligence.

"'TEPADA!'

exclaimed both of my companions at once; but the man, who was naked, except for a
breech-clout, took no notice of them. He put his hand heavily, but not unkindly,
upon my breast, gave me a piercing, long look, and said in excellent French, 'Are
you a brave man?'--'Try me!' I said. Instantly, without another word, he bandaged
my eyes with a part of the long white robe I wore; he snapped his fingers suddenly,
whispering in my ears, 'Not a word, for your life!' and the next moment I found myself seized in the hands of several strong men, and borne some distance along a
devious way, ascending and descending several times. At last I was put down; the
bandage was quietly removed; and I found myself squatted on a stone-floor, between
Soondatch and Woun-Tajac, who, with bowed heads, and faces partly shrouded in their
white robes, squatted like statues of Buddha, their knees and shins close to the
ground, their haunches resting upon their heels, their hands spread palms downward
upon their knees, their eyes deflected, and a look of devout reverence and abstracted
meditation in their countenances. The light was dim to my unaccustomed eyes, but
all around, as far as I could see, were white-robed worshippers crouched in the same
attitude of silent reverence.

"A WEIRD SCENE.

"By degrees, as my eyes grew used to the dim gloom, I began to look about me.
The place was a square vault, so lofty that I could not see the ceiling, and I should
say not less than a hundred paces long and wide. All around the sides rose gigantic
columns, carved into images of Buddha always, yet with a thousand variations from
the central plan, a thousand freaks of fancy, a thousand grotesqueries, through
which shone, the more effectively for the departures, the eternal calm, the
stagnant, imperturbed ecstasy of apathy of Buddha's remarkable face, with the great
pendant ears, and the eyes looking out beyond you into the supreme wistlessness of
Nieban--a face that once seen can never be forgotten. By degrees I came to see the
plan of this evidently subterranean vault, and to look with wonder upon the simple
grandeur of its massive architecture, which was severely plain, except so far as the
carving of the great columns went. At the farthest end of the hall, resting against
the columns, was a raised dais or platform, covered with red cloth. This stage was
raised between three and four feet above the floor of the vault, and was about
thirty-five or forty feet deep and one hundred and fifty broad. Behind it a curtain
of red cloth hung down from the capitals of the towering columns. In front of the
stage, just about the spot where the pulpit of the orchestra in a Greek theatre
would be, was a tripod-shaped altar, with a broad censer upon it, in which was burning a scented oil, mixed with gums and aromatic woods, that diffused through the
whole vault a pungent, sacramental odor.

" THE OPENING CEREMONIES.

"Suddenly there was a wild and startling crash of barbaric music from under the stage--gongs, drums, cymbals, and horns--and with wonderful alertness, and a really indescribable effect, a band of nakes, men came out from behind the curtains, bearing each a scented torch in his hand, climbed the columns with the agility of monkeys, and lighted each a hundred lamps, strung from the base almost of the columns sheer up to the apex of the vault, which, I could now see, rose in a lofty dome, that doubtless pierced far up into the interior of the pagoda proper. The illumination from these multitudinous lamps was very brilliant; too soft to be dazzling or over-powering, yet so penetrating and pervasive that one missed nothing of the perfect light of the day. The din of the horrible orchestra increased, and a band of old women came out from under the stage singing (or rather shrieking out) the most diabolical chant that I ever heard. The red curtain fluttered a little, there was a dull thud, and there, right before us, alongside the censer, stood a very old man, but wrinkled, with long hair and beard, white as cotton fleece. His finger-nails were several inches long, and his sunken jaws were horribly diversified with two long teeth, yellow and ogreish. He was naked, except for a breech-cloth, and his shrunken muscles shone with oil. He took the censer in his hands, and blew his breath into it until the flame rose twenty feet high, red and furious} then, with a sudden, jerking motion, he tossed the burning oil toward the crowd of squatting spectators. It shot toward them a broad sheet of terrible flame; it descended upon them a shower of roses and japonicas, more than could have been gathered in a cart. Turning the censer bottom upward, he spun it for a minute upon the point of his long thumb-nail, then flung it disdainfully away toward the audience. It struck the pavement with a metallic clang, bounced, and rose with sudden expanse of wings.

"A SHRIEKING EAGLE,

frightened horribly, and seeking flight towards the summit of the dome. The old man gazed a moment upward; then, seeing the tripod upon which the censer had stood, he sent its legs apart, with a nervous hand, straightened them against his knee, and hurled them, dartlike, toward the eagle. They glanced upward with a gilded flash, and instantly the eagle came fluttering down to the pavement in our midst, dead, and three horrible cobras coiled about him, and lifting their hooded heads defiantly, and flashing anger out of their glittering eyes. The music shrieked still wilder, the snakes coiled and plaited themselves together in a rhythmic dance, lifting the dead eagle upon their heads, and, presto! right in our midst there stood the tripod again, with its flickering flame, and its incense-savored breath. A more perfect illusion never was seen.

"'That is Norodom,' whispered Woun-Tajac in my ear. Another actor now came upon the scene, whom I recognized to be the tall athletic, Tepada. Behind him came a smaller man, whose name, Woun-Tajac informed me, was Minhman, and a boy, probably twelve years old, called Tsin-ki. These four began some of the most wonderful athletic exhibitions that can be conceived. It is

"IMPOSSIBLE TO BELIEVE,

unless you saw it, what work these men put human muscles to. I am not going to provoke the incredulity of your readers by attempting to describe the majority of them. In one feat Tepada seized Norodom by his long white beard, held him off at arm's length, and spun round him until the old man's legs were horizontal to the athlete's shoulders. Then, while they still spun with the fury of dervishes,

Minhman sprang up, seized upon Norodom's feet, and spun out a horizontal continuation of the ancient; and when Minhman was firmly established, the boy Tsin-ki caught to his feet in like manner, and the tall athlete, every muscle in him straining, continued to whirl the human jointless lever around. At last, slowing slightly, Tepada drew in his arms till the old man's white beard touched his body; there was a sudden strain, and the arm of men from being horizontal became perpendicular, Norodom's head resting atop of Tepada's, Minhman's head upon Norodom's feet, and Tsin-ki's head on Minhman's feet. A pause for breath, then the column of men was propelled into the air, and, presto! Tepada's head was on the ground, Norodom's feet to his, Mihnman's feet upon Norodom's head, Tsin-ki's feet on Minhman's head. Each had turned a summersault, and the column was unbroken!

"METAMORPHOSES.

"One trick which Minhman performed was a very superior version of the mango-tree feat of the Indian jugglers. He took an orange, cut it open, and produced a serpent. This he took down into the audience, and, borrowing a robe from one, cut the snake's head off and covered it with the robe. When the robe was lifted again, a fox was in the place of the snake. The fox's head was cut off, two robes borrowed, and when they were raised there was a wolf, which was killed with a sword. Three robes, and a leper appeared; it was slain with a javelin. Four robes covered a most savage-looking buffali, that was killed with an axe. Five robes covered in part, but not altogether, a lordly elephant, who, when the sword was pointed against him, seized Minhman by the neck and tossed him violently up. He mounted feet foremost, and finally clung by his toes to the capital of one of the columns. Tepada now leaped from the stage and alighted upon the elephant's shoulders. With a short sword he goaded the beast on the head until, shrieking, the unwieldy animal reared upon its hind feet, twined its trunk about one of the great columns, and seemed trying to lift itself from the ground and wrap its body around the great pillar. The music clashed out barbarously, Nerodom flashed forth a dazzling firework of some sort, and the elephant had disappeared, and Tepada lay upon the stage writhing in the folds of a great bos-constrictor and holding up Minhman upon his feet.

"During three hours the exhibition continued, feats of the sort I have described, each more wonderful than the one that preceded it, following one another in rapid succession. I shall content myself with describing the last and culminating wonder of the startling entertainment.

"THE BEAUTIFUL LUAN PRABANA.

"A perfectly formed and most lovely nautch girl sprang out upon the stage, and was hailed with universal exclamations of delight, everybody calling out her name, Luan Prabana, as if it were a word of good omen. Her only dress was a short petticoat of variegated feather-work. A wreath of rosebuds crowned her soft, short, black hair, and she wore a pearl necklace, as well as broad gold armlets and anklets. With a brilliant smile she danced exquisitely for some minutes to the accompaniment of a single pipe, then she knelt and laid her head on old Norodom's knee. The boy fanned her with a fan made of sweet-fern leaves, Minhman fetched a lotus-shaped golden goblet, and Tepeda poured into it from a quaint-looking flask a fluid of greenish hue. The old yogi-like Norodom held the goblet to Luan Prabana's lips, and she drained the contents with a sigh. As if transfigured she suddenly sprang to her feet, her face strangely radiant, and began to spin giddily around in one spot. First the boy, then Minhman, then Tepada tried to arrest her, but they no sooner touched her than that thrilled them as if she had imparted an electric spark to them. Spinning constantly, with a bewildering rapid motion, the girl now sprang off the stage and down the hall, along by the foot of the columns, Tsin-ki, Minhman, and Tepada in active pursuit. In and out among the crowd they spun, the three chasing. Tepada seized hold of the chaplet that crowned her; it broke, and as she was whirled along, a spray of rosebuds was scattered from her brow in every direction. Anything more graceful never was seen. And now a greater wonder. At the extremity of the hall the three surrounded and would have seized her, when, still revolving, she rose slowly into the air and floated gently over our heads towards the stage, scattering roses as she went. At the brink of the stage she paused in mid-air; then with a slight, wing-like motion of her arms, mounted up, up toward the loftiest arch of the vault overhead. Suddenly old Norodom seized bow and arrow and shot toward her. There was/wild shriek, a rushing sound, and the dancer fell with a crash to the flags of the floor, and laid there an apparent bloody mass. The music burst forth into a wild wail, and the chorus of old hags came tumultuously forth and bore her off in their arms.

"WAS IT A MIRACLE.

"Now, from behind the red curtains came a dozen strong men, bearing on their shoulders a great leaden box, which they laid upon the front part of the stage. As they retired the old women came out bringing a low couch, decorated with flowers and gold-embroidered drapery, upon which lay Luan Prabana, decked forth in bridal garments, and sweetly sleeping. The couch with its sleeper was put quietly down upon the front of the stage, and left there, while Norodom and Tepada went to the leaden box, and with hot irons attempted to unseal it. 'That is Stung-Tieng's coffin,' whispered Woun to me; 'the old saint has been dead more than half a millennium.'

"Quickly, eagerly it seemed to me, the two men broke open the fastenings of the coffin, until the side next the audience falling out at last, a teak-box was discovered. This was pried open with a small crowbar, and what seemed a great bundle of nankeen taken out. Tepada and Norodom commenced to unwind this wrapping, which was very tight. Yard after yard was unwound and folded away by Minhman, and at last, after at least one hundred yards of wrapping had been taken off, the dry, shrivelled mummy of a small, old man was visible, eyes closed, flesh dry and hard,--dead and dry as a smoked herring. Norodom tapped the corpse with the crowbar, and it gave a dull, wooden sound. Tepada tossed it up and caught it--it was still as a log. Then he placed the mummy upon Norodom's knees, and fetched a flask of oil, a flask of wine, and a censer burning with some pungent incense. Norodom took from his hair a little box of unguent, and, prying open the mouth of the mummy with a cold-chisel, showed that the dry tongue could rattle like a chip against the dry fauces. He filled the mouth with unguent and closed it, and anointed the eyelids, nostrils, and ears. Then he and Tepada mixed the wine and oil, and carefully rubbed every part of the body with it. Then, laying it down in a reclining position, they put the burning censer upon the chest and withdrew a space, while the drums and gongs and cymbals clashed and clattered, and the shrill, cackling treble of the chorus of old women rose hideously.

"A LA LAZARUS.

"A breathless pause ensued--one, two, three minutes--and the mummy sneezed, sneezed thrice, so violently as to extinguish the flame of the censer. A moment later the thing sat up, and stared, blinking and vacant, out around the vault--an old wrinkled man, with mumbling chops, a shrivelled breast and belly, and little tuffs of white hair upon his chin and forehead. Tepada approached him reverently, upon his knees, bringing a salver, with wine and a wafer-cake. The old man did not notice him, but ate, drank, and tottered to his feet, the feeblest decrepit old dotard that ever walked. In another moment he saw the nautch girl slumbering upon her couch; he scuffled feebly to her, and, mumbling, stooped as if to help his dim eyes to see her better. With a glad cry the maiden waked, clasped him in her arms and to her breast, and kissed him, Incomprehensible magic! He was no longer a monagenarian dotard, but a full-veined fiery youth, who gave her kiss for kiss. How the transformation was wrought I have no idea, but there it was before our very eyes. The music grew soft and passionate, the chorus of the old women came out, and with strange Phallic songs and dances bore the two away--a bridal pair. I never expect again to behold a sight so wonderful as that whole transformation, which, I may mention, my learned Jesuit friend, to whom I described it, regards as a piece of pure symbolism. His explanation is too long and too learned to quote, but he connects the ceremony with the world-old myth of Venus and Adonis, and claims that it is all a form of sun-worship.

"BACK TO THE TOMB.

"The show went on for some time longer with many curious feats. At the end of an hour the Phallic procession returned, but this time the Bayadere led it, a strange triumph in her eyes, while the youth lay upon the couch sleeping. The Phallic chorus sank into a dirge, the youth faded visibly; he was again the shrivelled dotard; he sighed, then breathed no more. Luan Prabana retired sorrowfully; Norodom and Tepada wrapped the corpse again in its interminable shrouds, restored it to the coffin, and it was borne away again. The attendants climbed up to and extinguished the lights. I was blindfolded and borne away again. I found myself once more at the doorway of the temple in the broad sunshine with my friends--as the mystic ceremonies of the great temple of Juthia were over, it may be for many years."

"With strange Phallic songs and dances born the two away--a bridal pair." "Venus and Adonis--a form of sun-worship." "The Phallic chorus sunk into a dirge." Can anything be plainer or more direct in confirmatory proof of what I had written in this book, than this excerpt from a newspaper, dated April 11, 1874, months after this book was completed,--but the appearance of which necessitated a brief additional page or two? There is no need to go to far-off Siam to witness such marvels, or to learn their strange principia, for I have not only witnessed displays of High Magic in this country, quite as marvellous, but different from the above, but have myself performed the feat of Fire-drawing, and came very near destroying the life of a woman who assisted at the rite, and but for the quick, brave, self-sacrificing action of Dr. Charles Main, of Boston, that woman would have been slain by fire drawn down from the aereal spaces by principles known to me. For fifteen years I sought a female of the right organization--an European or American Luan Prabana (the Fair and Virgin invocatress)--and not till March, 1874, did I find her. Her Self-will, and brother-in-law's (he was a Pupil) lack of decision, and his weighing of less than three dollars' expense against the possession of the loftiest Magic earth ever saw, determined me to seek elsewhere for the true material--which, it is needless to say, I have found again in my own personal circle. The Mysteries are all wrought through the Phallic, Discal, Yoni Principles, in unsullied purity, and the highest, noblest worship known to man. The great trouble with all whom I have partly taught in this land is that they--not one of them--saw anything nobler than the brilliant chance of sure gain, or opportunities to gratify Passion. Wherefore, of course, I dropped them all. The Phenomenal magic recounted in the extract given above, together with the equally startling things of Egypt, Negro-land, Japan, China, Tartary, and India--only distantly approached by the Fire-tests, materialization and the like, as seen in the case of Hume, the Baltimore negro and others, together with the air-floating of various persons, myself included, are, so far as real use is concerned, but secondary trifles compared to that loftier system of the far Orient, whereby persons are enabled to glimpse behind the scenes of life, and note what transpires on the further side. To the special consideration of that transcendent phase of high magic, I shall devote this concluding chapter of my book; observing, ere I do so, that I hope these things now written, will neither be scattered to the winds, or seized on in the interests of either dollars or lusts; for I cannot help utterly despising the worshippers of either Mammon or Priapus. One thing, however, is absolutely certain, and this it is; No one can succeed in either branch of high magic whose spur and motive is such as I deprecate above; but success is sure to eventually crown the efforts of the persevering student, whose aims are goodness and the acquisition of power for noble ends.

For many ages people have sought to penetrate through, or lift, the veil which hangs between the world we inhabit and that vast realm where causes reside and principles exist. To that end, recourse has been had to drugs, such as opium, cannabin, and camphora; to mesmerism, "Psychology," disks, magnets, and fasting; and in later times to circles and various so-called marvellous methods; all of which, in the end, have proved unsatisfactory, and the student and searcher has been, by them, left worse off than before. Not all persons can reach the interior sight by such methods, because all are not possessed of the essential organic attributes, or constitutional bias and tendency. To all such there is a surer, better, safer, and grander road, and that is self-development, by means entirely within the reach of every one, and which are within their will and control; and which require but the elements of Time, Patience, Assiduity, Persistence, and periodical effort to ensure, if not complete success in soul-sight, then in those other qualities, powers, and attributes essential to perfect human character.

That agency, I hold, is some form of the spirit-glass or lens,--not the "Urim and Thummim," or metallic breast-plates used for purposes of divination, and worn by the priesthood, as recounted in the Bible; nor the stones and crystals of later days,--but the perfected spirit-seeing or magic-glass, formed of materials prepared in the Orient, and fitted for use in Paris and France.

These are of two generic kinds, and also of diverse grades, sizes, sensitiveness, focal power, and magnetic planes,--because those made for, and adapted to, one line of use, are not so well suited to different lines: And First. The common kind averages about eight inches by seven, and is a true AEthic mirroe adapted to ordinary ends, such as invoking the dead; and the other purposes for which they have for ages been used.

The difference between the spirit-seeing mirrors, such as are described in "Seership," and the methods and materials of their construction therein set forth, and those hereinafter described, is the difference between a first-class gold repeater, and a common cylinder--escapement watch. Both are time-keepers, but one is vastly superior to the other. The materials of the two classes of mirrors are quite dissimilar; and the labor expended on those hereinafter described, is simply enormous, for after they come into the hands of us of America, they cost an immensity of toil, in cleaning, polishing, heating, bathing, and magnetic manipulation, and this it is that renders them valuable, and adapted to the uses for which from hoary antiquity they were intended. I have been a very small crystalline mirror, weighing less than a pound, for which the owner demanded $4,000 in gold coin, and was not at all anxious to part with it even at that price. Second. The larger and finer ones of the same sort; but which of course are far better, stronger, more perfectly magnetic, and have a great deal wider range. Formerly there were five sizes of this class; but it was found that but two could be depended on; as the rest were extremely liable to fracture by reason of the great climatic ranges of temperature in Western Europe and North America.

This class were also found better suited to beginners than to proficient seers; especially those who, not content with the limited ranges of the ordinary ones, were anxious for a perfected instrument of greater sensitiveness, magnetic calibre, focal range, AEthic basin, or magnetic reservoir, and of a capacity equal to the solution of almost any subject capable of demonstration by such means; wherefore that form was superseded, in 1874, by the ne plus ultra of all such things in that line;--fine oval magnetic polar ones, with deeper, broader, larger basins, or magnetic reservoirs, presenting a deep-sea surface, nearly absolutely perfect, and leaving almost nothing to wish for in any respect;--a beautiful, clear avoid, and of size, focal length and calibre seldom equalled and never surpassed. They go in grades, sizes, ranges, and cost according to their illuminant power.

In January, 1874, I received a few from Paris, and hung them on my chamber-wall to charge and fit them for their owner,--a lady; and there they remained till the morning of Feb. 8th, when they became suddenly illuminant, and no grander sight ever was beheld by human eyes than was presented on that memorable morning; for the whole starry galaxies; rolling world-systems of nebulae; vast congeries of stellar constellations; cities afar off on the earth; and scenes never before beheld by eyes of this world, were displayed to such a grand, sublime, and amazing extent that the soul panted with the weight of the transcendent Phantorama.* Such mirrors as these --would they were mine!--if kept free from promiscuous handling, treated judiciously, and rightly used, are capable of more psychic marvels than all the mesmerists on the globe! Very few of any grade are imported, save when expressly ordered; the risk of breakage in crossing the seas and by inland carriage being too great to admit of larger consignments, even were it possible to have such, which it is not.

Full directions for their general use and care are given in the book called "Seership," a work devoted exclusively to the subject. But those of the superior grades require suplementary advisements concerning their treatment. 1st. They should--when not in use,--be kept either with face to the wall in a dark place, else be covered with a board or plate (usually furnished with them) so as to exclude every

---

* They are, every one of them--(from the plain surface mirror, to the magnificent, golden-edged, Beauties; or the enormous 40-inch ones--fit for a Lodge!--worth a king's ransom!)--capable of mirroring correctly--and beforehand too! the MARKETS of the world. Here is a strange test, whose truth I solemnly avouch:--

A pregnant lady--and such are ever the most favored in all lines of celestial magic,--on the morning alluded to above--Feb. 8, 1874--gazed into one of the mirrors, and demanded to know the sex of her unborn child. The reply came instantly--"A Boy! and a great one! a vast soul!--the king-seer of FIVE THOUSAND YEARS!"

The result, so far as sex was concerned, was absolutely true; and there is but little doubt that the rest will prove equally so. This same lady was the only true mystic of her sex I ever saw in America. She was the best mirror-manipulator on the earth, and owned--still owns all the genuine ones on the continent. Through her I have obtained specimens of such rare value, that to part therewith was like the loss of the right eye.

ray of light. But about once a month they should be exposed to the full blaze of
the sun for at least an hour; while a similar exposure, but of longer duration, to
moon or starlight, invariably increases their power, and quite often adds new ones.
The larger ones may be used by a room full of persons at the same time; being fixed
immovably, and the people arranging themselves so that each san see the broad white-
black river flowing continually across the surface; but no one, save the owner,
should either touch, or sit, or stand closer than from four to seven feet or more;
and when the seance begins, no word should be spoken, no movement made; and it
ought to open with a prayer to the Most High, while special invocations, for any
given purpose or purposes, may be made to lesser potential intelligences. Those
which are now in this country are of an extraordinary character and degree of power;
their illuminant surface has never been equalled; while their _true_ cuspic-ovoid,
depth and breadth, is most admirable,--appreciable by those favored ones who are
true seers and born mystics, as being immeasurably superior to anything of the kind
seen since the days of the magi on the plains of Chaldea!--for great pains have been
taken with the glasses, which act as protecting-shields to the material beneath,--
on which material, the mode of its preparation, seasoning, application, and
magnetic manipulation, and _not_ upon the glass itself--their beauty and excellence
wholly _depends_; albeit the highest art is brought to bear in the making and shaping
of the crystal-shield, and in the construction of the frames in which they are
mounted. The GLYPHAE-BHATTAH, or Mirror surface itself is the _true_, and well-
factured bhatt from India, whence alone it can be procured even by the Mystic Brother
hood of Paris, France, where the mounting is done.

Due care is essential that they, like a child, be kept clean; to which end fine
soap and warm soft water, applied with silk or soft flannel, is the first step;
followed by a similar bath, whereof cologne, fresh beer, or liquor spurted from the
mouth, are the three ingredients: the second for the sake, 1st, of the spirit; 2d,
of the individual magnetism; and, 3d, the symbolism embodied in the ritual--so
palpably as not to need further explanation. _Write_ _for_ _other_ _information_ on this
delicate point.

"But why are these black-white, cuspic ovoids magnetic or magical in any degree?
or, if they are, why may not we of Western Europe or America fabricate the same?"
To which the reply is: You cannot! because you know not how to mingle the materials
--even if you knew them, which you do not--that enter as elements into the mysteriously sensitive substance wherewith the shields are covered, and which _alone_ constitutes the magnetic or magic film, of which and to which the lava-glass and frame
are merely protective covers.

People of the West (Europe,--America) are not subject to the same extremes of
passion (sexive) as are Orientals; and hence know not either its awful intensity,
or its terrible penalties, because they dwell far more in the Brain than in the
 gender, wherefore they have less _verve'elan_, and passional power than their brown
brethren and sisters of the far-off eastern lands; as a general rule, with occasional exception, they are unable to reach the magnificent goals of soul-vision and
magic power easily attainable by the sallow devotees of Sachthas and Saiva; and
therefore cannot realize the intense passional furore, essential both to the
successful invocation of correspondent AErial Potentialities, and the charging of
mirrors with the divine spiritual reflective powers which characterize them. I
here alluded to a profound mystery connected with their construction, known only
to the initiate, but which is vaguely hinted at in the subjoined quotation;--a
mystery at which dolts and fools may laugh--provided they sense its nature, but
which higher souls must reverence, honor, and adore.

Says Colonel Stephen Fraser, in his glorious volume entitled "TWELVE YEARS IN
INDIA," a magnificent book, which was kindly lent me by MR. W. G. PALGRAVE, of

London, who called on me in August, 1873, while on his overland route to China, via San Francisco, and whom I had known in England fifteen years before, as a polished gentleman and scholar, and one of the deepest mystics on the globe outside of the Orient:--

"We joyfully, gladly, went,--five of us, her Majesty's Officers, on a tour of military inspection, the toils of which were likely to be rewarded by an opportunity of witnessing the dance of Illumination, of the MUNTRA-WALLAHS, or Magic-working Brahmuns, whose strange miracles, worked apparently by the triple agency of Batta-shas (rice), Gookal (red-powder), and, strangest of all, by means of oval glasses or crystals, but black as night, in which it is reported, some very strange things were to be seen. We were all prepared to witness skilful jugglery, for which the residents of Muttra* are renowned, but fully resolved to ascertain, if possible, how ti was all done, rejecting, of course, everything claimed to be either supra-mortal or hyper-natural, so far as the underlying principles were concerned. . . It was sheer skill, but such as no European could pretend to equal; yet how the sleeping girl could tell our names, ages, place of birth, and fifty other true facts, she never having seen either of us before,--because the dust of Jubalpore was still upon our clothes, we having been but one day in Muttra,--was a problem not easily solved. They call it the Sleep of Sialam, and she passed into it by gazing into a dark glass.

"After reading Lane's story about the Magic Mirror in his 'Modern Egyptians;' what DeSacy says in his famous 'Exposition de la religion des Druses;' Makrisi's account in his 'History of the Mamelukes;' J. Catafago and Defremeny in the 'Journal Asiatique;' what Potter affirms as truth in his 'Travels in Syria;' Victor L'Anglois, in 'Revue D'Orient;' Carl Ritter; Dr. E. Smith; Von Hammer in his 'Hist. des Sasseins;' W. H. Taylor's 'Nights with Oriental Magicians;' the 'Gesta Magici' of Lespanola; 'Lettres Edifiantes et Curieuses;' 'Youett's Researches into Magic Arts,' and innumerable other unquestionable authorities,--it was far less difficult to believe in the existence of some occult visual power possessed by these mirror-gazers, of both sexes, all ages, and diversity of culture, than to attribute it all to chicanery and lucky guesswork. . . .'Sahib, it true,' said our Wallah, next morning, when speaking of the exhibition of the previous day; 'and now I s'pose you go see Sebeiyeh dance--(the Mirror Bridal-fete of a renowned Brotherhood of Mystics, Philosophers, and Magicians)--no doubtee?(Well, we all determined to go; and a three-hours' ride brought us to a plateau in a mountain-gorge of the Chocki hills. We were not too late, and were kindly offered vantage ground of view by the Sheikh, --a man of at least 125 years of age, judging from the fact that his grandchildren were white with snowy locks and beards waist long. . . . . The two brides entered

---

* "Muttra, a town in the province of Agra (India), on the west bank of the river Jumma, in latitude 27 deg. 31 min. North; longitude 77 deg. 33 min. East;--a place famous for the manufacture of Magical apparatus; and one of the only two places on earth where the Parappthaline gum is prepared, wherewith the adepts smear the backs of these extraordinary mirrors, so celebrated by the various authorities named in the text."--Twelve Years in India. Vol. 2, p.286.

the circle followed by the two grooms, all four bearing large earthenpots full of black, smeary, tar-like substance, which, on inquiry of the Sheikh, we learned was the product of the Volcanic springs of the Mahades hills, in the far-off province of Gondwana, in the Deccan; that it only flows in the month of June; is collected by girls and boys who are virginal,--that is, before puberty; and must be prepared for use within the ensuring forty-nine days, by similar persons on the eve of actual marriage, as it is supposed certain properties of a magical nature attach to it when handled by <u>such</u> person under <u>such</u> circumstances. Of course I, with my western habits of thought and European education, could but laugh at this, which seemed so very palpable and gross a superstition; and yet, strange to relate, when I expressed my sceptical views to the old Sheikh, he laughed, shook his head, handed me two parts of the shell of a large nut, and requested me to fill one with the crude material, and the other with the same after it had been prepared. I did the first, and reserved the empty shell for the other, taking care to hold both in my hand well wrapped up in a brown bandana. . . . . The circle had a pile of stones in the centre, upon which coals were brightly burning; and over this fire--which, by the way, is the Eternal sacred Fire of the Garoonahs, which is never allowed to go out from one year's end to the other--was suspended from a tripod of betel rods a coarse earthen vessel, into which the four expectant marriages poured about one-fourth of the contents of the simla gourds already mentioned; amid the din of an hundred tom-toms or native drums; the clashing of rude cymalos (cymbals) and wild, clarion-like bursts of the strangest, and, shall I, a staid Briton, confess it?--most soul-stirring and weird music that ever fell upon my ears, or moved the man within me! After this was done, the Sheikh's servitors erected a pole near the fire, around which pole was coiled the stuffed skins of the dreadful hooded snake of India,--the terrible Naga, or Cobra; while on top was an inverted cocoa-shell, and two others at its base--understood by the initiated as symbolizing the Linga,--the male emblem, or creative principle of Deity; while the suspended vessel over the fire represented the Yoni; or female principle; the tripod emblematizing the triple powers or qualities of Brahm--Creation--Preservation--Perpetuation;--the fire below corresponding to Love, or the Infinite Fire which is the Life of All! . . . . . And now began a strange, weird dance, to the wild melody of five hundred singing devotees of that wonderful Phallic, or sexual religion; mingled with the mellow breath of cythic flutes, the beating of tambours, the thrumming of various instruments, and an occasional ziraleet, or rapture-shriek from the lips of women and young girls, whose enthusiasm was unrestrainable, and who gave vent to it in wild movements of their graceful and supple bodies, and in shrill cries that might be heard long miles away, like voices from heaven awakening the echoes of Space! . . . . Advancing with a slow, voluptuous, rhythmic movement, not of the feet alone, but of the whole form from crown to toe, the girls--aged about fifteen, brown as berries, agile as antelopes, graceful as gazelles; lovely, with barbaric splendor, as an Arab's ideal houri;--they swayed, bent, advanced by twists and curves, by nameless writhings, by sweeping genuflexions, by movements the very poetry of passion, but passion of <u>soul</u> far more than of body, with suffused faces and moistly gleaming eyes, toward the taller emblem, round which they slowly whirled and danced, even and anon stirring with a silver spatula the dark substance contained in the vessels they bore. This by turns. While the two youths, bearing similar vessels, performed corresponding movements about the vessel which symbolized Nature in her productive aspect--until we five Europeans were lost in a maze of astonishment at the capacity of the human frame to express mutely, but with more meaning and eloquence than a thousand tongues could convey, the amazing heights, depths, and shades of passion, but a passion totally free from vulgarity or indecency; and as pure as that of the ocean billows when they kiss each other over the grave of a dead cyclone! . . . . . Observing my surprise, the old Sheikh touched my arm, and in purest Bengalee whispered:--'Sahib, ARDOR begat the Universe! There is no power on earth either for good or ill, but Passion underlies it. <u>That</u> alone is the spring of all human action, and the father and mother alike of all the good and

evil on the Earth! It is the golden key of Mystery, the fountain of Weakness and
of Strength; and through its halo alone can man sense the ineffable essence of the
Godhead! The materials in the vessels are charged with life,--with the very essence
of the human soul, hence with celestial and divine magic power! for O, Sahib, it is
only lust and hatred that keep closed the eyes of the soul!--and in the crystals
whose backs we cover with the contents of these five vessels, the earnest seeker
may behold, not only what takes place on earth, but also what transpires on other
globes, and in the SAKWALAS of the Sacred Gods!--and this is the only true Bab,--
(Door).'--'But,' I rejoined, 'we of the West magnetize people, who, in that
mysterious slumber, tell us amazing'--'Lies!' he said, interrupting the sentence,--
'for no two of them tell the same tale or behold the same things! Why? Because
they explore the kingdoms of Fancy, not of FACT, and give you tales of imagination
and distorted invention, instead of recitals of what actually exists Beyond! But
wait!' I acquiesced, and turned once more to the dances of the Aleweheh, who by
this time were moving in a more rapid manner to the quickened strains of the more
than ever wild and fantastic music. . . . . Three of them began stirring the contents of the cauldron, into which all the material from the gourds had now been
poured; murmuring strange, wild bursts of Phallic song the while; and the fourth,
the taller maiden of the two, stripped herself entirely nude above the waist and
below the knees; her long raven hair streaming around her matchless form--a form of
such superlative contour, proportions, lively peach-blow tint, and rounded beauty,
as made me blush for the imperfections of the race that mothered me! There were no
violent exertions of legs and arms; not the slightest effort at effect; none of
the gross motions in use in the West, on the stage or off it--whose palpable object
is the firing of the sluggish blood of halfblase spectators; but a graceful movement, a delicious trembling, half fear, half invitation;--a quivering, semi-long-
ing, semi-reluctant undulation of arms, bosom, form, eyes even--rippling streams of
most voluptuous motion; billowy heavings and throbbings of soul through body, so
wonderful, so glowing, that one wished to die immediately that he might receive the
reward of centuries of toil in the ravishing arms of the houris of the seventh,--
ay! even the first paradise of the Ghillim, and the resplendent Queens of the
Brahminical Valhalla. And yet there was absolutely nothing suggestive of coarse,
gross, animal passion in all this transcendental melody of hyper-sensuous motion;
on the contrary, one felt like seizing her by the waist, drawing his sword and
challenging all earth, and hell to boot, to take her away, or disturb her tran-
quillity of celestial--what shall I call it?--I am lost for a name!

"Presently both the girls joined the mystic sensuous-magic dance; and one of
them seized me suddenly by the arm and dragged me to the central vessel, saying,
'Look, Sahib, look!' I did so, but instead of a black mass of seething boiling gum,
I beheld a cauldron bubbling over with the most gorgeously pink-tinted froth that
imagination ever dreamed of; and while I stood there marvelling at the singular
phenomenon--for every bubble took the form of a flower,--lotus, amaranth, violet,
lily--Rose!--the old Sheikh drew nigh and said, 'Sahib, now's the time!' pointing
to the bundle containing the empty shell and the one already half filled. Acting
on the suggestion, I held forth the empty shell; into which the girl ladled about
a gill of the contents of the swinging vessel; and the Sheikh produced two perfectly
clean ovoid glass plates, over which he poured respectively the contents of the two
shells, and held both over the fire for a minute, till dry, and then handing them
to me, said, 'Look, and wish, and will, to see whatever is nearest and dearest to
your heart!' Internally I laughed, but he took the two shells, and while he held
them, I looked into the hollow face of the glass which was covered with the singular
substance first handed to me, and gazing steadily about half a minute,--the mystic-
dance going on meanwhile,--I willed to see my home and people in far-off Albion; but
nothing appeared. The old man smiled. 'Now look at the other one, which is a true
Bhatteyeh--full of divine light and imperial power, and you will--' Before he

finished, I glanced into the other, and--scarce hoping that the Western reader will credit me with anything loftier than a vivid imagination, fired almost beyond endurance, by the lascivious surroundings, in the midst of which I was, I nevertheless clearly and distictly affirm, on the hitherto unsullied honor of an English gentleman, and a colonel in Her Majesty's service, that I saw a wave of pale, white light, flit like a cloud-shadow over the face of the mysterious disk, and in the centre of that light a landscape, composed of trees, houses, lands, lowing cattle, and forms of human beings; each and every item of which I recognized as the old familiar things of my boyhood and youth, long ere the fires of ambition had turned my face toward distant India. I beheld the simulacrum of a dear sister, whom I had left in perfect health. I saw her to all appearance very, very sick,--the physicians, nurses, troops of friends, and faithful servitors, gathered round her; <u>she was dying! dead!</u> I saw the funeral <u>cortege</u> set out for the cemetery, and I marvelled greatly that they buried her by the iron ribs of a railway; because when I left, no road of that kind ran through my native town. I saw the silver plate on her coffin, and most clearly and distinctly read the inscription thereon; <u>but the surname was one I had never heard of!</u> I looked up at the Sheikh, who was eying me with strange interest and intensity, as if to ask in explanation; but he only smiled and repeated the one word,'See!' Instantly I turned my eyes to the ovoid again, as likewise did three of my European friends, and, to my and their utter astonishment, beheld a shadow, an exact image of <u>myself</u>, standing near the well-curb of my native manse, weeping as if its heart would break, over the prostrate form of my elder brother who lay there dying from a rifle-bullet through the groin,--the result of an accident that had just befallen him while in the act of drinking from the swinging-pail or bucket! Now came the most astonishing phenomena of all,--for each of the three friends who were looking with me, started in surprise, and uttered exclamations of undisguised astonishment, for each had seen things beyond the range or pale of trickery or the play of excited fancy. One beheld the three forms of his dead father, sister, and uncle,--the latter pointing to a sealed packet on which was inscribed the words, 'Dead--Will--heir--Oct. 11th. Go home!' The other beheld the drawing-room, and its occupants, of the old house at home,; and on the table lay a large pile of gold coin, across which lay a legend thus: 'Jem and David's winnings: Lottery: Paris: June 18th: 10,000 Pounds!' The third man saw a battle or skirmish waging in the Punjaub, and his senior officer struck down by a shot in the side, thus opening the road to his own promotion. Much more we saw and noted in that wonderful scene of diablerie, portions of which I shall detail at length hereafter. But it became necessary to attend to other matters. I did so (as will be hereinafter cited), and then accompanied the Sheikh to his tent, where the marriage was celebrated; and he told me there certain wonderful secrets in reference to the further preparation of the strange material composing the reflective surfaces of the curious Bhatts, which, while exceedingly mystic and effective, at the hands and <u>offices</u> of the newly married people, is yet of so singular and delicate a nature as not to be admissible to these pages; for while really of the most holy and sacred nature, yet the miseducation--in certain vital respects and knowledges-- of the divilized Teutonic, Anglo-Saxon, and Latin races, would render the matters to which I allude subjects of either not well-based blushes or outright mirth.*
. . . . . Seven long months after these memorable experiences, I parted with three of my then comrades, and, accompanied by two others, embarked on one of the steamers of the <u>Messageries Imperiales</u>, from Bombay, homeward bound. Before I left, one of my friends had sold his commission in consequence of having fallen heir to an uncle's estate, who, the letters of recall stated, had died in England, on Oct. 10th and <u>not</u> on the 11th, as the ovoid had stated! It had actually taken the differnces of Latitude, and was <u>correct to an hour!</u> The second man, on arrival in England,

---

* Exactly the reason why I have been unable to find a single true adept or adapt in the U.S.A.--P.B.R.

proved the truth of the mirror, for <u>Fane</u>, not 'Jem' as the glass stated, and
<u>Davison</u>, not 'David'--cousins of his--<u>had</u> fallen on a lottery-fortune of over a lac
of rupees in India money! The other officer was promoted in consequence of the
death of his lieutenant-colonel, in a skirmish in the Punjaub, which event was the
result of a shot in the loins, not the side. Arrived at home, I found my people
in deep mourning for my younger sister, the widow--after a wifehood of less than a
year--of Capt. H----, of Her Majesty's Navy, whom she had met for the first time
only a few months before their marriage. I had left for India five years before,
and though I had often heard of my brother-in-law's family, yet <u>we</u> had never met.
He went down in one of the new crack iron-clads on her trial-trip. The awful news
occasioned premature motherhood; she died, and her remains were deposited in the
hillside vault, skirting which was a railway just equipped and opened for traffic
a month or two prior to the marine disaster! Lastly: Within eight months after my
return I became sole male heir to our family-property in consequence of the death
of my brother by a charge of shot, <u>not</u> a bullet in the groin, as the Mirror showed;
--but full in the abdomen while climbing a fence for a drink at the brookside, and
not at a well. Every fact shown so mysteriously was proved strangely true, though
not literally so. I, just previous to my departure from the strange bridal, asked
the old Sheikh some questions; and learned that the material on the crystal surface
wherein we saw the strange miracles was but partially prepared,--as my readers will
also recollect; but some which he placed on a glass just before I left, and which
had been <u>fully</u> prepared, the finishing process being a secret one and conducted by
the newly wedded couples by a peculiar process--and nameless--never made a mistake
while in my possession; for I confess I lost it from a silly servant having shown
it boastingly to a gypsy, who stole it that same night, through the most adroit bit
of scientific burglary I ever heard or read of. The loss, however, was not irrepar-
able, for I have since that these strange Nuntra-Wallahs, as they are contemptuously
called by their Islamic foes in the Carnatic (but true magi in the opinion of better
informed people), have brethren and correspondents in nearly every country on the
globe--Brazil, China, Japan, Vienna, and even our own London; while they have a
regular Lodge in Paris, of some of whom the initiated, and favored ignorants even,
can and do obtain occasionally, not only well-charged and polished Bhatteyeh, but
actually, now and then, a gourd full of Moulveh-Bhatteyeh--the strangely mysterious
substance which constitutes the seeing surface, as mercury does in the ordinary
looking-glass, and the two are alike in all save that the latter reflects matter and
the living, while the former sometimes--but not at all times, or to all people,
or to the successful seers on all occasions--reveals only spirit and the dead,--ay,
and things that <u>never die</u>! Heaven help all whom a Muntra-Wallah hates!--or loves
either, for that matter--unless that love be returned; for the magician in one case
will bring up the hated one's bhadow,--and then strange horrors will seize him or
her; and in the latter case--well, <u>stranger things happen</u>, that is all."

     . . . .

    Thus much by way of information. Those who have read the works of MUNDT,
HARGRAVE JENNINGS, LAWRIE, PALGRAVE, MORIER, LANE, need not be told that these
Bhatts have been imitated often, but without avail; for, unless they be true, not
a cloud even can be seen. <u>There is another secret about them which can only be
revealed to such as have and use them</u>!--and not then till they shall have proved
worthy of the knowing.

    Now I wish right here to say, that some persons have been disappointed in such,
because all mysteries of the heavens, or gold in the ground, or hidden money, etc.,
were not <u>at once</u> revealed. I never used one for any such purpose; but I sat and
gazed upon it, awaiting <u>patiently</u> for aught that was vouchsafed in the way of visions
or phantoramas. This is their negative and immeasurably lowest use. The highest

is to sit gazing until the gazer shall pass into a transcendently lofty and most interior state--absolute, unequivocal supre-clairvoyent condition, and then, ah, THEN, as myriad glories untold and roll before the Soul's eyes the seer is every inch a king or queen, and can laugh this life and world, and all their trials, troubles, and infinite littleness to utter scorn, and, as it were, snap their fingers at life, death, and their copula--circumstance. And this is the positive use of a good Bhatteyah.

The facts of Psycho-Vision, Mesmeric lucidity, Somnambulic sight, and Clair-voyance, so called, are too numerous, palpable, and well authenticated in this age to be questioned. The old time animal magnetism and its marvels gave way to what was called "Electrical Psychology," which in turn receded before the advance of what were called "Seeing Mediums," but few of whom, however, could see the same facts alike; and all gave way before the better method of developing the inner vision; by a royal road the goal is reached in these days, and that too without the delays, dangers, and uncertainties heretofore attending all methods of attain-ing that strange soul-sight wherewith not a few have astonished the world. But a higher, broader, deeper clairvoyance is now needed and demanded by mankind, far superior to that displayed by the riff-raff pulings of half-crazed fanatics; the money-grabbing hordes of "Fortune-tellers" infesting all large cities; the "Biologists," "Psychologists," and others of the same order and genera. The new has become old, and the old new, and a better method of self-development is found in the revived practice than in all the others singly or combined. In India, China, Japan, Siam, Upper Egypt, Arabia, Central Nigritia, and on the far-off plains of Tartary and Thibet, the old usage still survives; and the seers divine through shells, and crystals, and diamonds, emeralds, or the plain and less expensive dark-ovoid--wholly surpassing the boasted clairvoyance of France, England, and America, and in the same identical lines too,--albeit some uses thereof are perversions from the true and normal, whether for mere financial ends,--as by the rising and the falling of a white or yellow cloud or spot on the mirror's surface, indicative of similar movements in the correspondent precious metals; the floating or the sinking of a fleece for "stocks;" the rising or lowering of a stalk or sheaf of wheat, declarative of the course to be taken by that cereal in the markets of the world, for, sometimes, weeks ahead; or whether the objects, purposes, and ends sought pertain to the higher, broader, or deeper ranges of human thought and speculation. Unquestionably this ancient mode of dealing with the dead, and rapporting the mystical worlds above, beneath, within, and around us, is as superior to modern "Circleism" as gold in beauty outvies rough iron; hence students and explorers of the mystical side of the human soul; those desirous of opening the sealed doors of strange new worlds, and realizing somewhat of the tremendous problem of Being, must develop, not merely "Progress;" and to such the process of self-culturement is by me considered absolutely indispensable, and worth more to an anxious, earnest, light-seeking, yet not impatient soul, than all the "circles," and magnetists on the four continents; because the developed man or woman grows CHARACTER; the "progressed" ones, merely memory and tact; and to be an Independent Seer is to be-come an absolute Power on the globe! whereas all forms of automacy, magnetic or otherwise, are but forms of serf-dom and Slavery to powers incapable of identifica-tion, and for that reason doubly dangerous!

But the question arises with many: "Can any and every one successfully use the Bhatts?" and the reply is, No! Yes! Not every one can see in them; but every one can develop by them the Nine characteristics of perfect man and womanhood: WILL; ATTENTION; CONCENTRATION; PERSISTENCE; SELF-RESTRAINT; RELIANCE; MAGNETIC ENERGY, and AFFECTION, by an hour's steady use per day, and thus develop soul, thereby growing the power of death-survival and ensuring immortality. For I hold that those who cannot see in them at all, or produce clouds, or other magnetic effects after fair trial, may rest assured that they lack the great essential to immortality, and unless they cultivate soul and strive for it, when death lands their bodies in the grave their inner selves will dwindle back to the monadal state or blank Nihility.

Others can see in them, if not at once, then in periods varying from six weeks to one year; and the slower the development, the grander will be the power when culture shall have brought it into play. I have known a few utter failures with them; but the successes outnumber them at least in the ratio of five hundred to one. Those who would learn more of these matters are referred to the special work on that subject, "Seership." But when that was written no first-class Bhatts were on this continent; now there are a few, and they may be used in a company, lodge, or circle of from five to one hundred persons. When used by a single one that front may be gazed at; but a glorious surface is presented edgewise, or obliquely. In lodge, the company, whether it be few or many persons, should sit in a semicircle; the mirror leaning against the wall, and the glare of a bull's-eye lantern be thrown full and round upon its glowing face. Let all be still and motionless, and then carefully note the result.

To conclude: I do not approve of the use of them for purposes of magnetizing the opposite sexes,--affectionally; for although easily done, yet I think Love thus gained is not apt to be enduring, by reason of its too ardent and too often passional character,--hence cannot fully satisfy the needs of the human soul; yet I do believe it good to stir the medicine for the sick, with the finger, in the Basin of the ovoid, for by such means it can be quadruply charged with the divinest and most loving, therefore healing difference of the tremendous soul of man.

CONCLUDING PARAGRAPHS.--Many will suspect from our true name--BROTHERHOOD OF EULIS--that we really mean "Eleusis," and they are not far wrong. The Eleusinian Philosophers (with whom Jesus is reputed to have studied) were philosophers of Sex; and the Eleusinian Mysteries were mysteries thereof,--just such as the writer of this has taught ever since he began to think, and suffered for his thoughts, through the unfledged "Philosophers" of the century, amidst whom only now and then can a true thinker or real reasoner be found.

Through the Night of time the lamp of EULIS has lighted our path, and enabled obscure brethren to illuminate the world. Before Pythagoras, Plato, Hermes, and Budha, we were! and when their systems shall topple into dust, we will still flourish in immortal youth, because we drink of life at its holy fountain; and restored, pure, healthful, and normal sex with its uses to and with us means Restoration, Strength, Ascension, not their baleful opposites, as in the world outside the pale of genuine science. Up to the publications hereof on this continent we were indeed secret, for not one-tenth of those tested and called "Rosicrucians," knew of the deeper, yet simpler philosophy. But the time has come to spread the new doctrines because the age is ripe. I--We--no longer put up difficult barriers, but affiliate with all who are broad enough to accept Truth, no matter what garb she may wear. But till then we shut out the world; now we open our hearts and hands to welcome all true searchers of the Infinite,--all seekers after the attainable. We have determined to teach the Esoteric doctrines of the AEth; to accept all worthy aspirants, initiate them, and empower them to instruct, upbuild, and initiate others, --forming lodges if so they please.

The doctrines and beliefs are broadly laid down in the series of books published from the same source as the present; but especially in the volumes noticed herein. Those who wish further and private instructions, and to obtain information, conditions, secrets, writings, etc., and who purpose to cultivate the esoteric and mystic powers of the Soul, may correspond with that object with the publisher hereof--(or his official successor when dead)--who possesses certain keys which open doors hitherto sealed from man, but which are ready to swing wide when the proper "Open Sesame" is spoken by those worthy of admission.

LASTLY.--"CANST THOU MINISTER TO A MIND DISEASED?" Yes! by teaching that mind the nature and principles of its own immortal powers, and the rules of their growth --not otherwise. For centuries we have known what the world is just finding out-- that all the multiple hells on earth originate in trouble, unease, of the love, affections, and passions, or amatory sections of human nature; and that Heaven cannot come till Shiloh does; in other words, knowledge positive on the hidden regions of the mighty world called MAN. Hence this partial uplifting of the veil between us and the people of the continents. MEN FALL AND DIE THROUGH FEEBLENESS OF WILL! Women perish from too much passion, none at all, and absolute, cruel love-starvation. This WE intend to correct. We shall succeed; for True Men NEVER FAIL!

CONCLUSION: THE LYMPHICATION OF LOVE.--I have already herein called attention to the various secretions--normal--of the human pelvic viscera, and named them lochia, exuviae, semen, Duverneyan lymph, prostatic and Cowperian fluids. I now call attention to another, different from all and far more important than either, and which is the only one common to both sexes alike. I refer to that colorless, viscid, glairy lymph, or exudation which is only present under the most fierce and intense amative passion in either man or woman. This lymph has been noticed by M.D.'s, and regarded as a vaginal or prostatic secretion, but it is neither. They sought for its point of issuance, but fount it not, because, prior to its escape, per vagina and male urethra, it is not a liquid at all; but the liquid is the resultant of the union of three imponderables, just as common water is the result of the union of two gases and an electric current. Just so is this lymph the union of magnetism, electricity, and nerve-aura,--each rushing from the vital ganglia and fusing in the localities named. When it is present in wedlock's sacred rite then Power reigns and Love strikes deep root in the soul of the child that then may be begotten. If it is absent, the world is sure to receive a selfish, mean, small, contemptible thing in human shape,--a terror, or stalking crime and pestilence,--a partial man or woman, of little use to him or herself, and none at all to others, the world, or God. Wherefore the IMPERATIVE LAW--the violation of which entails horror, crime, and suffering, through at least a dozen lives--is: Absolute self-mastery in certain respects unless the presence of this divine fluid is God's permit for the holiest of all human enjoyments and duties. It is often present when it ought not to be, and when so, many a man has forgotten his manhood and triumphed over a similarly tempted girl; and many an honest girl and woman has fallen to rise no more. When this fluid is abundantly secreted the only safety is in instant flight, for, unappeased, it begets an insanity and furore too dreadfully intense and imperative to be successfully resisted even by an archangel, much less poor, weak, erring sons and daughters of men. If flight do not take place, and the leakage goes on, Soul itself is wasted, and Madness, with Horror at his gorgon side, waves his cruel baton, and another victim takes his or her place among the awful ranks of the Impotent, Barren, or Insane. It is the loss of this through personal vice solitary, and from the reading of infernal books and plates of damnation, that so many rush into bagnois and the madhouse. Could my readers but visit, as I have done, the magnificent Institution for the Insane at Nashville, Tenn., most ably presided over by Dr. J. H. Callander, a man who knows more about Madness and its cure than all others in the world combined, and witness the soul-harrowing spectacle of splendid people reduced to drivelling, soulless idiocy, wild mania, or absolute dementia from sex perversions, I am sure that no one would allow himself or herself to stand an instant in the presence of a temptation which, if successful, means havoc and destruction to the human soul. May God long preserve Dr. Callender, for the world will need him and such for centuries to come, until the race shall learn that "Love, indeed, lieth at the foundation," and whosoever infracts its laws must pay the dreadful penalty. I have spent the best years of my life in the endeavor to awaken mankind to a realizing sense of the real meaning, the words just quoted, and in ministering to those who had suffered from violations of that fundamental law; and I trust that when I am gone others will take up and carry on the good work. As will be seen in my work, "The New Mola," I desire to leave my system in good hands after my death, or at once, if need be; and I trust that through such, and other means, the great evil of love infraction and perversion may be put a stop to, measurably, if not altogether. So may it be.

P. B. RANDOLPH.

<u>Toledo</u>, <u>Ohio, June</u>, 1874.

NOTE.—The Provisional Grand Lodge of Eulis established in Tennessee, was dissolved by me—the creating, appointing and dissolving power—on June 13th, 1874. I intend to re-establish Eulis in organic form before I pass from earth, and as soon as the Brethren of over one year's standing, constituting the C.S. Grand Lodge, shall assist me in codifying its laws. The Supreme Grand Lodge is re-transferred to these head-quarters of the Order, and Eulis has none other on the globe.

P. B. RANDOLPH,
Supreme Grand Master of Eulid: Pythianae and Rosicrucia and Hierarch of
the Triple Order.

I here tender my thanks to the Brothers Lumsden for aid in issuing this work—their purchase of part of the edition; and to Ernest A. Percival, Esq., who came to the rescue, and contributed toward completing it,—after others' promises, solemnly made, were ruthlessly broken! And yet God reigns! and my book saw the light despite the blows aimed at me and it by the rule or ruin policy of—Never mind! The Book Survives and Thought Prevails.

PARTIAL LIST OF WORKS

BY THE SAME AUTHOR.

_____

I.

PRE-ADAMITE MAN. Seventh edition. Demonstrating the existence of the Human Race upon this earth 100,000 years ago. $2.00.

"A remarkable book." "We hail this shot from the Fort of Truth! Shows that men built cities 35,000 years ago! . . . Extra valuable volume." "Great grasp of thought! . . . Proves Adam was not the first man, nor anything like it! . . . Engrossingly interesting."

"The literary and philosophical triumph of the century, written by one of that century's most remarkable men."

II.

AFTER DEATH; or, DISEMBODIED MAN. Sixth and enlarged edition; with notice of the author. $2.25.

"No modern work ever created such astonishment and surprise, especially among Ministers and Theologians."

"This new work is, by far, the most important and thrilling that has yet fallen from the author's pen, inasmuch as it discusses questions, concerning our state and doings after death, that heretofore have been wholly untouched, and, perhaps, would have been for years had not this bold thinker dared to grapple with them. For instance, do we eat, drink, dress, sleep, love, marry, beget our kind, after death? These and many other most astounding and thrillingly interesting subjects are thoroughly treated in this very remarkable volume."

"No other living man could have penned such a work as this. The immortal tenth chapter, concerning sex after death, is alone worth a hundred ordinary books."

III.

THE NEW MOLA! THE LAWS AND PRINCIPLES OF MAGNETISM, CLAIRVOYANCE, AND MEDIUMISM.

This is unquestionably the most important monograph on Mediumship ever yet published in any country on the globe.

How to obtain the Phenomena in all its Phases. Conglomerate Mediumship. New and Startling Doctrine of Mixed Identities. A hand-book of White Magic. Explicit forms for all Phases of Cabalistic, Incantatory, and Thaumaturgic Science and Practice.

SYNOPSIS.

White Magic an actual fact. Identification of the dead. Conditions essential to their reappearance. Essentials of Mediumship and Clairvoyance. Blonde and Brunette Media. Curious reasons. A vast discovery of inestimable importance. Conglomerate Circles. The YU-YANG. Psychic Force. Medial Aura. Spanning the Gulf of Eternity! Electric People. To get the Phenomena when alone. Odyllic Insulation. To form a splendid Circle. Double Circles and new arrangement of the sitters. MATERIALIZATION OF SPIRITS, and how to bring it about! The Phantom hand of Toledo. The Spirit-room. MACHINERY ESSENTIAL TO PHYSICAL MANIFESTATIONS! AN ASTOUNDING IDEA--ATRILISM! Mergement of Identities--A dead one walks, talks, eats, drinks, and does what it chooses while occupying another's body, while the latter's soul is quiescent, and consciousness and identity wholly lost!--a most momentous problem, or enormous importance to every Physician, Judge, Juror, Minister, husband, wife, in short, to every human being. It is the most astounding thought yet evolved --as it accounts for much heretofore wholly unaccountable.

PART II.--How to Mesmerize. Clairvoyance. Psychometry--their differences. The Eastern Mystery of obtaining Seership. The Mystical Mirror--in a drop of common ink. The Breath-Power. An Arab Secret. Magnetic Spells. "VOODO-ISM" Black Magic. Price, postpaid, 60 cents per copy.

IV.

THE SECOND REVELATION OF SEX; LOVE, WOMAN, MARRIAGE. THE WOMAN'S BOOK. FOR THOSE WHO HAVE HEARTS. Prive, $2.50. Postage free.

SYNOPSIS.

CHAPTER I.--Love, Wealth, Power,--a mighty Lesson. The two Sphinxes: Woman, Fascination. True and False Love,--their lines of difference. Some very peculiar ideas about women. Female nature superior to male, and why. Test of a genuine Love. Passion-love. Curious notions of Noyes, Smith, Swedenborg, and some spiritualistic affinitists on love,--and bad ones,--some of them. "Women suffer less and are more cruel in love matters than men." Is it true? If so, why? Signs of a false love and a true one.

CHAP. II.--The one great human want is love. Why? Happiness impossible without a love to crown life. Women worse off than men. She must have love or die! Men satisfied with Passion, but women never! Why? Magnetic attraction. Physical aspects of Love. Its celestial chemistry,--a grand secret and hint to every woman, and lover, and husband, too,--not to be neglected. One of Love's Hidden Mysteries, and a wonderful one. Conditions of Love. Why we are not loved. Divorce Sharpers. "Passional Attraction." The Miser on the Desert. A Wonderful Dream. Why a Seduced Wife can never be happy with her Seducer. The Laws of Amatory Passione.

CHAP. III.--Strange Love-origin of crime,--curious. Why a loved wife can never be Seduced. No wife who is loved can ever be led astray. Why no husband can prevent her going aside unless he does love her. A hint for Husbands,--and a terrible fact. A fallacy exploded. Marks of LOVE,--THE MYSTERY OF MYSTERIES! How wives are slain; how husbands make them false! Seduction by condolence! New readings of old words The quietus of Anti-Marriageists. Whoever cannot weep is Lost! Why Libertinage can never satisfy or pay. The death-blow to "Free Love."

The <u>Home</u> <u>argument</u>! A Love Pang worse than triple death. Jealousy. From Parent to Child. Theories of Soul-origin. A curious thing about Parentage. A Strange Mystery of Fatherhood. Secret and Mysterious cause of Adultery.

CAHP. IV.--Necessity of returned Love. Who wins a body loses; who wins a soul wins ALL!! a strange, but mighty rule of Love! The Vermicular Philosophers. Why Free Lovers <u>always</u> come to grief! The 11th and 12th Commandments. Passional dangers of Eating-houses! "The long and short of it." Moments of very strange, wonderful, and mystic beauty in all women. The mystery of Vampirism,--a terrible revelation! Picture of a love-laden woman. True Womanhood, and its counterfeit. A true woman's Love. Men cannot call out love; but can kill it quickly. Why? The three things essential to call out woman's love!!

CHAP V.--A strange, weird Power of the human soul. The sunbursts of Love in heart-reft and lonely! The Solar Law of Love. A Vampire. The Better "Something." The Bridal Hour, and the fearful "<u>afterwards</u>." An <u>unsuspected</u>, terrible counterfeit of Love. Legend of the Wandering Jew, and Herodias, his mate. "Circles," "Sorosis, and the Circean Sisterhood. Protection from Vampire Life leeches. How these are created by Parents not loving each other. Singular fact and a Plea for the fallen woman. Actual Vampirism, a case described. Spiderwomen. Kidney troubles indicate Love troubles also. The triple form of Love,--a new revelation. The kind of Love that sets us crazy! LOVE TIDES! Proof of Love-adeptedness. Love and Friendship, --the difference. Eternal Affinityism dissected. A grand Love-Truth.

CHAP. VI.--New definitions of Marriage,--Love a fluid AEther!! Origin of Vampire Life, how they destroy plant and animal life. Why loving wives and husbands fail. A Test. Genius, Love, and Passion go together. Why? The Genius-producing Law. The Law of Social Joy. A chapter full of redemptive counsel for those wrecked on Love's storm-lashed rocks. Vivat!

CHAP. VII.--Love's Chemistry,--<u>very</u> curious, but very true. Love's double nature. Magnetic, Electric, and Nervous bases of the grand Passion! Law of Tidal Love. The Poison flow. Attraction of Passion. Chills and Fevers of true Affection! IMMORTALIZATION. Difference between male and female existence. Strange. What a woman never forgets or forgives. To Husbands and Lovers. Words never to be forgotten by either.

CHAPTER VIII.--Goodness alone is Power. Brain versus Heart! Knowledge is strength, <u>not</u> power! Head versus Heart Women. Grooves, Moods, Phases of Love. How Love requires but one second to change to deadly Hatred. A Mystery. Isabella of Spain, and Marfori, her lover. How the Franco-Prussian War resulted from their loving. Singular fact about a woman's Magic Photographic power. Darwin of the "Monkey-origin of Man" on trial. His acquittal. A Hint to Parents.

CHAP. IX.--Why women are ill, but should not be. Confectionery and Love. Drugged Candy. An unsuspected rock on which lovers are wrecked. Mental Sex, not physical, is what men love most. About woman's dress, as Love creators. A mistake about women which most men make. Another word for the "Strange Woman". Why women complain, and why wives die early! Extremes: Shakerism--Freeism, Caution to all.

CHAP. X.-- Divorce: Hereditary Bias. The Love-cure. An Old Friend in a New Dress. Why boy-babies are kissed more than girl infants. Why girl-babies reverse the business after the second year. Camp-meeting and Ball-room Loves. Another Mystery. People who are Love-starved. The Affection-Congress,--the Conductor, the Train, the Passengers, and the Arrival. A splendid series of FACTS FOR THE MARRIED.

CHAP. XI.--A New Discovery in Love, and a great one too! To a husband! To a Lover! Jealousy exists without Love! Love may exist without Jealousy. Gems of rare truth. How to recover when Love-exhausted. Beginning of Souls. Why Foeticide, at any stage, is worse than adult Murder! Freezing of Affection. The Sad Story of a Heart! What a man said about it. A Persian Poet's plea for "Free Love." Its Refutation. Rome before the Caesars.

CHAP. XII.--"The age of Brass." Why Mutilates cannot Love! Why a Woman recognizes Genuine Manhood. "The Origin of Eveil." "Organic"Love. Why no Man can respect a "Mistress." Why a Mistress" CANNOT BE HAPPY! Something concerning Wedded Life, very seldom thought of.

CHAP.XIII.--A Pice of a Man! Wife versus "Kept Miss." Selecting Partners: the bad rule and the good one. Pre-nuptial Familiarities. Marie and her "Husband!" Keep cool. How a wife bore a Christ-like Infant! Amativeness, tame and wild,-- their effects. Eternal Affinity is infernal nonsense! Why? A novel idea of how Eternity may be Passed. An idea of a new and better method of divorce. "Complex Marriage" in Heaven,--a curious notion. Why Great Men and Women are often Sensualists. Did ever a woman forgive a man's preference of a Rival. Can she?

CHAP. XIV.--A Penny's Worth of wit, and what came of it? Dimity vs. Divinity! One-sided Love, and Single-sided Marriage. The Piggitude of Husbands" (⚥) What a Sensible Woman said about Love-making Men!! Wives Beware! How to make Him Love Her!! Denial,--its fruits. The Great Question Direct. Its answer! How to Make Her Love Him!! No Ugly Women. All are Beautiful somehow! All Women Demand Home and Homage. No one can Seduce a Loving Woman. Why? Potiphar's Wife. How to Conquer by Stooping. Why a Coarse Person can Resist Temptation better than a Fine one. Old Maids! Old Bachelors! What Sappho said on Love; her Poem.

CHAP. XV.--The Long-haired Philosophers on Love; Mr. Boarland and Miss Green. Ascent, Descent; a Great New Truth for Wives and Husbands. How the Coarse Feeds upon the Fine,--the Stronger on the Weaker one. Who are Strictly Human, and who are not. Anatomy of several grades of Professional Love-ists. Homeymoonness versus Settle-downity! Definitions: Strength, Force, Energy, Power, Esteem, Friendship and Passion. Unless you love you can't be great, or even good. How to Reconstruct a Wife. Love and the other,--in ancient Pompeii.

CHAP. XVI.--Antagonisms. Stormy Love; its uses. A Defense of Adam,--premier. Who Falls by Love by Love must Rise!! Skeletons in People's Closets,--and our own. Copy-ists. Hero-Worship,--its Folly. Why? Anatomization of a Hero! Picture of a Modern "Husband!" Why Lincoln was a great Man. St. Peter and Paddy O'Raffety! What befell an Affinityist in Same Company. JAMES FISK, JR. His Love-power and Career. His Parentage, Nature, Character. The Grand Secret of his wonderful Success! What the Feronee Lady said about Fisk, Vanderbilt, Butler and Forney.

CHAP. XVII--Woman's Eyes, and how to read them. The curious conditions of Winning a Woman. Her rule of Safety,--Powerful. The Grand Magnetic Law. The Rule and Law of Ruin; also the Rule and law of Right. How a false step photographs itself and the Party--in her eye--an Egyptian Secret! The distrusts of Love-life, and their causes. The deeper meanings of Love! Descensive and Ascensive Passion. "The mother-in-law Curse." Admiral Verhuel--the father of Napoleon III. The Louisana Belle and what befell her! The Male and Female Worlds distinct. New Fact --Woman's rights destroys marriage. "Who's been here since I've been gone?" Chemical Love. Secret of absolute love-power.

CHAP. XVIII.--"Spiritual or Mediumistic marriages," a concubinic Sham! Madame

George Sands' Consuelo Love-theory--rejected. Personal Earthquakes and Periodic Excesses. True Love renders us malaria-proof--Singular Fact! Debauchees and the Parasites that attack them! Why insects and beasts prefer human prey to all other --A STRANGE AND VAST DISCOVERY! LUST PRODUCED BY ANIMALCULAE. Another Discovery --and how some little worms brought on the War in Europe! How to make Home happy! --a new recipe. Want, and what it does! The Seducer's Wiles. A Woman's Story, and a sad one. The 1st, 2d, and last grand duty of every husband living.

CHAP. XIX.--How meat hurts our souls at times unless properly slaughtered-- which it seldom is!! A fact for Legislation--How a wicked cook magnetically injures our food. Ethereal action of Love. An Extraordinary Love Mystery revealed. How Slovenliness kills affection! The Suffrage Problem. The New Departure. About Relationship, very curious! Touch! Good women get the worst husband; Bad men, the worst wives. The general mixed-upness. Boy and Girl love. Something for everybody.

CHAP.XX.--The Girl and Bride of the Period. What's up? Why Honeymoons turn bitter so quickly! Curious causes of Female Whims and Oddities. Scarcity of real Friendship. The Love Key. The Seven Devils. The King Passion. Amative Love Passion beyond the grave!! Woman's Grand Power. Ben Eli's Marrowy letter.

CHAP. XXI.--Dead-level love. Tiffs and spats. Husbandic Rules, which husbands neglect--any pany for doing it. Married celibates. Angularities. More about Eyes. BLONDES and Brunettes--their relative love-power and value as Wives--A very curious analysis worth much to those concerned!! Black Eyes, and the "De'il." Blondes resist outward pressure better than Brunettes. Brunettes fall from within quicker than Blondes. Why, in both cases. Singular! Astounding theory concerning Brunettes one only,--their Fire-Packed Souls! Their relative love and revenge power! A Brunette's love. Its intensity. Blonde-love--its superior delicacy. Disadvantages of the Ruddy. Brunette love, Sense-subduing; Blonde love, Soul-Subduing! Brunettes never vampiral. Blondes are, and a startling fact! Their relative immunity from varied diseases! A widow's and widower's chances of marriage better than those of single persons! Curious reasons. Cotton-Aids. How to win a true man! A "Case." Male Vampires. Little women have advantages. Why? Reconstruction of Dead-Loves. How? Loftier Gospel. New England Love! Comparative deaths of the wives of light and dark men. Whose children live longest--and Why!

CHAP. XXII.--How we sigh for the old loves! Prodigal Wives and Husbands. Meddling "Friends." Dangers of unrequited Love! The Awakening. Never Make your loves Public! Watching a wife--and what came of it!! What befell Mr. Connor--and his trowsers--while watching his wife!--The place of sighs!--a touching story of "Lost Souls." The "All-Right" fallacy exploded. The Social Evil!--a chapter of which the Author is proud--and his readers will be glad.

CHAP. XXIII.--Pre-nuptial Deceptions sure to be found out! Complaining Marriages. Necessity of loving some one. Dissection of an Atheistic Libertine. The Upper Faith. The Dog Nature. Temptation. The True Bill. Bad Marriage-horrors! The Magic Power of dress. Wife-neglecting husbands. Woman's love--a Poem. Evidences of high civilization from a savage's point of view. A rebuke to the 19th Century. Ignorant offers, and foolish acceptances. Wedded Licenses-- Impure brides,--Discovered. The Married Rights of Man. What a Turk told the Author about Women--New, and very good! How the great are fooled by the little. How the best women must act queer and offish at times.--A Hard "Case." No Atheist a full man. Hopes fixed on inappreciates. No man can endure neglect. A powerful female advantage! A powerful male one! Stingy husbands! How husbands can rewin the wife's love! A splendid resort!!

A story and sermon concerning "the animiles what went out for to fight." The fight, and what came of it. Singular fact about jealousy. "Only once!--that won't count much!" Won't it? Can a lover trust a woman who deceives her husband? Social Brigands--their own worst foes. Why? A bit of the author's life history. What love is like. Human Responsibility. Vastness of the human soul! "She was all the world to Me!" A Heart Poem. No libertine can evoke real Love. Modern Love! Sensitiveness--its advantages. The seven Points--this alone is worth the cost of the book to every woman. Something for wives; do. for husbands. "When her soul's at work!" The distributive Offices of woman's Being. The human Telegraphic system. Its wonders. Sexburg and Scoundrelton. Counterfeit kisses. "Opportunity." THE REAL KISS! ITS MEANING. GRAND! When friendships fail! "Bitter Beer!" Home! Sweet Home! Its Joys. "Like a gentle summer rain!" A Poem. The twain who truly love. Vive L'Amour! Finis.

V.

THE FIRST REVELATION OF SEX. LOVE: ITS HIDDEN HISTORY. TWO VOLS. IN ONE. A BOOK FOR WOMAN, MAN, WIVES, HUSBANDS. THE LOVING AND THE UNLOVED. ALSO FEMALE BEAUTY AND POWER. THEIR ATTAINMENT, CULTURE, AND RETENTION.

> "Hearts? Hearts?
> Who speaks of breaking Hearts?"

Price $2.50. Post free.

Of this volume, reprinted from the large octavo edition, nothing need be said; for "Seventh Edition" tells its own story. It differs entirely from the preceding work, and covers totally different grounds.

CONTENTS.

CHAPTER I.--What is Love? Reply--All of us born with a certain amount of Love in us. Passion is not love, but love is Passion! "Free Love" Infernalisms. Life and Love a desperate game. True Love and its counterfeits. Prudery. Why young girls "Fall." Magnetic Love. Why the wedded disagree--a curious cause--and un- suspected! ABORTIONISTS-- the infamous tribe Love's Hidden Mysteries. The TEN great Rules and Laws thereof! She stoops to conquer! Dress--Silence--as Powers of Love. Vampires life-teachers. Soul-devourers. Test of True Love. Jealousy. Suspicion. When woman is divine, and how to make her so.

CHAP. II.--The wife's great fault and oversight. Adultery. The kiss. A woman's idea of Love. Doggish husbands. Blind Tom and the Monkey boy. Love an Element. Why she "can't bear him!" Why he "hates her!" Divorce. "Spirit-medium" frauds. "Love powders." "Dragon's blood." The Heart Song. Barn-yard Love Philosophers. "I've gallen--again!" Passion in Men and Women. Song of the Forsaken. Laughing Scandal. Sunshine. Sugar-life.

CHAP. III--Perverted Magnetisms. Magnetic Poisons. Uterine diseases; undreamed -of causes of such. Complaints of women. Vulgar natures. Love dependent on victuals and drink. The Song of Wedded Misery. Vicarious Love--Wretchedness. Real Marriage--What it is, and is not! Meddling People. Love-song of the Soul!

CHAP. IV.--Power of words--A startling truth. AIR; the supreme joy of life. Curious, but true!--Oxygen!!--a Love creator! The two Babies. A sad, sad story. Nellie and the flickering candle. Consumption. Affection; Love; the difference between. Love and provender! The secret sin! The Proper Study of Mankind is --Woman!

CHAP. V.--Origins of the Black, Red, and White races. Differences between the Sexes. "Blue Pill for Breaking Hearts." Unwelcome Love no Love at all. Forced _attentions_ and _other_ Poisons. Dark people healthier than light ones. Why? Modern marriage _not_ a Bed of Roses. Why? The wonders of a woman. Nuts for married people. False Divorce. Helplessness of woman. Men of lofty soul love simple women best. Why? Actual Marriage means reciprocateness. Why a woman who bears a child by a dark man can never thereafter bear a light one. Transfusion. Temptation--and how to resist it. Magnetism. Mingling.

CHAP. VI.--How to win a husband's love. The Three Oriental Love Secrets. An excellent, but strange, revelation. Magnetic Will and Love Power. Love Starvation --and how to cure it! The Seven Rules of husbands--good ones to the wise. Mrs. Grundy. Free will. John and Sally. "Animality." The other side. Tides of Passion and Love. The Social Evil. "When it is dark"--a mournful tale. Incompatibility. Why relations hate each other. Physical basis of human love. Seven Laws of Love. Vampires. The author's experience. Why he loves a pretty woman. "When the Sultan goes to Ispahan!" Funny, but dangerous.

CHAP. VII.--Woman is Love Incarnate, only men don't realize it. Dimity _versus_ Divinity. Hearts for sale! Woman fails to know her Power. Love, an Art. The Magic Ring--very strange. The Love-cure. Mother-in-law--the trouble they make. Once in a whilish love of husbands. Lola Montez. The Christ-imaged child. Wonderful law. Love-storms, gales, tempests. How to subdue wild husbands. Woman's second attack wins, and why.

CHAP. VIII.--Love not to be forced on either side. What Leon Gozlan said about women. "Infernal fol-de-rolisms," "Legal" _violence!_ How Love-matches are broken off. The Lesson it teaches. The French "Girl's curious Prayer. Beauty; its laws. Insanity. An invaluable Chapter on the arts and means of increasing Female Beauty; translated from the French of Dr. Cazenave. Special instructions for beautifying the skin, hair, eyes, teeth,--in short, the Perfect Adornment of Women.

CHAP. IX.--Good -Humor. Home. The true life. Heart _versus_ Brain. The Woman condemned to be strangled, and how she was saved. The Three Lessons. A latter-day Sermon--Text: "Jordon _is_ hard road to travel." The Castaways. Singular. Magdalen. Scandal and Gossip. What Echo said. The Baby World. A thrilling Sermon by a reformed Prize Fighter. A splendid Poem--Swinburn.

CHAP. X.--"Eternal Affinityism," and Church-ortion. Honeymoons _versus_ sour Syrup. Marriage in 1790. One happy man; the curious reason why. "Doctors." Science--a wonderful case of its mighty Power. Cyprians not all bad or lost. Why? Monogamy and Amative Stimulants. The finest race upon the Planet. Propagation of Heroes--how it is accomplished! The Eye as an Index of character--Gray, Blue, Hazel, Black eyes. The Laughcure in a new phase. Matrimonial career. Gossiping. Healthy Love. Sex in Nature. Marriage of Light and Matter. Music is Sexive. Three classes of Women. Whom _not_ to Wed.

CHAP. XI.--Married Celibates. Friendliness. Fretting. "Lip-Salve." Boston. Philosophy--Soul-Marriage! A Fashionable Lady's Prayer. Prayer of the Girl of the Period. Hottentot's Heaven. Voudoo John, and Female Subjugation by Black-magic Arts. Breastless Ladies. How Wives are Poisoned!

CHAP. XII.--The Fountain of Love. How to remedy vital exhaustion. What to eat to gain Love-Power. Power of a Loving Woman. Her child. Excess. Promiscuous "Love." "When Sweetness reigns in Woman!" A half man; and how to pick him out. Ankles. Genius and Wedlock. Why the Talents are generally Wretched in the Marriage State. Singular facts, and Singular Faults in Women. Bitter Experience. A

Singular Paper upon Incest. Non-reciprocation--and its cause--and cure. Childless Couples--Causes--Cure. Fault-finding. Jealousy; its cause and cure. The Rule and Law of Human Power, or Genuis.

The book also contains special articles concerning why wives hate their husbands. Singular causes of wedded misery, and its cure. A hint to mothers. Hint to unloved wives. Gusty Love. When woman has most conquering power. The stormy life. The magnetic attack. Sex and passion after we are dead. Old-maidhood, and how to avoid it!

VI.

THE MYSTERIES OF THE MAGNETIC UNIVERSE. SEERSHIP. NEW EDITION. A wonderful series of discoveries for self-development in all branches of Clairvoyance, including the astonishing agency of MAGIC MIRRORS; and how to use them.

CONTENTS.--PART I.

Somnambulistic lucidity. Genuine clairvoyance a natural birthright. Two sources of light, astral and magnetic. Why mesmerists fail to produce clairvoyance in their "subjects." Vinegarded water, magnets and tractors as agents in its production. Specific rules. Clairvoyance is not spiritualism. The false and the true. Psychometry and intuition are not clairvoyance. Mesmeric circles. Eight kinds of Clairvoyance! Mesmeric coma and magnetic trance. The difference. Effect of lung power. Effect of amative passion on the seer. Dangers to women who are mesmerized. Oriental, European, and American methods. The mirror of ink. How to mesmerize by a common looking-glass. The insulated stool. The electric or magnetic battery. The bar magnet. The horse-shoe magnet. Phantasmata, Chemism. Why "Spirits" are said to take subjects away from magnetizers. Curious. Black Magic. Voudoo ("Hoodoo") spells, charms, projects. Very Strange! "Love Powders." The sham, and the terrible dangers of the real. How they are fabricated. Astounding disclosures concerning Voudooism in Tennessee. Proofs. The cock, the conches, the triangle, the herbs, the test, the spell, the effect, the wonderful result. White science baffled by black magic. Mrs. A., the Doctor, and the Voudoo Chief. Explanation of the mystery. The degrees of Clairvoyance, and how to reach them. The road to power, love, and money. Self-mesmerism. Mesmerism in ancient Egypt, Syria, Chaldea, Nineveh, and Babylon thousands of years ago. Testimony of Lepsius, Botta, Rawlings, Horner, Bunsen, Champollion, and Mariette. The Phantorama. Advice to seekers after Seership.

PART II.--THE MAGNETIC MIRROR AND ITS USES.

Dr. Dee and his magic mirror. Strange things seen in it. Not a spiritual juggle. George Sand. The Count St. Germain, and the Magic Mirror of Spirit-Seeing glass. Jewels used for the same purposes. Hargrave Jennings (the Rosicrucian), On fire. Curious things of the outside world, and divine illumination. Cagliostro, and his Magic Mirror. Frederick the Great Crystal-seeing Count. American Mirror Seers. Dr. Randolph, in April, '69, predicts the Gold panic of September. Its literal fulfilment. Business men use mirrors to forestall the markets. Their singular magic. Better and more effective than animal magnetism. Why. Extraordinary method of holding a psycho-vision steady as a picture. Two kinds of mirrors. Crystals. The pictures seen in a magic mirror are not on or in, but above it. Dangers of "Spirit control." Facts. Theory. Constructors of magic mirrors. Failures. Success. Chemistry of mirrors. The Life of Dream, and the Street of Chances. The Past, Present, and Future are actually now, because there can be no future to Omniscience. The future embosomed in the Ether, and he who can penetrate that can scan unborn events in the womb of coming time. It can be done, is done, and will be by all who have the right sense. Sir David Brewster, Salverte, Iamblichus, and Damascius. A magic mirror seance extraordinary. The Emperor Basil's sons is brought to his father in a magic glass by Theodore Santa Baren. Mr. Roscoe's account of a strange adventure of Benvenuto Bellini. What death really is. A new theory! The phantasmagoria of real things. Absorption. Its use and meaning. Platonic theory of vision. Theory of spiritual sight. Magic and magnetic, one and the same. Statement of the seven magnetic laws of Love. The blonde wife rewins her straying brunette husband from a brunette rival--from a blonde rival. Polarites. Caressive love. The antagonal polar law of love. Backthrown love. A singular principle. Egyptians. Magic mirrors. Mrs. Pool and Mr. Lane's testimony. How a maiden discovers a lover--a rival--a wrong-doer. Awful magnetic power of an injured woman's "magnetic prayer." Oriental widow finds a husband-- having seen him--never having seen him. "The Master Passion." "After death." Rules and laws of magic mirrors. How to clean and charge them magnetically. The Grand Master, De Novalis. The celebrated "Trinius" Japanese magic crystal globe of San Francisco, Cal.

The price of this work has been fixed at two dollars. It is the only work on the subject now extant in the English language, and incontestably excels either the French, German, Arabic, Syriac, Hindostanee, or the Chaldaic treatises upon the same topic, and is, probably, the fullest and most perfect compilation and exposition of the principia of the sublime science ever penned. A work of this extraordinary character is, indeed, rare. It can only be had direct from my office.

VII.

The WHOLE, instead of a part, of the quite Extraordinary ANSAIRETIC MYSTERY-- the fourth Rosicrucian Revelation Concerning Human Sex, and, as thousands can testify, the most astounding that has ever yet appeared anywhere on earth; and while there is not a word or line or suggestion in it, or in the third Revelation, that favors anything that could make an angel blush, yet they go to the very food of the subject. Said a celebrated agitator, on hearing a portion of them read: "What do you charge for that astonishing writing?" alluding to about one-fifth of the whole. "Five dollars; as it is hard work to write it out." Five dollars! Why, it is worth $500 to any one on earth with an ounce of brains, or a thrill of Man or Womanhood left in them!" Well, I looked up the Oriental MSS., and copies can be had of me, and if the mighty things therein--things not even dreamed of in these cold, practical lands--are not found to be worth ten times the sum, then the sublimest secrets the world ever held must wait another century for appreciative souls.

To those whose orders hereafter reach $5 at one time, a fine likeness of the author, by Poole, of Nashville, Tenn., will be sent as a premium, and the Ansairetic Mystery will be given gratis, and without any charge whatever, but only when requested in letter of remittance with return stamps.

Address this Publishing House, Toledo, Ohio.

THE CURIOUS LIFE OF P. B. RANDOLPH! "The Man with Two Souls!"--A Revelation of
the Rosicrucian Secrets! The Oath! Their Initiation! Strange Theories--Very.
His Birth, Blood, Education, Adventures, Secret of his Power! His Glory and Their
Shame! The Scandal and Sensation!

Part I. The Bright Side. What the People say.
Part II. The Ordeal. The Accusation. His Experience. Behind the Bars. He
loses all he has made in Life-time!

Part III. The Charge and Trial! The Witnesses. Curious Testimony. Speeches
of the Attorney against Randolph, and Selden's the Free-Love Champion.--A Caution
to Masons, Odd-Fellow's, and other Secret Societies. (See Part 3.) Randolph's
Defence, and Address to the Jury. He makes a Clean Expose of the Whole Thing!
These three masterly efforts are undoubtedly the strongest and ablest ever delivered
for and against Free Love.

The Verdict! Startling Disclosures! "The Mysteries and Miseries of Love."
Talk about Novels and Romances! Why they are tame nothings beside this man's life
and career. It reads like a romance. The strange oaths of the Rosicrucians regard-
ing all females. Extraordinary comparison between Agapism and Free-Love! The
Rosecross initiation,--the officiating girls--and what they do. "Doctor" BAY and
his "BUG" theory! "When the Band Begins to Play!" What was said concerning
Randolph's Book about Love and Women, Affection, the Sexes, Attractions, Vampirisms,
Infatuations, Friendship, Passion, Beauty, Heart, Soul, Lost Love, Dead Affection,
and its resurrective law, True and False Marriage.

One of the first writers in the country, when asked his opinion of the MSS.
from which it was printed exclaimed: "All I can say to the people of America is
Buy the Book! Price only 75 cents! and that will tell the whole strange story!"

LaVergne, TN USA
22 September 2009
158682LV00004BA/52/A